Oliver Statler's interest in Japan started when he arrived there in 1947 as a member of the United States Army. After retiring from service in 1954 he remained in Japan, where he immersed himself in the culture and history, becoming one of the first Western specialists on contemporary Japanese prints. Since 1977 he has been associated with the University of Hawaii as an adjunct professor and a fellow in Asian studies, which enabled him to research and write the sequel to *Japanese Inn*, entitled *Japanese Pilgrimage*, which is also published in Picador.

D1216132

Also by Oliver Statler
in Picador

Japanese Pilgrimage

JAPANESE INN

BY *Oliver Statler*

PICADOR published by Pan Books

First published in Great Britain 1985 by Pan Books Ltd,
Cavaye Place, London, SW10 9PG
9 8 7 6 5 4 3 2 1
© Oliver Statler 1961
ISBN 0 330 28560 2
Printed and bound in Great Britain by
Cox & Wyman Ltd, Reading

All illustrations, with the exception of the following, are used by courtesy of the Art Institute of Chicago: page 65, from the fourth edition of Dening's work, 1935, the Hokuseido Press, Tokyo; page 139, by courtesy of the Metropolitan Museum of Art (Fletcher Fund, 1929), New York; page 203, from the James A. Michener collection, Honolulu Academy of Arts; page 232, from the collection of Abbot Shutara Ryocho, Jogyoji Temple, Tokyo; pages 33, 128, 307, 328, from the author's collection, in the Art Institute of Chicago.

To

James A. Michener

Seikenji

Okitsu

Saionji's House

TO SHIMIZU AND KYOTO

Satta Mountain

Tokaido Road

Minaguchi-ya

TO YUI AND TOKYO

Suruga Bay

Miho

Shimizu Harbor

Contents

List of Illustrations

JAPANESE INN

CHAPTER ONE

In which the inn is introduced

The crest of
the Minaguchi-ya

ONCE AGAIN I am driving southwest on the great Tokaido Road that runs between Tokyo, the present capital of Japan, and Kyoto, the ancient capital. Once more, as I have done many times in the past twelve years, ever since the American Occupation brought me to Japan, I am seeking escape from the turmoil of Tokyo, and relaxation in a gentler place.

I am headed for the dream-haunted calm of the old inn called Minaguchi-ya. The *ya* means that it is a place of business, but even its owners confess they do not know the significance or origin of *Minaguchi*. Perhaps, they say, it refers to "water" and "mouth." Perhaps, when long ago the inn was named, it was named for a nearby source of fresh water, but they make this suggestion without conviction.

Unlike the quaint hostelries that pop up in fiction, my inn has a name that eludes colorful translation, but there is no question what Minaguchi-ya means to me. Through the years, I have come to treasure it as the most Japanese place I know, the place most sure to wrap me in the time-honored courtesy of a country I have grown to love. Yet at the same instant, it is the Minaguchi-ya, stubbornly holding on to the old ways of Japan, that reminds me of the fact that no matter how many Americans come and go, Japan will remain Japanese.

For at the Minaguchi-ya, resting with fertile hills behind me and the changeless face of Suruga Bay before me, I can conjure up visions of the strange history this inn has known. I can sense the spirit of that tough, cool warrior Ieyasu, who three and a half centuries ago laid the foundations of modern Japan. I can imagine that artful conspirator, Yui Shosetsu, once more storming into the inn as he did three centuries past. And I can visualize, standing on the sea wall, that most appealing of all modern Japanese figures, Prince Saionji, who lived almost next door to the inn and who as the nation's elder statesman fought the militarists and helped stave off war, as long as he lived.

I do not have to be an imaginer of history to see these visions at the Minaguchi-ya, for this inconspicuous rural inn has participated deeply in its country's history, and when I am within its quiet confines that history storms back into consciousness. Here in these walls, so often burned, so often changed, yet always owned by one continuing family, the history of Japan resides, and in time subtly envelopes the visitor.

On this day I have already progressed along the old Tokaido Road to the village of Yui. A new highway has been built a few hundred yards inland to avoid the congested main street of the village, but leaving Yui it swings back to the shore and runs between the sea wall on my left and the sheer face of Satta Mountain on my right.

It is here, as I drive almost into the sea, that my spirits always quicken, for only Satta Mountain divides Yui from Okitsu, the next village, where my inn lies. I know that in a few moments I will slip within its gate and be at home in Japan. I am almost at the end of my journey, and my nerves, taut from the ebullient anarchy of Japanese highways, relax a bit. I notice men and women diving around the offshore rocks, sharp knives in hand, hunting for abalone. Beyond them, fishing boats dot Suruga Bay.

In old days, too, men and women dove for abalone, and fishing boats dotted the bay, but then this was a dangerous and unpleasant stretch of road, with rocks falling from the cliff and waves surging over the path. Just short of the wide Okitsu River bottom, the mountain jutted angrily into the sea, so that there was no path at all. There a traveler had to plunge into the ocean, fighting the rocks and the swift undertow. It was every man for himself, and many were lost. The point was well named, "Parent-forgets-child-and-child-forgets-parent."

4

Travelers high on Satta Pass pause to drink in the view of Mount Fuji and Suruga Bay (*a print by Hiroshige*)

In these last minutes of the tiring drive—Yui is a hundred miles from Tokyo but I have only one more mile to go—I always pause to remember a memorable vista, one of the highlights of the entire length of the Tokaido . . .

At my right rises the rude bulk of Satta Mountain. In 1655 some Korean envoys were to pass this way, and the Japanese government, with more consideration than might be expected from present-day relationships with Korea, ordained that the perilous old road that dipped into the sea be replaced by a new one which climbed strenuously up and over Satta. Today all those collectors around the world who treasure Hiroshige's color prints of the Tokaido prize in particular that vivid and daring design which shows the precipitous mountain pass from Yui, with the bay blue and handsome below.

At the highest point of the pass, where the path breaks out of the pines and into the open, there is a breath-taking view, and anyone who finds himself there must turn to drink it in. He faces the great sweep of Suruga Bay and the open Pacific beyond, while waves break into flowers on the rocks far beneath his feet. Yui lies on the shore at his left and Okitsu at his right. Beyond Yui, bathed in mist far off on the left, looms the mountainous coast of Izu. Beyond Okitsu, on the right, is one of the loveliest sights in Japan, for the harbor that lies there is protected by a long arm of curving black sand, covered with ancient and twisted pines. This is the fabled beach of Miho. Lovely in itself, an arc of pine-laden beauty, it is also the scene of a famous legend. It was Miho's beach that so entranced an angel that she came down from the sky for a swim, leaving her feathered robe on a branch of a wind-bent pine. A fisherman discovered the robe and refused to give it up until the angel danced for him. Fortunately, the heavens provided music.

But travelers have always loved Miho not so much for its abstract beauty, or for the legend which illumines it, but rather because from its sand and pines one can obtain the only perfect view of Mount Fuji. From almost any spot on Miho, one looks northward to see Fuji's noble presence looming beneath some arching arm of pine, mirrored in the bay, and set off by glistening sands. Until one has seen Fuji thus he has not truly seen it, but if he has caught this vision he carries it with him forever. I have seen Fuji from Miho, so that now as I pause at Satta and look across the bay I see not only that lovely sweeping shore but Fuji, too, within me.

Putting thoughts of Fuji aside, I zip around the point that used to be so dangerous. The old footpath down from Satta's crest winds inland here, hugging a gentler slope. In former days, a traveler rich enough to ride instead of walk would be jostled down this path in a rude mountain palanquin borne by two sweating carriers, each naked but for a scanty loincloth, straw sandals, and a twist of towel tied around his head. As they scrambled down the pass they might chant to keep in step,

> "Last night I crept
> To where she slept
> When supper was done
> And had some fun."

The inn is introduced

At the foot of the pass prudent travelers paused at a small, weather-beaten Buddhist temple housing the stone Jizo of Satta. It is a much revered little statue, miraculously hauled out of the ocean by fishermen in 1185, or so they say. It was providential to find Jizo by Satta Pass, for he is a Buddhist god of mercy and the patron saint of travelers, not to mention children and pregnant wives. A traveler could use some help on Satta in the old days. The going was rough, and robber bands sometimes struck from the woods.

I swing onto the bridge that crosses the wide gravelly bed of the Okitsu River. In old bridgeless days, river coolies loitered near this spot until some traveler came to cross the swollen stream. A traveler's requirement for coolies depended on the style in which he was traveling. He could, of course, wade across with no help, and he could drown in the process. Many did. He could wade with one or two coolies holding him by the hand. He could perch on stout shoulders, or on a ladder-like contraption that was itself carried on shoulders. He could even stay in his palanquin and have that carried on the ladder. At the Okitsu River many a pompous official suffered a wet bottom to get to the opposite bank.

I cross the bridge and approach the Minaguchi-ya. Here the old Tokaido becomes a wide paved street. Okitsu town lies strung out along this street as it has been for a thousand years, its narrow strip of precious level land squeezed between the sea on my left and the mountains on my right, mountains cut off from Satta only by the great trough of the Okitsu River.

The street is lined with shops, and behind each shop, or sometimes spilling over into a second story, live the shopkeeper and his family. Here and there a bright enameled sign makes a spot of color, or a gay banner announces a sale, but the dominant tone is the dull brown of stained and weathered wood. These files of much-used buildings marching down the street give an impression of neatness, but each shop is a little jumbled, and the lithographed displays are mostly faded and flyspecked. When my Japanese friends walk down this street for the first time they are likely to exclaim, "Old! Ah, this is an old town."

At the far end of the town, on an imposing slope of its own so that it stands well above Okitsu and commands all that goes on below, is the temple of Seikenji (the suffix *ji* means temple, so that it is redundant to say "temple of Seikenji," but the name Seiken by itself rings unnaturally on the ears). It is one of the notable Buddhist temples of this district and one cannot stay long at the Minaguchi-ya without becoming aware of it. Here great Ieyasu studied as a boy, and the principles he mastered under this towering roof helped him weld Japan into a single nation. Here aging Prince Saionji climbed from his little house on the shore, to sit in the light of the warm sun or the cool moon, gazing across the bay to the sand and pines of Miho stretching out towards Fuji.

The noble old temple, burned again and again through the years and always rebuilt in some new fashion on its slope, stares down as one climbs the long flight of stone steps to its domain. It stands to-

Travelers fording a Tokaido river: a man of importance in his palanquin, lesser men perched on coolies' shoulders (*detail from a print by Hiroshige*)

day gray and hushed, coated with history and steeped in the passions of its land, for Japanese temples were never aloof from the power struggles of any age, and Seikenji was one of the foremost.

This is the setting of the town of Okitsu, and as I drive slowly down the street I feel this setting closing in about me, friendly and familiar.

In the old days inns stood shoulder to shoulder here, and when the afternoon sun slipped behind the mountains, dozens of girls used to line the road, crying, "Please lodge in this house, gentlemen. The bath is quite ready. There's a vacant room especially for you. Stop here! Stop here!"

Without their pleading I am prepared to stop. And now on my left, towards the bay, I see a high gray wall broken by a low, dark-stained wooden gateway. I leave the Tokaido, turn through the gate, and before me, stretched out to the very edge of the sea, is the Minaguchi-ya. I drive across the white stone of the courtyard, and I am home.

Gratefully I switch off the motor, and in this momentary quietness the inn of Minaguchi-ya springs to life.

A kimono-clad maid comes running, calling back messages to the interior, and sinks to her knees on the straw matting of the entrance hall. Bowing almost to the floor, she cries, "You are welcome to the Minaguchi-ya."

Round-faced Yoshi, his bald head gleaming, rushes out to take forcible possession of my bag. "You are welcome! You are welcome!" he cries.

And from the interior appears buoyant, bubbling Isako, the mistress of the inn, tall, slender, and young in heart. She too slips to the floor and bows. *"Shibaraku!"* she says, and she smiles. *"Shibaraku! Shibaraku!"*

"Shibaraku," I reply, signifying that it has indeed been too long a time since I was last at the inn.

"Please come in. Your room is waiting. It is your home." Isako rises to lead the way.

I climb out of my hot shoes and into cool slippers. I follow my little procession of friends as they lead me down dim corridors marked by gleaming, polished floors. The door to my room slides open. I kick off my slippers, feel the springy mats beneath my feet, and drop to the cushion that has been placed for me. Isako bows, the maid bows, and I bow. We murmur more greetings and inquire after each other's health. *"Shibaraku! Shibaraku!"* we agree.

Another maid appears with tea and cakes. Then I am left alone in my quiet room. Great glass doors have been slid open to the garden and I rest my eyes on its cool greenness. Beyond I hear the sea, and a drowsy hum from the bustling Tokaido, crowded today as it has been for hundreds of years.

Soon Yoshi taps quietly at my door to tell me that my bath is ready. I follow him to the scoured-wood room, where he scrubs my back as we exchange notes about mutual friends who have also known hospitality at the Minaguchi-ya. Then I recline full length in the big hot-water pool and let tension soak away.

Later there is good food, fish from the sea, vegetables from the hills, rice from the countryside. My bed of soft pads is laid upon the woven mats, and I willingly slip between crisp white sheets. The Minaguchi-ya enfolds me, as it has travelers for centuries. In the darkness I see them: warriors marching across Japan, lovers fleeing to a new life, pilgrims on their merry expeditions, great men going to or from the capital. I fall asleep to the sound of the sea.

First and Second

Generations

CHAPTER TWO

In which the inn is founded

PRINCIPAL CHARACTERS

Takeda Harunobu (Shingen), *chief of the mountain clan of Takeda*

Imagawa Yoshimoto, *chief of the coastal clan of Imagawa*

Sessai Choro, *abbot of Seikenji Temple, general and strategist of Imagawa's army, and tutor to young Ieyasu*

Tokugawa Ieyasu, *chief of the rising Tokugawa clan*

and among the people of the inn:

Mochizuki, *samurai retainer to Shingen, who, having been moved from his mountain homeland to the coastal village of Okitsu, unintentionally founds the Minaguchi-ya*

His son

*The crest of
Takeda Shingen*

SO MUCH of history seems pegged on battles that I see no need to apologize for beginning the Minaguchi-ya's story with one. They call it the Battle of Okitsu. It took place on the Okitsu River in the winter of 1569.

It was a fragment of the fighting that swept Japan all through its bloody sixteenth century, for the central government had rotted away and each of the great clans was struggling for supremacy. The Battle of Okitsu was fought between a clan of the mountains and a clan of the coast.

Actually, it was too cold for enthusiastic fighting. The two armies glowered at each other across the wide, flat river bottom, and some-times small bands sallied out to skirmish.

The chief of the mountain clan was called Shingen. He had taken this name, along with the title of Archbishop, when he became a Zen Buddhist monk. This move reflected his love for learning and the arts, but it did not diminish his ambition. In those days it was not considered incompatible for a priest to be a warrior.

He was an old campaigner. When his troops had slashed out of their mountain stronghold towards the coast, he had thoughtfully ordered his commissary officer to seize all the saké, the good rice wine, that could be found. This had been toted to the chill new en-campment on the river bank, and the villagers around Okitsu had been relieved of their iron kettles so the wine could be heated the way the Japanese like it.

Shingen demonstrated his generalship one bitterly cold night by breaking out the liberated saké and giving his troops a generous, warming drink. Then he inquired whether they still felt cold, but when they all thirstily replied in the affirmative, he delivered not another round but an exhortation. "If you still feel cold after hot saké," he bellowed, "think how much colder the enemy must be. They may even have left their positions. Charge, and we shall take them!" They did charge, and right enough the coastal warriors had left their forward camps, and Shingen's men captured quantities of weapons and supplies.

This sort of thing, however, did not happen often enough and, as winter softened into spring, Shingen's stores ran low, a condition aggravated by the peasants' uncomfortable ability to smell a loser and hide their rice from him. So Shingen slipped his army back through the hills to his mountain-locked home provinces, and the army of the coastal clan, when they found out what had happened, tramped back to their own capital.

Not a very conclusive campaign, it is agreed, but next summer Shingen was back. This time he gave his enemy a businesslike beating and took firm control of the coastal province, called Suruga after

Takeda Shingen
(*a book illustration by
an unknown artist*)

the bay it hugged. Suruga was a handy acquisition, for it gave his mountain people access to the sea.

Shingen pushed a few miles south of Okitsu to investigate the peak known as Kunozan, which juts out like the prow of a ship to dominate the low-lying coast, and finding that its sheer face made it an almost impregnable position, he promptly fortified it. He was not one whit dissuaded by howls from outraged priests whose temple had to be moved from the heights to the lowlands. Then, winging out from Kunozan, he built a string of strong points along the coast to supervise the collection of salt and fish that his people needed. That was what he had been after all along.

One of these little forts was at Okitsu, and there he installed one of his samurai, a two-sword man, a liegeman and warrior named Mochizuki. Looking after salt and salted fish is not very warlike activity, but Mochizuki's post was a responsible one, since Okitsu lies at the junction of the coastal Tokaido highway and one of the main routes to the mountains, the road which runs inland along the Okitsu River. Mochizuki filled his post capably, for as a samurai of a great clan he was a responsible man.

Soon, with Shingen's permission, he sent for his family. His aging mother refused to make the change, clinging to her younger sons at the family home in the mountains, and so only Mochizuki's wife and son came to Suruga and moved into the fort. The boy adapted quickly, as the young do. He learned to swim, and spent hours on the beach until he was the color of old bronze. He listened to the tales of fishermen as they mended their nets in the sun, and he investigated their catches when they hauled them in.

He watched as the women made salt. Endlessly they trudged from sea to shore, buckets of water straining from a pole over an aching shoulder. They sprayed the water on smooth sand beds to evaporate, raked up the saturated sand, filtered out the salt with more sea water, and boiled the concentrate in great iron pots until there remained only the gray, coarse, indispensable crystals which his father sent back to the mountains. The boy soon took for granted the smoke from the salt fires and the resulting haze which seemed a permanent part of the landscape.

He roamed with new friends in the high hills back of the village, and found that it was quite useless to belittle those hills with talk of the great mountains he had come from, for the other boys weren't interested, and neither, he discovered, was he. At home he spoke familiarly of the local Shinto spirits around whose shrines he romped, and he seemed to have quite forgotten the gods of his homeland peaks.

Salt-makers (*detail from a print by Hiroshige*)

He learned his lessons, too, going almost daily for instruction in calligraphy to one of the Buddhist temples, though not Seikenji, for Seikenji is a temple of the Zen sect, and the Mochizukis were not of that sect. And his father taught him to ride and to use a sword, skills that the sons of samurai had to master.

The inn is founded

For the Mochizukis at Okitsu, the years passed peacefully enough, though they were not peaceful years for their clan. Shingen was acquisitive, and he was soon quarreling with another neighbor. A couple of years after the Battle of Okitsu he was besieging one of that neighbor's fortresses. It was ably defended and the siege dragged on for weeks. As an added attraction, one of the defenders began appearing on the ramparts night after night to play the flute. He played very well, and Shingen, who loved music, often went out to listen. One night he went too close, and a sharpshooter put a bullet through his head.

Whether Shingen's death had been schemed by someone who knew his fondness for the flute, or was merely his enemy's good luck, no one knows, but at any rate the destinies of the clan fell into the hands of Shingen's son, who was not the man his father had been.

The son was brave enough, perhaps overbold, but he was autocratic and self-willed. He antagonized his father's veterans and alienated his father's allies. Nevertheless he stood off powerful enemies for almost ten years, and all that time (for there was no fighting around Okitsu) Mochizuki commanded his little fort and shipped salt and fish to the mountains along the road that follows the Okitsu River.

Calligraphy master
(*a book illustration by Jichosai*)

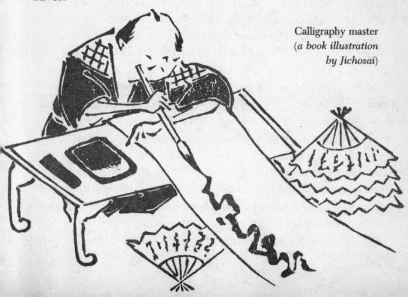

Mochizuki liked the sunny, fruitful coast as much as his son did. His family expanded. He sometimes remarked to his wife that their oldest son had quite forgotten, and the younger children had never known, the long harsh winters of the mountains. They were really, he said, natives of Suruga.

But while those were good years for the Mochizukis, they were not good for their clan. The news from their mountain homeland grew worse and worse. There finally came a day, an early spring day, when Mochizuki buckled on his armor and his two swords and went out to face the enemy. His oldest son went too, for he was now sixteen, a warrior's age. But they did no fighting. They were two against an army. They kneeled and surrendered.

They surrendered to a stocky, unsmiling man on horseback. That was Mochizuki's first glimpse of Ieyasu, the man in whose hands his fate and the fate of all Japan would lie. The first words he heard Ieyasu utter were a crisp command to burn the little fort. Mochizuki, head bowed to ground, caught his breath in what was almost a sob.

That was Mochizuki's first glimpse of Ieyasu, but Ieyasu was no stranger to this place. Long before Shingen had swept through and stationed Mochizuki in Okitsu, Ieyasu had known this province and this village. He had spent most of his boyhood in Suruga, and on this spring morning, as he had pushed towards Okitsu with his troops, he had recognized each familiar turn of the highway. It had seemed like coming home, and his mind had kept darting back to the years when he had galloped over the same road as a boy . . .

He had been six years old when his father had sent him off to Suruga. His father had been a daimyo, one of those dozens of feudal lords like Shingen who ruled their fiefs with despotic authority, commanded allegiance from hundreds of samurai and thousands of peasants, and warred amongst themselves for eventual supremacy. But compared to Shingen, Ieyasu's father had been a comparatively minor daimyo, one who maintained his relatively weak clan in a state of precarious semi-independence under the protection of a much more powerful daimyo named Yoshimoto. Suruga had then belonged to Yoshimoto, and young Ieyasu was going there because Yoshimoto thought it would help insure his father's good behavior. It was a common enough arrangement in an age when a man could not trust his own brother: the six-year-old was to be a hostage.

His father had provided young Ieyasu with a staff of servants, and twenty-seven youngsters of his own age to keep him company, and an escort of fifty samurai. The fifty were not enough. The party was ambushed, and the boy kidnapped and carried off into enemy hands.

There was talk of ending his short life then and there, but other counsel prevailed, and two years later Yoshimoto was able to make a trade with the enemy, and the boy was released to complete his original journey. In Suruga at last, he was installed in a suitable house with a suitable entourage, and he lived very well.

Everybody lived well at Yoshimoto's capital. His wife was the daughter of a court noble at Kyoto, and she had transplanted to a warrior's headquarters the atmosphere that surrounded the effete and powerless Emperor. She had brought a great many relatives, who were delighted to come, money being more plentiful at Yoshimoto's capital than at the Emperor's, and they had done their best to soften the hardships of living in the provinces. They had set up a lavish program of poetry-making and flower-viewing, they had named all the beauty spots after famous landscapes near Kyoto, and they always saw to it that ceremonies were impressively proper, never mind the expense. They also had a hand in raising Yoshimoto's son, and it should have been no surprise that he turned out to be more courtier than warrior.

They had nothing to do with Ieyasu's education, and his first formal appearance must have been a shock to them. It was at a New Year's reception in Yoshimoto's mansion, a very stately and ceremonious occasion. A group of elders had been arguing about who the new boy was, when, amidst all the pomp, he rose and unconcernedly made his way through the assembled nobles to the edge of the veranda. There, in the words of A. L. Sadler, "he proceeded to assume the attitude of the famous mannikin who is the oldest citizen of Brussels. In quite a natural and unflurried manner he finished his business and returned to his place"—and that ended the argument about who he was, because the old men knew that his grandfather had possessed just such icy poise.

Ten years he lived and grew up in Suruga. He hawked and swam and rode, and he practiced swordsmanship, and marksmanship with both bow and matchlock. For in the same year of 1542 that he had been born, just fifty years after the Western Hemisphere had frustrated Columbus's attempt to reach the fabulous Indies, the Portuguese had "discovered" Japan, and simultaneously the Japanese had discovered the gun. On both sides it was love at first sight. The Japanese, being, as one early visitor put it, "naturally addicted to the wars, wherein they take more delight than any other people we know," were enchanted by the newfangled weapons, and the visitors were enchanted by the Japanese. "The best people so far discovered," pronounced Francis Xavier, for hot on the heels of the merchants came the missionaries.

But as a youngster in Suruga, Ieyasu had more immediate problems than barbarians from the Western world. His father was now dead, and he was very conscious that the battered fortunes of his clan were in his hands. So, though he was not the studious type, he paid attention to his lessons, and this was not difficult, because he felt more than a touch of hero worship towards his teacher. That man, Sessai, was, like Shingen, not only a priest and a learned man, he was also a general, and he had commanded Yoshimoto's armies when they were most successful. So whenever the boy had a chance, he led his tutor to discourse on tactics and strategy, and those early lessons must have been effective, for Ieyasu later became a very skillful general himself.

It was his teacher who first brought Ieyasu to Okitsu. Sessai was the abbot of two temples, one of them Seikenji in Okitsu, and when he came to stay there for a while to supervise more closely its dozens of priests and acolytes, the old abbot brought along his charge. Today at Seikenji one can still see the room where the boy studied. It was a little apart from the bustle of the great temple, in the rear of the main hall, tucked in behind the altar. It is small but handsome, and it faces the garden which is built against the side of the mountain. In later years Ieyasu often came back to Seikenji and this garden.

By his eighteenth year he had already proved himself as a commander of troops. It was about then that Yoshimoto decided the time had come to take over the country. Under the rules of the game it was first necessary to march to Kyoto and take over the Emperor. Then, having extracted an Imperial mandate to subdue all the other daimyo, one tried to do just that.

Sessai was dead now, and so Yoshimoto assumed personal command of his armies. It is evident that he was not equal to the task, for his campaign was barely under way when he was caught by a surprise attack. Before he knew what was happening, his head rolled on the ground.

As suddenly, Ieyasu seized his independence, because he saw that Yoshimoto's son could never replace his father. The courtiers from Kyoto had played too big a part in his education, with results that were shocking to his martial contemporaries. They said that he was given up to drink and dalliance, and, even worse, to football. Ieyasu kept up friendly relations because they had grown up together, but he did not let sentiment interfere with the hard business of getting ahead, and a few years later he helped carve up Yoshimoto's territories.

That suggestion had come from Shingen, Mochizuki's fiery old chieftain. Yoshimoto's son held two provinces, Shingen pointed out, which would work out nicely at one for himself, Shingen, and one for Ieyasu. Ieyasu could see that it was only a matter of time until somebody took over those territories, so he agreed to Shingen's attractive proposition and in an easy campaign lopped off one province.

Shingen had not quite such an easy time of it, for that was when he bogged down in the wintry battle at the Okitsu River, but next year, as we have seen, he took the province he had marked for himself, Suruga, and shortly thereafter installed Mochizuki at Okitsu.

After Shingen and Ieyasu had divided between them the territories that once were Yoshimoto's, there was no longer much reason

for them to remain friendly. They had, in fact, good reason to become enemies, because now they were neighbors. Since Shingen
was stronger and more irritable, he was soon on the march. It was
one of Ieyasu's forts he was besieging when he fell victim to his
love for music played on the flute.

Now, after long years of fighting, Ieyasu was pushing Shingen's
son out of Suruga, out of the coastal province that the mountain
clan needed so desperately as its source of fish and salt. Today, a
day in early spring, Ieyasu had returned to Okitsu. Samurai Mochizuki was kneeling on the ground, and black smoke was twisting
into the sky, marking the end of his little fortress.

While Mochizuki and his family watched what had been their
life burn away, Ieyasu wheeled his horse and rode back to Seikenji.
There he dismounted and climbed the steps he had climbed many
times as a boy, thirty or so years before. He was received privately
by the abbot.

When Ieyasu emerged he spoke briefly with an aide, remounted,
and rode away without a backward glance. Soon other great col-
umns of smoke writhed upward, joining the soot from Mochizuki's
fort to smear the sky. It was the third time in history that Seikenji
had been burned because it dominated a strategic point on the
highway. Even with victory apparently certain, Ieyasu was not a
man to take chances. He would rebuild the temple if things went
his way, he had told the abbot, but in the meantime it had to go.
At the abbot's pleading he spared only the central hall, and with it,
incidentally, the little room where he had studied as a boy.

A few weeks later Shingen's son, the last chieftain of his clan,
took his own life deep in the mountains. Suruga was firmly in
Ieyasu's hands, and Mochizuki's career as a samurai of the mountain clan was finished. When a daimyo fell, his samurai lost their
status as members of the military class; unless they could attach
themselves to another daimyo, they reverted to being commoners.
Mochizuki had been a man with position and authority. Now he
had neither. He had been entitled to wear two swords. Now he

must put them away. He was a warrior with no army to fight in, a man adrift.

What next? Mochizuki thought hard over his situation. He could return to his own people, to his chill mountain homeland, and settle down as a repatriate farmer; but he had grown attached to the warm and fertile coast. Or he could seek a position as samurai with some other clan—he thought of petitioning one of Ieyasu's subordinates; but he knew that even if he were successful the rewards were likely to be scanty: there were too many men in the same predicament as he.

In the end he remained in Okitsu. Perhaps he made his decision when the Headmen of the village, old Ichikawa and even older

Travelers on the Tokaido
(*detail from a print
by Hiroshige*)

Tezuka, called on him to tell him, solemnly, that he would be welcome. Ichikawa recalled that his own family had immigrated from the mountains four generations back. They had found life better here, he said.

Mochizuki's neighbors helped him build a new house where the fort had stood, a large and impressive house, for he still commanded respect in Okitsu. And all the servants elected to remain with the family. In their minds, Mochizuki was still a samurai.

Because his new house was large and impressive, important travelers were likely to stop there and request lodging when they found themselves in Okitsu with night coming on. As peace came to the area under Ieyasu's firm control, travelers became more frequent and so did their requests for lodging.

Mochizuki was not aware of becoming an innkeeper, and it is difficult to say when his house became an inn. All we know is that it was the spring of 1582 when Ieyasu burned the fort. The new house was built that summer, and, shortly after, Mochizuki acceded to the first request for a night's lodging. Whoever he was, that traveler was the first guest in what was to become the Minaguchi-ya.

1582–1605

CHAPTER THREE

In which a reluctant Mochizuki is pushed deeper into innkeeping

PRINCIPAL CHARACTERS

Oda Nobunaga, *who, with Ieyasu as ally and Hideyoshi as chief of staff, begins the unification of Japan*

Toyotomi Hideyoshi, *who, with Ieyasu's help, finally achieves unification*

Tokugawa Ieyasu, *who replaces Hideyoshi as master of all Japan and founds the dynasty of his own Tokugawa family*

Sen Rikyu, *tea master to Hideyoshi*

and among the people of the inn:

Mochizuki
His son

The crest of
Toyotomi Hideyoshi

TO SAY that Mochizuki was not aware of becoming an innkeeper is to put the case mildly. He insisted that his home was not an inn and never would be. Of course if some man of rank requested accommodations, there was no choice but to be gracious about it. One could not expect a person of importance to put up at some vulgar little inn where he would be bitten by bedbugs and vexed by caterwauling commoners. And so the Mochizukis would vacate their best rooms, in the rear of the house around the garden, and would retire to the big kitchen fronting on the highway. These concessions to nobility were unavoidable, he explained to his son, but they did not mean that the Mochizukis were going into business.

"Going into business"—Mochizuki winced at the phrase. In today's world it is difficult to conceive what a fall it was from samurai to businessman. In Mochizuki's world it was from top to bottom, from gentleman to huckster. Fate had been unkind, he frequently remarked. He had lost his samuraiship, he had lost the privilege of bearing arms, but, and he took a deep breath, there was no reason to lose all honor.

His son was silent but he had other ideas. He was impatient with his father's clinging to past glory. Every year more people thronged the highway, people who had to find a place to sleep at night. Why shouldn't the Mochizukis help them? A big house and plenty of servants could be turned to advantage, the young man reasoned, and he vowed that things would be different when he took over as head of the family.

Inn or not, Mochizuki's house by the side of the road gave him a ringside seat to some of the most stirring events of a stirring period,

27

and a look at some of the towering figures who shaped those events.

He did not, however, see anything of the first of the three giants of the time, a savage Titan named Nobunaga, a wild, bold man possessed by a vision of a unified Japan. Nobunaga and Ieyasu had been allies in crushing Shingen's son. It had been one more step toward unity.

But before Nobunaga could reach his goal, one of his own barons did him in. It was a short-lived rebellion. Within two weeks Nobunaga's chief of staff, a little monkey-faced military virtuoso named Hideyoshi, had disengaged his army from its current campaign and brought it home to crush the insurgents.

Then there were two—Ieyasu and Hideyoshi, Nobunaga's greatest

Oda Nobunaga (*a book illustration by an unknown artist*)

ally and his greatest retainer. They fought each other in a campaign which neither could win, and because each had the sense to realize this, plus a deep-seated belief in diplomacy rather than war, they called off the fighting and settled down to make the best of things. Hideyoshi had firm control of Nobunaga's armies, but Ieyasu could afford to wait. He was not to be trapped into fighting the wrong war for the wrong reason, and so he became Hideyoshi's ally as he had been Nobunaga's, and the task of unifying the country went forward.

About this time Ieyasu created excitement in Suruga by moving his headquarters to Yoshimoto's old capital, where he had spent much of his boyhood as a hostage. There, in the city now called Shizuoka, he was closer to the center of his growing territories, and he was a scant ten miles from Okitsu.

Mochizuki's son was quick to point out new bustle on the highway. Couriers and tradesmen thronged the road, and the family found they were living more and more in the kitchen while some arrogant guest lorded over the best part of their house.

Mochizuki caught frequent glimpses of Ieyasu as that stolid lord rode out to his favorite sport of hawking, and in 1590 the almost-innkeeper at last had an opportunity to see Hideyoshi. The occasion was the final campaign to unite the country. Every clan had bowed but one, the Hojos, who held a vast territory northeast of Ieyasu's. Hideyoshi accomplished nothing by diplomacy, so he went to war.

As neighbor of the recalcitrant clan, Ieyasu was called upon to lead the attack, and Suruga soon stirred with preparation. Old warrior Mochizuki chafed because he would not march out as a soldier. Instead, a village elder, he was put in charge of one section of the highway. The Tokaido would bear the main thrust against the enemy, and word had come from Shizuoka that the potholes had to be filled in and the underbrush cut back. It was said around Okitsu that Mochizuki handled his work detail of peasants in very military fashion.

The reconstruction of Seikenji was also pushed to completion, because Hideyoshi was to rest there after his journey from Kyoto until his field headquarters was ready. Ieyasu had put off keeping his promise to rebuild the temple after he had burned it, for he never enjoyed spending money, but there was no help for it now.

Out at sea there were dozens of sails. A fleet went by to blockade the coast, and other ships moved up huge stores of rice and artillery and gunpowder. Then troops started marching through Okitsu, column after column, day after day, and Mochizuki, his stint on the highway done, spent hours watching them.

With Ichikawa, Tezuka, and the other elders of the town, he was at Seikenji in formal dress to await Hideyoshi's arrival. They had heard of his spectacular exit from Kyoto, over a bridge especially rebuilt for the occasion and along a road lined for two or three miles with stands so the populace could cheer him off in comfort. They had heard of his triumphal tour up the Tokaido, through the fresh green and bloom of April. He had paused at all the famous beauty spots to compose verses in their honor.

Mochizuki and his friends had agreed in advance that by the time Hideyoshi reached Seikenji he would be somewhat travel-worn. His magnificence would certainly have dulled since he left Kyoto. But when he appeared he dazzled them.

There were guards and banners in the van, and high officers, more guards, and more banners in the rear, but it was Hideyoshi who dominated the scene. He had been born the son of a foot soldier, but he had clawed his way to the top. Now he wore scarlet-laced armor, a great wig, and a shimmering gaudy helmet shaped like a Chinese headdress. He carried a massive gilt quiver on his back and a scarlet-lacquered bow in his hand, and his teeth were blackened, courtier fashion. His horse stepped proudly in golden-tasseled mail with ornaments of green and gold. The awed men of Okitsu, kneeling by the side of the road, let their mouths fall open.

The priests of Seikenji met the great man at the highway. The old abbot, his pink scalp gleaming, wore his robes of ceremony, sheer purple over white with a golden stole. His priests, more than twenty of them, massed behind him in black over white. Together

30

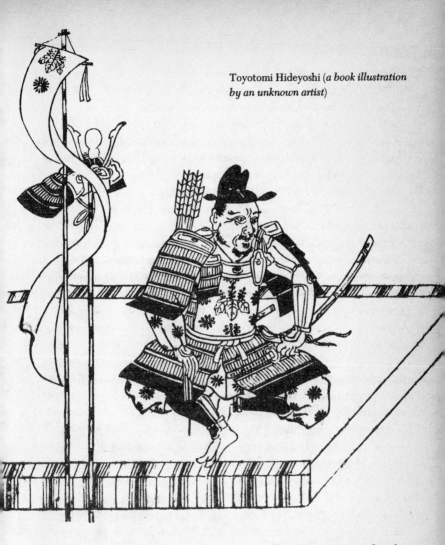

Toyotomi Hideyoshi (*a book illustration by an unknown artist*)

they escorted Hideyoshi and his party up the stone steps under the arching cedars and into the temple.

Back home, Mochizuki almost stuttered as he attempted to describe this scene to his family. A man used to the stubborn reticence of Ieyasu had to grope for words to describe a spectacle like that he had just witnessed. His wife and son interrupted him to report that more guests had imposed themselves then ever before; their demands for service kept family and servants scurrying. While Hideyoshi was in Okitsu most of the rest of Japan seemed to want to be there too.

All of the mighty daimyo who were involved in the campaign came to pay their respects, and first among these was Ieyasu.

Mochizuki watched from his gateway as Ieyasu came riding back from the front. His uniform was drab as ever. He had a handful of dusty companions and no banners at all.

Next day Mochizuki had it straight from a friend who lived near Seikenji, who had it straight from an acolyte who had served at dinner the night before, that Hideyoshi had interrupted the conversation to suggest that Ieyasu now had a golden opportunity to wipe him out, since he was almost unguarded in the heart of Suruga. In the raw silence that followed, reported the acolyte, only Ieyasu had seemed unperturbed. He had looked at Hideyoshi, laughed, and gone back to his fish.

There was another encounter at Seikenji which Mochizuki did not learn of, though the story is now known. Of all the visitors, none created a greater stir in Okitsu than Rikyu, who was neither lord nor warrior. Rikyu was the greatest of all tea masters, the man who perfected the quiet ceremony of drinking tea, and made its ritual the heart of an aesthetic code of restraint and naturalness which was to permeate all Japan. Hideyoshi was a man whose taste ran to gold chamber pots, and yet he sought out this priest of the perfectly simple. Perhaps he needed an antidote for luxury and a balm for war. At any rate he wanted the tea master near in any campaign, and so Rikyu came to Okitsu.

But he came late. By the time he reported to Seikenji, Hideyoshi's temper was frayed. What had kept him, he demanded of Rikyu. The tea master's reply was not meant to be flippant, but it certainly sounded irreverent. He answered that he had been drinking tea.

Hideyoshi was furious. Seizing one of Rikyu's cherished possessions, a delicate bamboo tea scoop that had been fashioned by his teacher, he snapped it in two. They say that Rikyu wept at this wanton destruction of something beautiful.

Seikenji still has this scoop, its slender bamboo handle patched with gold. In many ways, it embodies the essence of the tea ceremony—the simplest of natural materials chosen with consummate care and molded with unobtrusive artistry. Because Rikyu wept, it is called "Tears."

The bell tower of Seikenji (*a print by Hiratsuka*)

While Hideyoshi was staying at Seikenji he could not help hearing the temple's bell, for it was struck eighteen times at dawn and eighteen times at dusk. In those days the temple had no clock, and in the evening the bell was rung when failing light blurred the lines in the palm of the priest's hand. The villagers went to bed earlier on a cloudy day.

Seikenji's bell is famous for its tone, and it occurred to Hideyoshi that those of his soldiers who were besieging a stubborn outlying fort needed just such a bell to keep their spirits up. He wrote a note,

33

still in the temple archives, asking that it be loaned to him for the duration. The abbot had little choice but to comply.

A work party was organized among the villagers. Mochizuki offered the assistance of his gardener, which was accepted, and a great deal of advice, which was not. With a hubbub of fussing and shouting, men lowered the bell from its tower and inched it down the face of the hill. There were almost no vehicles on the Tokaido, which was mightily congested anyway, and so the bell was borne on timbers to the beach and lashed to barrels. The fishermen of Okitsu towed it across Suruga Bay for a short haul inland.

There was muttering in Okitsu, for the villagers were proud of Seikenji's old bell and had regulated their lives by it, but all agreed with Mochizuki that the abbot could not have done otherwise.

Hideyoshi stayed almost a week at the temple before word came that his headquarters was ready. Then he moved on to join his armies, a hundred and fifty thousand men who had circled the enemy's central fortress at Odawara.

But the traffic in Okitsu continued unabated. Couriers galloped through, looking resolute. Tradesmen hustled by, their pack horses loaded with everything from daily necessities to exotic European goods fresh from Portuguese ships. Women moved towards the front, eager to relieve the army's tedium. Mochizuki judged there would be no shortage of things to buy.

The pressure for accommodations was heavy as ever, and for the first time Mochizuki took an interest in his guests. He sought out those who were returning from the front, and through the long evenings of early summer he talked with them about the campaign.

On the beach he gossiped with the fishermen of Okitsu, who daily delivered their catches to Hideyoshi's commissariat, grumbling all the while. They had counted on these hostilities to make them rich, but the price of fish never did go up. Mochizuki's son said that the low prices were a sign of Hideyoshi's generalship, and the same thought must have occurred to the besieged Hojos. They had believed it impossible to supply so vast an army.

So summer ran its course, and at last on one hot August day in

A reluctant Mochizuki is pushed deeper into innkeeping

1590 word sped down the Tokaido and buzzed through the streets of Okitsu to reach Mochizuki where he was napping in a cool room off the garden. The embattled fortress of the Hojos had fallen. A few days later it was learned that the elders of the defeated clan had acted on a broad hint and disemboweled themselves. Japan was a united country.

To the people of Okitsu, the victory meant a change of overlords. Ieyasu took over the enemy's great territories, relinquishing his capital at Shizuoka to found a new one in the scrubby village of Edo, which speedily exhibited the growing pains that have marked so much of its history, and still do, now that it is called Tokyo.

Suruga was parceled out to Hideyoshi's generals. It was the third change in twenty years: Shingen had snatched the province from

Fishermen with their nets
(*a book illustration
by Kyuran*)

Yoshimoto, Ieyasu had wrested it from Shingen's son, and now Ieyasu was moving on to bigger things. The news was received in the village streets with general indifference. The people's concern was how to meet their taxes, not who pocketed them at the top.

But Mochizuki felt differently. He might have carried a burning hatred of Ieyasu, for Ieyasu's victories had cost him his status as a samurai, but instead he developed a pride in Ieyasu's triumphs. "This is the man to whom I surrendered," his attitude seemed to say, "and a very great lord he is—worthy of any man's surrender." Mochizuki felt a sense of loss at Ieyasu's leaving.

Hideyoshi started back to Kyoto, and again he stopped at Seikenji. The morning after he left, Mochizuki, Ichikawa, Tezuka, and the other elders of the village trooped to the temple. They knelt stiffly in an anteroom while a priest brought out the scroll that they had come to see. He deigned to tell them what they already knew: that on Hideyoshi's return visit the abbot had asked him to set down his impressions, and that the great lord had graciously dictated a record of his two stops. Clearing his throat importantly, the priest read:

"Leaving the capital in early April, I came to the temple of Seikenji in the province of Suruga. The scenery was superb there. Especially lovely were the pines at Miho, the moonlight on the bay, and the snow on Fuji. Attracted by flowers seen through the green leaves of the garden, I stayed my palanquin and dallied there for five or six days. Abbot Daiki is a priest who has attained the true spirit of a Zen monk, and has risen so high above the common herd that I invited him to join our circle in the guest room.

"After defeating my enemies, I went far into the northeast, subduing the local inhabitants to my heart's content, and then on my way back to Kyoto I returned to the temple in the middle of September. The trees which were adorned with flowers in April had leaves of crimson now. I was reminded of the poem written by Priest No-in about his own journey —

> I left the capital behind
> When it was wrapped in springtime mists
> But now the autumn wind blows here
> At Shirakawa Barrier.

A reluctant Mochizuki is pushed deeper into innkeeping

—and so I wrote some poems myself:

> Seikenji's bright flowers,
> Bidding welcome from a distance,
> Nearer, become autumn-crimsoned leaves.

and

> I praise again the view of Tago Bay,°
> Waves white against the shore,
> Snow white on Fuji-san.

Dictated by
Toyotomi Hideyoshi"

When he had finished reading, the priest unrolled the scroll and held it up for the men of Okitsu to see. They gazed at it, sucked in their breaths reverently, and bowed deeply.

Despite Hideyoshi's promise to return Seikenji's bell, the priests themselves had to go and fetch it back. Again they organized a work party, and again Mochizuki released his useful gardener to help. The bell was floated back across Suruga Bay, hauled up the face of the hill, and raised into its tower. Its only scar from wartime service is that from being dragged overland on the other end of its journey, part of its inscription is worn away, but the year of its casting, 1314 by the Western calendar, is legible. Today it is still struck eighteen times at dawn and dusk, and at midnight on New Year's Eve one hundred and eight times, for that is the number of the sins of man.

After the victory that made Japan one country under one ruler —ostensibly the shadowy Emperor but in reality Hideyoshi—there was new spirit in the land. Mochizuki felt it himself and he found it in the travelers who came his way. The nation had new energy, new optimism, and it gazed at new horizons. Japan was eager for adventure and ready for conquest. Conquest was what Hideyoshi had in mind.

When word reached villages like Okitsu that Hideyoshi had determined to conquer China, no one doubted he would do just that.

° Tago Bay is an old, poetic name for Suruga Bay.

Mochizuki, for one, quoted with approval Hideyoshi's pronouncement: "I shall do it as easily as a man rolls up a piece of matting."

This time the burden of supplying manpower for the campaign fell on southwestern Japan. Only a few fishermen's sons were drafted from Okitsu to help ferry the army across the straits to Korea, for that hapless kingdom was to play its usual role as battlefield before the gates of China. Mochizuki envied these lads their participation in what everyone was certain would be a triumphant adventure.

It may have been villages like Okitsu that felt the first chill doubts of victory. Their fishermen's sons never came back. They were caught in the fateful first disaster of the war.

It had not occurred to these young sailors that they might have to fight. Fighting was a job for the land. They delivered their troops, and then lolled in the harbor at Pusan, caught in the age-old hurry-up-and-wait of war. They were probably swapping fish stories when a Korean navy no one had given any thought to, headed by an admiral no one had ever heard of, struck at them, scattered them, and sunk them. The Koreans had a fearsome ship with a dragon's mouth that belched gunfire and flaming arrows, and more important, with armored sides and an armored roof to protect its fighters while they rained destruction on a fleet of fishing boats. Hideyoshi had made a classic mistake. He had attempted an oversea invasion without a navy.

The Japanese armies never reached the China frontier, but the war dragged on for six years, until the country was heartily sick of it. When it ended, Hideyoshi was dead, though not in battle, for he vacillated and procrastinated but he never did go to Korea himself. At his death, all his hopes of dynasty were pinned on a five-year-old son. And whether those hopes would ever come to fruition depended on Ieyasu, who was now the country's strong man.

He fought one great campaign to convince a few skeptics and, that over, he had the Emperor appoint him Shogun. To give him his full title, he was now Seii-Tai-Shogun—Barbarian-Quelling Generalissimo—and the country's military governor. It was a title Hideyoshi had never dared appropriate, for he was not of the right blood. Confirmed as the real ruler of the empire, Ieyasu set about to found his own dynasty, the dynasty of his own Tokugawa family. As for Hideyoshi's son, the boy growing up in Osaka Castle, he left his fate to the fullness of time.

Now that Ieyasu's capital, Edo, was to all intents the capital of the country, it began to grow at a dizzy pace. The daimyo, the great lords, flocked there. Naturally they wanted to be close to the center of things, and, besides, there was a very good chance that Ieyasu would construe absence to be unfriendly. He welcomed them to the city of the Tokugawas, and gave them the privilege of making themselves poorer by constructing his vast castle and all its fortifications.

Mochizuki felt a vicarious sense of fulfillment. All of Japan had surrendered to Ieyasu now, and in doing so had wiped the last stain from Mochizuki's honor. There could be no disgrace in having bowed to a man to whom everyone else bowed. But Ieyasu's triumph, while it salved Mochizuki's pride in one way, wounded it in another: it pushed his family further into innkeeping.

Daimyo strutting with mettlesome pomp to and from Edo, they too had to sleep at night. Of course Ichikawa and Tezuka were Okitsu's Headmen, and since their houses were even larger than Mochizuki's, one of them was first to be called on when some daimyo decided to spend the night. But Mochizuki had to take care of lesser lords, and he took the overflow from the entourage of any daimyo who stopped at Ichikawa's or Tezuka's, for an entire retinue could not be accommodated under one roof. And when the highway was congested and both Ichikawa's and Tezuka's houses were already reserved, Mochizuki sometimes found himself playing host to some difficult daimyo.

Mochizuki habitually referred to these visits as temporary afflictions, but his son pointed out that they gave every sign of becoming permanent. All the daimyo were building mansions for themselves in the Tokugawa capital of Edo, and it seemed they intended to divide their time between that city and their home provinces.

Of the country's two hundred and fifty daimyo (the number varied from time to time according to the whim of fate and the Shogun), about one hundred and fifty traveled the Tokaido to reach Edo. Their journeys would make the highway busier than ever before in time of peace, the younger Mochizuki argued, and, as if to bear him out, the government—the Tokugawa government, Ieyasu's government—issued a series of laws to make travel safer, more comfortable, and, bureaucrats being bureaucrats, more systematic.

In 1601, the government established fifty-three stations along the Tokaido between Edo and Kyoto. Each designated town or village was directed to set up a transportation office where privileged travelers could obtain horses and men to relay them on their way; inevitably inns and restaurants clustered around these transportation offices. Okitsu was station number seventeen, numbering from Edo.

Of course it did not take fifty-three days to travel the three hundred and five miles from Edo to Kyoto. Fifteen days were usually ample for a leisurely journey, and a man passed through several stations during one day. It was only about three miles from Yui, the sixteenth station, to Okitsu, and about the same distance past Okitsu to the eighteenth station, Shimizu.

Before the daimyo had anywhere near finished building the great walled castle in Edo, Ieyasu gave them another project. He had decided to honor the old Japanese custom of retirement. His son would be appointed Shogun in his place, thus establishing the succession of his Tokugawa family, while he himself retired to Shizuoka to pull the strings from there. So the daimyo were permitted to build another castle at Shizuoka, and since it burned just as it was being completed, they were doubly honored.

When one of his mistresses wondered aloud why they were moving to Shizuoka, Ieyasu told her. Of all Japan, he said, he loved Suruga best: first, because it had Mount Fuji; second, because it provided good hawking; and, third, because its balmy climate brought the season's first mad-apples, the fruit of the eggplant. Mad-apples, hawks, and Fuji form a prominent triad of lucky symbols. Ieyasu was stepping out of character to be clever for the lady, but there is no doubt he loved Suruga best.

With Ieyasu's retirement a fact, Mochizuki felt that he could post-

A reluctant Mochizuki is pushed deeper into innkeeping

Changing horses and bearers at a Tokaido post station, while one of the post-house staff supervises from the right (*a print by Hiroshige*)

pone his own retirement no longer. He had long procrastinated about releasing headship of his family, for he knew that there was a gulf between himself and his son. It was not that retirement itself would make such a difference. He knew that his son would defer to him as long as he was around to be deferred to. But he knew also that his retirement would foreshadow change. He had been, though he no longer was, a samurai, and he would think as a samurai and carry himself as a samurai as long as he lived. But he had lost his status when his son was only entering on manhood. To Mochizuki it seemed that the boy had adjusted all too easily; painlessly he had dropped a samurai's bearing; he had become a commoner, he now thought as a commoner. In rare moments when Mochizuki felt old and tired, he let himself think the whole bitter thought: his son was a commoner and he thought like a tradesman.

Mochizuki knew in his heart that his home was an inn. From the time that Ieyasu had retired to Shizuoka, only two stations away, the congestion in that city was so great that a wise traveler seldom attempted to stay there. A station like Okitsu was a much more sensible choice, and the Mochizuki house was usually filled. The old man knew in his heart that his home was an inn, but he wrapped himself in dignified silence and pretended to ignore the strangers.

1947 *and* 1605–1621

CHAPTER FOUR

In which I become acquainted with the inn—three and a quarter centuries after its establishment is formally acknowledged

PRINCIPAL CHARACTERS

1947

Among the people of the inn:

Isako, *mistress of the inn today*
Mochizuki Ryozo, *her father*

1605–1621

Gen'emon, *ancestor of the Shimizu Mochizukis (the family of Isako and her father), Headman of his village, and friend of Ieyasu*

Tokugawa Ieyasu, *who rounds out his life and is enshrined as deity of the new Japan*

Will Adams, *the first Englishman in Japan, friend to both Ieyasu and Mochizuki*

Don Rodrigo de Vivero y Vellasco, *shipwrecked Spanish governor of the Philippines*

and among the people of the inn:

Mochizuki
His son

The crest of
Tokugawa Ieyasu

THERE ARE TIMES, during long quiet nights at the Minaguchi-ya, when something wakens me—a change in the rhythm of the waves scouring the beach, or the watchman's wooden clappers as he makes his rounds. I lie relaxed, at peace, and sometimes in the friendly darkness I can see Ieyasu riding out with a band of his retainers for a day's hawking. Sometimes I can sense the mounting chagrin of that first Mochizuki of Okitsu as more and more travelers forced him deeper into innkeeping. Sometimes I think back on my own first visit to the Minaguchi-ya . . .

By the time I arrived in Japan in April, 1947, General MacArthur's headquarters had placed almost all public places "off limits" to members of the Occupation. Theatres, restaurants, and hotels, not to mention banks and bathhouses, were denied to us, and a large and energetic corps of military policemen were enthusiastically enforcing the order.

It was true, of course, that the Army had appropriated some of the best Japanese theatres to show us American movies, that its mess halls dispensed ample if unexciting food, and that it had taken over most of Japan's "Western-style" resort hotels so that we could spend an occasional holiday in chummy togetherness, safely apart from what Headquarters called "indigenous personnel."

But as a warm spring evolved through a sultry rainy season into a hot summer, I found that I was unsuccessful each time I applied for a reservation at any of the Army's hotels near enough to Yokohama for a weekend jaunt. And, though it may have been sour grapes, I became increasingly cool to the idea of military-supervised recreation in a military-operated establishment. I listened agog as old-timers told of bacchanalian or idyllic (depending on the old-timer) weekends at some Japanese spa before the Occupation became so well organized, and I told myself that I wanted to break through the hedge of restrictions to get closer to Japan and the Japanese. Quite truthfully, like many of my co-workers, I was captivated by what I could see of the country.

At the time when I was feeling most frustrated, I found in the Nippon *Times* a little advertisement stating that the Minaguchi-ya, an inn in Okitsu, had been placed "on limits," and was therefore open to Occupationaires. Investigation revealed that Okitsu was a seaside village southwest of Tokyo about five hours by train. I enlisted my roommate and made a reservation.

Members of the Occupation paid nothing to ride Japanese railroads in those days, but a weekend trip was not simply a matter of getting on a train pointed in the right direction. Orders had to be applied for and authorizations obtained, all in good, complicated military form. Our project was not simplified by the fact that the special second-class coaches (there was no first class), which were hooked onto Japanese trains for the exclusive use of Allied personnel, stopped about an hour short of Okitsu. Without these special coaches to ride in, it was considered in some quarters legally questionable whether we had any right to go there.

On top of everything else, we were required to carry with us food for our entire weekend. That order had considerable logic behind it. There was scarcely enough food in Japan for the Japanese, and there was little point in allowing any of it to be diverted to well-fed Americans. The campaign to keep us from eating the Japanese into starvation was zestfully reinforced by the Army Medical Department, who devised a propaganda barrage to convince us that Japanese food, because of the human fertilizer used to grow it, was so unsanitary as to be almost instantly fatal. Stories were rife concerning individuals whose health was undermined for life by consumption of a local tomato.

As I now recall the difficulties then involved in such a safari, it seems a little incredible that we ever went anywhere. But early on a hot and humid Saturday afternoon we climbed aboard a train, clutching our travel authorities and feeling like pack horses beneath great bags of food. We had no intention of going hungry.

Nearly four hours later we lugged off our stuff at the railroad division point of Numazu, as far as our Allied cars traveled. The Army had an RTO, or Rail Transportation Office, there, and we opened discussions about going on to Okitsu. Fortunately, the staff of that office was, at least at that moment, entirely Japanese. We convinced them that we really wanted to go to Okitsu, and, further, that we bore bona-fide military orders directing us to go there. It was an inevitable corollary that if we didn't get there, General MacArthur was going to be displeased. On this basis we came to speedy agreement that we must simply ignore the legal difficulties raised by there not being an Allied car. Unbefitting though it was, we would have to complete our journey on a strictly indigenous train.

The coaches used by the Japanese were badly run-down and hopelessly crowded. We were therefore ushered to the baggage car. The crew received us with ceremony and became positively cordial when I offered a few American cigarettes. This was not an entirely unselfish gesture on my part. I am a nonsmoker and I found the aroma of early postwar Japanese cigarettes so upsetting that I almost believed the unbelievable rumors concerning their ingredients.

The standard Japanese packing material is rice-straw matting. This makes baggage ideal to loll upon. We stretched out in front of the wide-open doors of the baggage car, and as the train rolled along the coast we reveled in the lush green of the rice paddies backed by the sea on one side and the magnificent cone of Fuji on the other.

Any qualms about our arrival in Okitsu were quickly dispelled. Our friends back at the RTO in Numazu had telephoned ahead. When our train pulled in, the station master was planted opposite the doorway of our car, defying the heat in black uniform, red-banded cap, and white gloves.

Delighted to exercise his English, he bowed us to his office for a cup of fragrant green tea while we waited for the bicycle-cart from the Minaguchi-ya to carry our paraphernalia. And his second-in-command personally escorted us up the main street to the inn.

It was then I first experienced the Minaguchi-ya's gracious welcome. The quick gathering of the staff, their expressions of pleasure that we had honored their house, the low bows and warm smiles conveyed a greeting which seemed very personal even on our first visit.

Our room, the Pine Room it was called, was open to the garden on three sides. We heard the surf just over the wall and felt the fresh salt breeze. Cool damp towels were brought so that we could wipe sweaty grime from face and hands. Tea appeared with little cakes.

Maids brought kimonos of crisp cotton, helped us into them, and led us through rambling corridors to the bath. There Yoshi was in charge, wreathed in steam, stocky, bald, and smiling. He carefully invited us to read the neat sign that advised novices like us that Japanese bath etiquette requires one to soap and rinse before entering the tub. He scrubbed our backs with a vegetable sponge and tempered the hot water until he thought we could stand it. We doused off the last bit of suds and climbed into the big pine tub. The water at first was almost unbearably hot, then blissfully relaxing. That smooth, fragrant old tub, which has since given way to a sparkling tile pool, could easily accommodate four or five. Two of us stretched full length.

Back in our garden room, our bodies cool and clean and free in kimonos, we lay utterly relaxed on the smooth *tatami*, thick straw mats that form the loveliest floor covering yet devised by man.

From the hallway there was a soft *"Gomen nasai"* ("I beg your pardon"), and our hostess, Isako, made her appearance. She welcomed us and we tried to tell her how happy we were to be there. We turned over to her our canned rations with perfect confidence that no matter what came back we would eat well. The Minaguchi-ya had put us serenely at ease, but Isako was worried. She was worried about the language problem. To us there seemed no problem at all. Hospitality flowed around us. Our miserable Japanese and her scanty English seemed perfectly adequate, but she let us know that rescue was at hand. We had never felt less like being rescued, but we were unable to tell her so. Her papa, she explained, spoke English, and he was on his way.

A little later she was back with him. We saw at once where Isako got her height. Her father was taller than I, thin and almost boyishly gangling. His face crinkled with good humor.

We exchanged bows and he presented his card. His name was Ryozo Mochizuki. He lived in the neighboring city of Shimizu, he said, only three or four miles away, and when his daughter had phoned he had come by bicycle to assist us.

We assured Isako, through him, that we wanted for nothing and that we placed ourselves in her hands as far as dinner was concerned. We had, we hurriedly emphasized, no special affection for any of the food we had brought.

She withdrew, looking relieved, and we talked with her father. He excused himself when our dinner appeared—fat shrimp and fresh vegetables *tempura*, dipped in batter and cooked golden brown in sweet oil, sliced ripe tomatoes and cucumbers, white rice, and for dessert, cool red watermelon. I hadn't eaten so well since I reached Japan. We justified our banquet with the thought that the food we had brought might be a nice change for the people of the inn.

The next morning Mr. Mochizuki was back before we were up, to make sure our breakfast eggs were cooked the way we wanted them. Fresh eggs—my first in months (the Army was struggling to exhaust its stocks of the powdered variety): I still remember that breakfast.

Our Sunday was full, in a lazy way. We swam in the surf. We ambled along the village street, window-shopping the meager stocks and trying to keep up with a chorus of "hellos" and "good-byes" from a multitude of small fry. And we chatted with Mr. Mochizuki, fascinated by his stories of that part of Japan.

In my subsequent visits to the Minaguchi-ya I talked often with Mr. Mochizuki. He was one of those who opened Japan to me.

It was he who first told me of that mountain warrior Shingen.

"Mochizuki is a mountain name," he told me. "It means full moon. It's a very common name in Suruga. My family are Mochizukis and the family of this inn are Mochizukis, but we weren't related until Isako married here. Finding mountain names hereabouts shows how mountain people kept pushing towards the sea."

And it was Mr. Mochizuki from whom I first heard of Ieyasu. He pointed out the Tokugawa crest, used to decorate the Minaguchi-ya's finest suite: three hollyhock leaves in a circle. After my eyes had been opened to that crest I saw it everywhere. The Tokugawa descendants of Ieyasu ruled for two and a half centuries and left their mark all over the country.

Mr. Mochizuki has a warm regard for Ieyasu, and with good reason, for he traces to that great lord his own family's once substantial fortunes. It seems they were acquired by an ancestor named Gen'emon, who was lucky enough to be friendly with Ieyasu and smart enough to make the most of it.

It happened after Ieyasu had relinquished the title of Shogun to his son and had retired to his new castle in Shizuoka. Gen'emon's village was not far away, off towards a range of foothills.

Gen'emon was a commoner, but nevertheless a substantial citizen. He was one of the landed gentry, the solid stock from which the great daimyo families had risen. He was Headman of his village, as his father had been before him and his son would be after him. He kept the law and he collected taxes, and since he was expected to reward himself suitably out of the taxes before he passed them up the ladder, he lived very well and managed to put something aside. In later times, many a village Headman became a banker with his capital, and so did Gen'emon's descendants, but that is another story.

His village consisted of a few houses and a large range of paddies, bamboo groves, and rough wooded lands. It made ideal hunting ground, and Ieyasu, whose only real pleasure was hawking, came there often.

When the First Lord of the Empire went hunting it was no minor excursion. Most of his retainers went along, because Ieyasu liked to observe how they stood up to a rigorous day on foot, climbing steep places, wading streams, and maintaining a hard pace. He took the ladies, too, a few in sedan chairs, but most of them on horseback, sitting on crimson cushions with wide country-women's hats to shade their faces. Naturally there were servants, and, of course, the falconers with their hawks.

The hawks, like the ladies, rode. Each was carried on the arm of his trainer, hooded until released to fly. The Japanese are good at training birds. When the command was given, the bird took to the air like a thing of vengeance, and moments later the hapless prey felt great claws strike deep in its back. Often the game was bigger than the hawk, but the bird was trained to hold on till its master arrived, one claw deep in the animal, the other anchored to some solid thing. It was a great dishonor to a trainer if his hawk lost its prey. It happened very seldom.

Sometimes on these expeditions the servants would go ahead and

A falconer
and his attendant
(*a book illustration
by Jichosai*)

prepare a meal in the open, but when they hunted in Gen'emon's territory Ieyasu liked to stop at his house and eat simple country dishes, such as potatoes baked in the coals.

Gen'emon was always asked to join the party, for Ieyasu took a great liking to this frank and open country man, and no doubt he also approved of the way the village was run.

For instance, they never found traps in Gen'emon's area. Ieyasu disliked intensely to have other people go after game in the grounds where he hawked, and he was inclined to be huffy when they encountered anyone there without good reason. Once they came across an oil-seller who compounded his crime by being insolent, so Ieyasu handed his sword to a retainer and told him to cut the fellow down. It was done, but the man went on walking a few paces before falling divided into two. This, of course, was a great testimonial to the sword, which they promptly christened "Oil-seller."

Along with earning respect for the way he managed, Gen'emon also had the ability to make Ieyasu laugh, and Ieyasu was not a man who laughed easily. No doubt it was the Headman's earthy humor that turned the trick, but Ieyasu, when he was with Gen'emon, laughed loud and often.

There was one day when he stopped by to find the village chief laid up with a painful affliction in which his scrotum was swollen to prodigious size. Even in this predicament, Gen'emon was able to laugh at himself, and Ieyasu was vastly entertained, so entertained that he thought the ladies ought to share in the fun. Gen'emon was understandably reluctant, but Ieyasu had a way with him, besides being an all-powerful monarch. So the ladies had a peek at the spectacle, and as a reward Ieyasu told Gen'emon he could have all the land he could walk around in one day.

Gen'emon was not a man who would let pain balk an opportunity like that, and by a sunrise-to-sunset hike he acquired a sizable fortune, one which was kept intact until the generation before Isako's father's found that by diligent efforts they could squander most of it, appropriately, perhaps, on women.

With Mr. Mochizuki I have visited that house in which Gen'emon entertained Ieyasu. It was rebuilt a hundred and fifty years ago, and is probably smaller than it was in Gen'emon's time, with a tile roof now instead of heavy thatch. Still it is a great sprawling farmhouse, set in the bamboo grove which gave Gen'emon his local title, "The Bamboo Lord."

The village name is Mizunashi. It was christened by Ieyasu after Gen'emon gave him an especially delicious water pear, *mizunashi* being the Japanese name for that fruit. In the main room of the house, in the place of honor, stands a big, plain wooden chest, all that is left of Ieyasu's gifts. No one today is exactly sure what is inside—a few kimonos, a sword or two. There is a family belief that whoever opens the chest will be blinded. The great-grandfather of the present owner did open the chest, and he did go blind, though not immediately, and no one has seen fit to test the superstition since.

Once there was a warehouse filled with treasures. There were three hundred swords, chest upon chest of kimonos, dozens of scroll paintings by great artists. There were solid-gold braziers, with solid-gold tongs to handle the charcoal. All these things are gone now, including the warehouse. There remain only the old chest in the place of honor in the house, and the name Mizunashi, as reminders of the days when Ieyasu hunted and laughed there.

Ieyasu went to Okitsu, too, drawn by old associations. He was partial to Seikenji's classical garden, to which his eyes had often strayed when as a boy he was supposed to be studying his lessons. Very likely it was his boy's imagination that saw in certain stones the shapes of animals. One was a tiger, another a cow, and a third a turtle. Now that he ruled the empire, a light-hearted reminiscence was enough to christen those stones for all time, and so they are known today as the stones that Ieyasu named—the Tiger, the Cow, and the Turtle.

He planted five saplings in the garden. The plum, the oak, and the persimmon still live, but the pine and the tangerine have died.

The abbot sometimes planned entertainments for him, like a performance of Noh dance-drama. Ieyasu was not an ardent devotee of Noh, but it was part of his age and like others of his class he sometimes took a role, though his stocky figure and inability to keep time generated more laughter than applause. On one occasion the abbot asked him what plays he would like to see, and so he wrote out the program of his choice, a program still cherished at Seikenji. He listed eight dramas, for this was to be an all-day affair. Understandably, his attention wandered from the stage at times, and once he leaned to an aide and remarked, "What I was thinking was that it is just about the right time to cut bamboos for the banner poles." Certainly his mind was never far from military matters and he could not forget his unsolved problem, that son of Hideyoshi's, growing up in Osaka Castle.

Whenever Ieyasu visited Okitsu, the elder Mochizuki always made a special effort to catch a glimpse of him, and then Mochizuki family and servants steeled themselves for a flood of too-familiar reminiscence. Between Ieyasu's visits, Mochizuki enlivened his retirement by watching the crowds on the Tokaido. They were to him a never-ending parade: the daimyo and their strutting retainers, the beggars and the peddlers and the priests, and now a new and exotic element—foreigners.

The first big show was put on by the Koreans. Ieyasu worked very hard to mend relations after Hideyoshi's disastrous invasion, and by 1607 the Koreans were sufficiently mollified to send a mission to formalize the peace. Both sides had reasons to promote friendship. They liked to trade across the straits, and each used the other to play off China.

The Shogunate went all out to impress its guests from the mainland. The highway was cleaned and repaired, cisterns were dug so that farmers and villagers could lay the dust, and new rest houses were built at short intervals. In each of these, men in formal dress waited with tea, tobacco, cake, and fruit. To brighten late-evening arrivals and early-morning departures, villagers were ordered to hang lanterns in front of their houses, and cheering bonfires were set along the way. Pontoon bridges were built across rivers, and at the swift-running Oi, where a bridge was impossible and fording unavoidable, fourteen hundred coolies were mobilized as a human dam, to slow the current with their bodies. (It was for one of the Koreans' later missions that the new road was built between Okitsu and Yui in 1655, straight over Satta, replacing the hazardous coastal path; the route over the mountain was steep, but it averted the dangers of being washed into the sea or hit by falling rocks.)

The procession was worth coming miles to see. The Koreans sent about three hundred men, but their party was so swelled by escorts which the Shogun ordered the daimyo to provide, that the daimyo themselves were told to stay off the highway.

Leading off were massed streamers and flags, and a guard armed with bows and arrows, crescent-shaped swords, and three-pronged spears. Then there was a thirty-piece band of flutes, trumpets, and gongs. All of these were on horseback, as were the even larger guard that followed. Then came a column of pages, the palanquin of the chief envoy, more pages and the palanquin of the chief senior offi-

The Korean ambassador in his procession (*a print attributed to Moronobu*)

cial, more pages and the palanquins of the envoy's adviser, the envoy's physician, and another adviser. Sixty mounted officials and two drums brought up the rear.

The chief envoy was always lodged in a temple and so in Okitsu it was Seikenji that played host. But Mochizuki got much more than a spectator's view of the Koreans, for his house, along with Ichikawa's, Tezuka's, and every inn in town, was pressed into service to house the lesser lights. The dinner ordered for the guests was elaborately formal and Mochizuki's son spared no effort to make it as impressive as possible; he knew that in Edo the chefs of the city's finest brothels had been drafted for the Koreans' kitchens and he was determined that his food should not suffer by comparison.

The Ryukyuans were next to provide spectacle on the Tokaido, though not exactly of their own accord. In 1609, as a part of Ieyasu's drive to promote foreign trade, the powerful daimyo of Satsuma, whose fief was the southwest corner of Kyushu, led an expedition against the islands. He went in virtuous anger, for the Ryukyuans had for a long time carelessly neglected to send tribute. Their oversight was understandable, since they considered themselves a part of China.

The Lord of Satsuma disillusioned them on this score. He got his tribute, and he also brought back the king and his two sons. The next year he escorted them to Shizuoka and presented them to Ieyasu. The king made a splendid gift of silver and silk, and promised to keep his ports open to Japanese merchantmen, and not to forget what nation he was a part of.

Then the whole expedition started for Edo to repeat the performance before Ieyasu's son, the Shogun. Before they reached Okitsu, it became apparent that one of the young princes was ill and so they halted at Seikenji. It was an unscheduled stop and the Mochizukis were thrown into a frenzy when they and the others along the street were suddenly ordered to accommodate members of the party.

Everything possible was done for the boy, but he died in the temple and was buried on the mountainside under tall cedars.

In the years that followed, whenever the Ryukyuans sent a mission to Japan they stopped at Seikenji. They called on the abbot and offered the gifts they had brought, incense, or lacquerware, or perhaps a stone lantern. Then they were guided to the prince's grave and they did reverence. There were many such visits, for, like the Koreans, the Ryukyuans continued to send missions for more than two centuries.

The Ryukyuans, who came not as equals but as vassals, did not get the lavish treatment accorded the Koreans, but their processions were even larger. This was because they were always escorted by the Lord of Satsuma, who was much more important than the daimyo who escorted the Koreans, and wanted no one to forget that fact. He considered that the Ryukyuan party of less than a hundred was not impressive, and so he invariably mustered about four thousand of his own men to round out the procession, and each station where they stopped along the way had to provide five thousand men and a thousand horses to move them to their next stop.

Not only was the Ryukyuan procession larger than the Korean, but their music was more appealing. To flutes, gongs, and drums they added a number of samisen, a guitar-like instrument which so charmed the Japanese that they adopted it for their own. The Ryukyuans always entered Edo behind a couple of handsome youths playing the samisen. It was a very stylish touch.

But Koreans and Ryukyuans were in a sense cousins of the Japanese. It was Europeans who created the greatest interest along the Tokaido.

The Jesuit priests of Portugal had been in Japan for sixty years, and as the center of power shifted to Edo and Shizuoka, Mochizuki saw their black-robed figures more and more frequently. Lately they had competition, for brown-robed Franciscans had entered the picture. One of them came frequently to Okitsu, and talked in the street to whatever curious crowd gathered. It was reported to Mochizuki's son that one of his maids, an impressionable girl of fifteen, frequently slipped out to listen to this priest, and later held forth in the kitchen about the new doctrine.

Soon after Ieyasu moved back to Shizuoka, Jesuits and Franciscans each built a church there, and, in not very friendly rivalry, set about to propagate the faith, reaching even within the moated walls of the castle.

But not all foreigners were missionaries. Old Mochizuki's favorite was a doughty Englishman straight from the London of Queen Bess and Shakespeare. His name was Will Adams, but to the Japanese he was Anjin-sama, "Mr. Pilot," the first Englishman in Japan. He was more than that to Mochizuki: he was the first European to stay in his home, and the old man took such delight in Adams's company that he was almost grateful that innkeeping had made it possible.

They took a great liking to each other, and Mochizuki never tired of hearing Adams's stories, though they were hard to believe. Here was a man who had started as an apprentice seaman at Limehouse, who had commanded a ship when Drake defeated the Spanish Armada, and who ended as a Japanese samurai.

Mochizuki especially liked to hear about the calamitous voyage that had brought Adams to Japan, and whenever the Englishman stopped at the inn his old host would soon join him, calling for the maids to bring saké and keep on bringing it.

"Your cup, Anjin-sama," Mochizuki would cry as he finished the preliminaries of formal welcome, and he would hardly set the bottle down before he would ask, "Tell me about the voyage."

"But I've told you all that many times, my friend," Adams would reply, downing his wine.

"Tell me again," Mochizuki would beg, refilling the cup.

"Ah, well," Adams would begin, "you know that I had risen through 'prenticeship to be master and pilot in Her Majesty's ships —to good Queen Bess!" And then Englishman and Japanese would drink a toast to a great red-headed Queen on the other side of the world.

When, on a particular afternoon in 1609, the two men had toasted Elizabeth, and thoughtfully added a toast to Ieyasu, so as not to play favorites, Adams took up his story.

"When the Indish traffic began from Holland, I was desirous to make a little experience of the small knowledge which God had given me. So, in the year of our Lord 1598"—Mochizuki blinked, and Adams substituted the Japanese year-name—"I was hired for Pilot Major of a fleet of five sail, which was made ready by the Indish Company.

"Being June ere we set sail, it was too late ere we came to the line to pass it against contrary winds. About the middest of September we found southerly winds, but our men were many sick then, so that we were forced to go to the coast of Guinea—Africa, d'ye remember?" Adams was not convinced that his Okitsu friend had mastered the elements of geography he had tried to teach.

"Yes, yes," Mochizuki answered. Africa was in truth a foggy concept but he didn't want the story interrupted.

"Ah," said Adams doubtfully. "Well, let this tray stand for Africa, and this for South America, and this bottle—" he took a porcelain bottle in which hot wine had been served, and shook it to make sure it was empty "—shall stand for Japan."

And so, stabbing at the trays and tracing a course across the *tatami* mats, Adams once more told his friend a story of horror at sea. The five ships had landed their sick on Africa's sweltering Guinea coast, but many died and few recovered in that miasmic climate. Leaving, they came upon the island of Annabon. The enemy Portuguese controlled the place and forbade them to land, but land they did and took the town. While the Portuguese harassed them from the interior they refreshed themselves with "oxen, oranges, and divers fruites," but the air was so unwholesome "that as one bettered another fell sick." When they left the island they burned the town to teach the Portuguese hospitality.

It was a voyage of five months across the South Atlantic. One ship's mast fell overboard, and it gave them much trouble to set a new mast at sea. They reached the Strait of Magellan on April 6, 1599.

For six days winds were favorable. They might have gone through the Strait, but they used the time to gather wood and provisions on shore. Then the winds shifted and they were bottled up for the long southern winter. Snow lay deep, the cold was bitter, and food was scarce. Many died of hunger.

It was late September before they left the Strait. They had set a meeting place in case they should be separated by storms, but when that happened one ship turned tail and sailed back to Holland, one continued across the Pacific and was captured by the Portuguese in the East Indies, and one made her way up the coast of South America and was captured by the Spaniards at Valparaiso.

Adams's ship waited for a month alone at the rendezvous point, then struck out for the coast of Chile to forage for food. A shore party of twenty-three men including Adams's brother Thomas was ambushed and killed by natives.

Sailing back to the appointed meeting place, the survivors were overjoyed to find the fifth ship of their fleet waiting there. Both crews were by now so understrength that the sensible thing would have been to sail one ship and abandon the other, but the two captains could not agree on whose ship would be sacrificed and at length both set out across the Pacific for their original destination, Japan. In February they encountered a violent storm. One vessel was never seen again and Adams's ship sailed on alone.

Adams hated to talk about that last terrible lap of the voyage, but Mochizuki could imagine it. Supplies of food and water dwindled and no land was sighted where they could be replenished. Men died one after another until but twenty-four were left, and they were so weak that they could only crawl about the ship to sail her. A few more days would have finished them all, but on the nineteenth of April, 1600, they sighted Japan.

Boats surrounded them and curious Japanese scrambled all over the ship. Adams and the others were too weak to resist. Their ship was towed into harbor and the exhausted crew was taken ashore and given the kindest treatment, but succor came too late for six, who died there.

Word of the new ship's arrival was rushed to Ieyasu, then in Osaka making arrangements for a vigilant watch over Hideyoshi's young son, and Ieyasu promptly sent galleys to bring the ship's captain to him. But the captain was still too ill to travel. It was pilot Adams who faced Ieyasu and whose blunt honesty saved all their lives.

When Adams reached this point, Mochizuki was no less entranced than by the wild adventures of the voyage. To be able to talk with someone who knew Ieyasu first-hand put the old Japanese in the glory seat.

"As soon as I came before him," Adams told Mochizuki, "he demanded of me, of what land I was, and what moved us to come to his land, being so far off. I showed unto him the name of our country, and that our land had long sought out the East Indies, and desired friendship with all kings and potentates in way of merchandise, having in our land diverse commodities, which these lands had not: also to buy such merchandises in this land, which our country had not. Then he asked whether our country had wars. I answered him yea, with the Spaniards and Portugals, being in peace with all other nations. Further, he asked me, in what did I believe? I said, in God, that made heaven and earth."

Mochizuki nodded in agreement as he filled Adams's cup, and let Adams fill his in return. This statement of belief was wide enough to appease any man, and no doubt it had satisfied Ieyasu.

"He asked what way came we to the country," Adams went on. "Having a chart of the whole world, I showed him, through the Strait of Magellan. At which he wondered, and thought me to lie. And having asked me, what merchandise we had in our ship, I showed him all. Thus with one thing and another, I abode with him till midnight. So he commanded me to be carried to prison."

Mochizuki registered dismay. He knew this story and its outcome, but he was a good audience. This was a moment of crisis, and he felt it with his friend. He refilled his cup.

"But two days after, he sent for me again, and enquired of the qualities and conditions of our countries, of wars and peace, of beasts and cattle of all sorts, and of the heavens. It seemed that he was well content with all mine answers unto his demands. Nevertheless, I was commanded to prison again, but my lodging was bettered in another place.

"Thirty-nine days I was in prison, hearing no more news, neither of our ship, nor captain, whether he was recovered of his sickness or not, nor the rest of the company. Every day I looked to die, to be crucified as the custom is in your country, as hanging is in our land."

Mochizuki sighed sympathetically. The cups were filled again.

"And all the time of my imprisonment, the Portugals gave many evidences against me, that we were thieves and robbers of all nations, and that we should be put to death. But God showed mercy unto us, and in the end, Ieyasu gave them answer that we as yet had not done to him nor to none of his land any harm or damage: therefore against reason and justice to put us to death. God be praised."

The two men drank to that.

"Ah, they were evil men, those Portugals," said Adams, "papists, you know," and he speared a morsel of dried and salted octopus.

Mochizuki thought this was a good moment to confide the errant behavior of the young maid who had fallen under the spell of the Franciscan.

"You had best watch her closely," advised Adams. "Those Spaniards are strange ones, and I doubt not their power over the ignorant."

And so the two men talked and laughed and drank together until the day died and maids came bearing supper and flickering oil lamps that cast deep shadows.

This visit, Adams told Mochizuki, was occasioned by a shipwrecked Spanish nobleman. He was ex-governor of the Philippines, homeward bound by way of Mexico, and a storm had driven his vessel on the coast north of Edo. He had already been received by the Shogun in Edo, and now was on his way to pay his respects to Ieyasu. Tomorrow he would pass through Okitsu and reach the city of Shizuoka. Adams had been hastily summoned to act as intermediary.

The thought of another stranded European, even a Spaniard and a papist, made Adams sentimental. As the moon climbed out of the sea, he talked of home and England, and he wondered aloud if ever again he would see the wife and children he had left there. It was late when Mochizuki excused himself and slipped along the moonlit veranda to the family quarters and to bed.

There he lay awake for a long time pondering his strange friend's strange career. He did not doubt that the Englishman was on terms of intimacy with Ieyasu that few Japanese could boast of. He knew that Adams was to Ieyasu interpreter, shipbuilder, counselor on foreign affairs, tutor in geometry and mathematics and geography, and adviser so trusted that in the Englishman's own words, "I pleased him so, that what I said he would not contrarie." Pleased him so that the Englishman had made himself a prisoner, for Ieyasu would not let him sail back to his own country. Mochizuki knew all this to be true, for had not Ieyasu given Adams an estate with more than a hundred peasants to farm it, and made him a samurai so that he carried the two swords of the upper class—swords that Mochizuki himself had been forced to relinquish.

The old Japanese groaned at that bitter memory and twisted in his bed. With all that Adams had been given, including even a wife—for Ieyasu knew that a man needed a wife and had provided one—with all of this why did the Englishman want to return to his own country? What must that strange faraway land be like? A country ruled by a woman—to Mochizuki it seemed quite incredible. Could this be one of Adams's fantastic lies? He wished he could untangle fact from fiction in this foreigner's tall tales. And Africa, could he believe in Africa? He fell asleep pondering Africa.

Next morning he was up before dawn to bid his friend good-bye. He watched in the gray light as Adams's palanquin was jockeyed into position by the six bearers sent from the Okitsu post station. (The road was level to Shizuoka; had Adams been bound in the other direction, over Satta Mountain, there would have been ten men to carry him.) Another man drew in behind, leading a horse should the Englishman choose to ride awhile.

Adams signaled. A man with a tasseled pike shouted, "Make way!" and dashed off to clear the road. The bearers stooped to put their shoulders under the poles, grunted, and raised the swaying carriage. They thumped their staffs in unison, marked time, and then with a sharp "Hup!" trotted off.

"Come soon again!" cried Mochizuki.

It was not far to Shizuoka and Adams knew the way well. He knew, for example, when to hold a handkerchief over his nose: at the edge of the city was an execution ground, and crosses hung with corpses, some of them slashed to pieces by men who had tested their swords upon them.

When that unsavory passage was behind him, he had reached the noisy outskirts of Shizuoka. "This citie," he had once written in a letter to England, "is full as big as London, with all its suburbs. The handi-crafts men wee found dwelling in the outward parts and skirts of the towne; because those that are of the better sort, dwell in the inward part of the citie, and will not be annoyed with the rapping, knocking, and other disturbance that artificers cannot be without."

By the time Adams reached the better part of the city, and the castle at its center, his friend Mochizuki, back in Okitsu, was taking up a position in the crowd that had gathered to gawk at Don Rodrigo de Vivero y Vellasco. The Don was not surprised at the throng. In Edo he had been unable to sleep until guards were posted around his inn to keep the people back. It had been the same all down the Tokaido. In his diary he wrote, "On whichever side the traveler turns his eye he perceives a concourse of people, as in the most populous cities of Europe." He bowed as he rode through Okitsu and on towards Ieyasu's castle. Mochizuki bowed back.

The next time Adams stopped in Okitsu, he told Mochizuki how Ieyasu had received Vivero.

"One week I taught the Spaniard the manners of the court," the Englishman explained, "and then the invitation came.

"They bore him to the castle in a palanquin with an escort of two hundred matchlockmen. At each gate he was handed over to another company of guards, until he reached the palace. Then he was led through eight or nine apartments, their ceilings bright with gold and their walls bold with diverse animals, trees, and flowers.

64

Ah, I could see that he was dazzled. In the last room there was a crowd of ministers, and a graybeard told him he would be honored as no man had been honored before him."

Later Don Rodrigo himself wrote an account of his reception: "In the center of a spacious apartment was a dais of three tiers. Round it was a double railing. In Spain such things are only gilt, but in Japan I understand they are of pure gold. Around the monarch were nearly twenty grandees in long silk robes with trousers so long that they entirely concealed the feet."

Ieyasu sat on the dais on a round velvet cushion of green. "He wore loose robes of green satin ornamented with gold brocade in a pattern of stars and moon. In his belt were two swords, and he had no hat on his head, but his hair was done up in a knot with a colored band. He was a stout, heavily built old man between sixty and seventy years old, with a most dignified bearing and a pleasing expres-

Tokugawa Ieyasu *(by an unknown artist)*

sion. I stopped a few paces in front of him, and he signed to me to put on my cap and be seated. He said that he was pleased to see me, and trusted that my shipwreck had not perturbed me, and urged me to submit any requests as freely as to my own king."

After a bit of conversation, the Don prepared to leave as Adams had instructed him to, but Ieyasu told him to wait a bit. And so Vivero was allowed to see how his own reception had differed from that of a Japanese lord. A daimyo of high rank was introduced, accompanied by a retainer who carried a tray piled high with gold pieces. Just inside the apartment they prostrated themselves, apparently kissing the floor in humility, and they remained in this posture for several minutes, neither Ieyasu nor any of his chamberlains offering a word. Finally they retired. Don Vivero was told that the gold was worth one hundred thousand ducats.

Mochizuki sucked in his breath when Adams told him of this scene. "Ieyasu has come a long way," he said. "As a boy he was a hostage in that same city, and no one then would have guessed that some day he would rule all Japan. Have I ever told you how I surrendered Okitsu to him?"

He had heard that story, Adams replied.

Mochizuki was momentarily crushed, but he quickly recovered. "And what requests did the Spaniard make of Ieyasu?" he asked.

Adams looked as though he had bitten an unripe persimmon. "They were three," he answered, "—that papist priests be granted freedom of the land as are your Buddhist priests; that Spanish trading ships be welcomed from Manila; and that the Dutch be driven from the country, for, he said, not only are they enemies of Spain but on the high seas they are pirates."

"And what answer did Ieyasu give him?"

"He looked pleased," said Adams grumpily. "He told his ministers the Spaniard might serve as example to them: he asked nothing for himself, only for his God and his king. And he granted all, save driving out the Hollanders, for he said they had his word they might remain for two years."

Don Vivero had reason to be pleased with himself. When he

sailed from Japan on a ship that Adams had built, he left confident that the busy priests, Jesuit, Franciscan, Dominican, Augustinian, and all, would be given no trouble. Things did indeed look bright for them. Years before, Hideyoshi had turned on them, demolished their churches, and ordered them out of the country. But he had seemed little concerned with enforcing his edict, and they had come back even stronger. Now, only sixty-six years after Francis Xavier first touched Japan, they had half a million converts, a very respectable share of a population probably less than twenty million. And Ieyasu had a reputation for broad-mindedness.

They misinterpreted his attitude. Ieyasu was a great believer in trade between nations, and though he was a devout Buddhist he was willing to put up with Christian priests because, for a time at least, they seemed essential to that trade. But his Japanese merchant fleet was growing swiftly, making him less and less dependent on foreign traders, and not two years after Vivero sailed away, Ieyasu's tolerance snapped. Scandals, corruption, and intrigue erupted within his own palace, and they all seemed to involve Christians. The tempest broke.

In Okitsu, the impressionable young maid in Mochizuki's house heard of it and rushed off to Shizuoka. There she joined a band of common people who were noisily demonstrating in front of the castle, publicly confessing their faith and demanding the same punishment as the fourteen members of the court who had been sentenced to exile. She returned crestfallen, for Ieyasu had ordered that the common people receive no punishment, but her dereliction earned her a thundering lecture from the younger Mochizuki.

It did little good. A few days later when one of the palace culprits, the Lady Julia, was led along the highway to exile, the maid once more left her work to follow the procession far out of town, lamenting for the victim and protesting her own faith. This time the girl was packed home to her parents on their tiny farm, where no doubt she was beaten to within an inch of her life.

Two other ladies of the court, Claire and Lucia, were also banished, but it was Julia's case that gave Ieyasu greatest pain. She had been a Korean princess and she was a great favorite of his, and some say his concubine. He appealed to her himself, but she refused to give up her religion. She lived out her days on a stark and craggy island far out to sea, "the only woman," said Ieyasu, "I ever lost to."

Two years later Ieyasu banned Christianity entirely. By now he was convinced that the priests were a fifth column. Each nationality spoke viciously of all the others. Plots, real or fabricated, kept coming to light. And anyone could see that Christians made heroes of their martyrs instead of respecting the law that condemned them.

The edict that outlawed Christianity in Japan for two and a half centuries was issued on January 27, 1614, and was promptly posted in every city and village in the land.

Mochizuki read it in front of the Okitsu post station: "The Kirishitan band have come to Japan, not only sending their merchant vessels to exchange commodities, but also longing to disseminate an evil law, to overthrow true doctrine, so that they may change the government of the country, and obtain possession of the land. This is the germ of a great disaster and must be crushed."

It was a signal for bloody persecution. In Okitsu, those who had been converted by the Franciscan were routed from their homes and herded to Shizuoka. On the banks of the Abe River their fingers were chopped off and the cords of their legs split. Helpless in agony, they lay until death took them.

Shizuoka's two churches were pulled down, and as a final act of degradation the area was licensed for brothels. The image of Mary gave way to a statue of Benten, the only female among the seven gods of good luck, patroness of women and the arts, and naturally the favorite of prostitutes. The errant maid from Mochizuki's ended here, for her father could not afford to feed her and before the persecution struck he had sold her to a sharp-eyed madam from Shizuoka. Somehow she held to her belief, and in the only way she could think of to express it, she brought flowers to Benten on the great holy days of Christianity. For generations after, the women of the quarter followed her example, preserving a living remnant of an almost forgotten faith.

I become acquainted with the inn

Actually, Ieyasu only began a persecution that was to gather in bitterness over the next three decades. He had more important business, and time was running out for him. Hideyoshi's son was now a handsome youth of twenty-two, and far from turning out badly, as Ieyasu had hoped, he had become a formidable menace. There were still many in the country who considered Ieyasu a usurper.

So Ieyasu led his armies out for a last campaign. Old Mochizuki watched them march away, and once more felt a martial thrill. Once more he was looked to as an expert as he analyzed reports from the campaign. It took a winter and a summer but, as Mochizuki said all along, the youth in Osaka never really had a chance, and when it was over Hideyoshi's line had been exterminated.

Then Ieyasu came back to Shizuoka, back to his hawking in the countryside, his library, and his long talks with Will Adams before a screen which mounted a map of the world. They talked of trade and ships and faraway places, and they talked, as many men have talked, of a northwest passage.

The old ruler fell ill after eating some fish *tempura*. He went over every contingency with his son, the second Shogun, and with his counselors. He reviewed the plan to maintain the dynasty of his own Tokugawa family. He reaffirmed the legacy of law and precept that he had drafted to maintain the peace that he had won. He directed that he should be buried on Suruga's salient peak of Kunozan, and a year later enshrined in the central mountains, among the cedars above the village of Nikko. There he would stand guard, tutelary spirit of the new Japan that he had founded.

Very quietly, at noon on the seventeenth day of the fourth month, 1616, he died, and in the evening of the same day he was carried up Kunozan.

One man wrote in his diary: "There was a slight drizzle. The coffin was carried up the hill by relays of lesser personal attendants. In complete silence they proceeded on their way. Honda Masazumi walked beside in straw sandals, and whenever the bearers stopped to rest a while he would crouch down by the coffin and say, 'At your service, my lord.' And when they took it up again to resume the journey he would look up at it and repeat, 'We are all here, my lord.' Just as though his master were alive he waited on him."

The soft rain blotted out the flare of their torches, and on the shore below, only a few miles away, Mochizuki was unaware of the silent procession, or even that the old man was dead.

He had his chance to render homage a year later when the cortege moved towards the mountains and Nikko town. A thousand footmen and all the great vassals marched with their lord again. They moved slowly, quietly, with banners furled. Long after they had passed through Okitsu, and the crowd had silently dispersed, Mochizuki sat alone and still. Memories crowded in on him, and he felt old.

He saw little of his friend Will Adams after that, for Adams returned to the sea and captained voyages to Asian trading ports. But he never found his way back to England, and in 1620 word drifted up the Tokaido Road that he had ended his days not far from the place he had first touched Japan. Mochizuki was too ill to be told, and he died without knowing that his English friend had made his exit first.

The family that Mochizuki had left went through their year of mourning, and faithfully prayed for his departed soul. On the day that year was over, his son marched to the front of the house and there he hung a carefully painted sign. It read, "Minaguchi-ya." For the first time the house was in name what it had long been in fact, an inn.

He went then to the family shrine in the heart of the house, and kneeling before the name-tablets of his ancestors, including the new one of his father, he reported what he had done and tried to explain it. "If I have brought dishonor on this house, I beg forgiveness. I have seen great changes from the time I was a boy. There has been change in the status of our family, change in the body of the empire. These are changes I am powerless to oppose, changes which must be acknowledged. If I have offended you, if I have failed our family, I am humbly sorry. I shall pray for the peace of your souls. I shall pray daily for the peace of your souls."

He rose slowly and called the family into conference. He announced that he was releasing headship of the family to his eldest son. He himself would go into retirement to prepare himself for the next world, and to pray for those who had gone before him.

That evening he went to the beach and sat there alone. He thought of himself as a samurai's son, playing on this beach, long ago. He thought of his father, gallant fighter against the inevitable.

The smoke from the salt fires made Miho hazy, and then darkness dissolved its shadowy form.

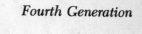

Fourth Generation

1651 and Today

CHAPTER FIVE

In which the inn becomes involved in a rebellion against Tokugawa rule

PRINCIPAL CHARACTERS
1651

Yui Shosetsu, *rebel*

Marubashi
Kato } *his aides*

Priest Kakunen, *who served the rebels*

and among the people of the inn:

Mochizuki, *fourth master of the Minaguchi-ya*

Today

The owner of the Shosetsu Dye Shop in Yui
The priest of Shohoji Temple in Yui

The crest of
Kusunoki Masashige

IT WAS the night of September 7, 1651. Wind exploded against the Minaguchi-ya, sheets of rain slapped it. Waves roared and smashed at the sea wall. The storm had threatened in the morning, struck in the afternoon, and now was at its height.

Few travelers had ventured out that day, and most of them had found shelter early. The shutters of the inn were closed, and Mochizuki—the fourth generation in Okitsu—was about to order the doors latched, when, with a gust of wind that almost blew out his lamp, they clattered open. Three men burst into the entry, then fought the doors until they closed again.

It was strange that men should be traveling on a night like this, and Mochizuki was tempted to turn them away. The inn was full, he would explain, there was no more room. But at that moment the wind screamed, and as he waited to speak he looked into the eyes of the one who was obviously their leader. When it was quieter, the innkeeper heard himself saying that he had one room left. The maids came, and took the men's soaked kimonos, and dried their feet and legs, and led them up the stairs.

The men were quiet enough. They took their baths, ate some supper, drank only enough saké to ward off a chill. They did not ask for women. As soon as the quilts were laid on the floor, they went to bed.

One of them, the swarthy, stocky one, rolled over, rasped a snore, and was asleep. The second, the young one, lay for a long time, tensing and untensing his sword arm, listening to the sea roar, feeling the inn shudder. He wondered about tomorrow, and the day after that, and, especially, the day after that. Finally he too fell asleep.

75

The third lay quietly. He was hardly conscious of the storm, but his mind would not rest. Once again he reviewed the plan, probing for some flaw that might undo them.

At least, he thought, they had got through Yui. Not that anyone there would have been likely to recognize him, for he had been just a boy when he left. Much more danger in Kambara, the village just before Yui, for there he had lived in his uncle's house until he was seventeen. But now both towns were behind them, and they were across the Okitsu River. The waters were high and swift, and crossing was forbidden after dark, but those dangers were minor. In stormy blackness they had clasped hands and waded through. Luckily, too. By morning the rains would raise the river past the danger point, and crossing would certainly be prohibited all day. He hoped that all the others had got through. They must have. They started before him. Probably they were already in Shizuoka.

The plan was in motion now. In another day they would be poised, Marubashi in Edo, Kato in Kyoto, and he, between them, in Shizuoka. On the tenth, if it was windy—if not, on the first windy night thereafter—Marubashi would strike.

Within hours, minutes perhaps if things went well, Edo would be in flames, and the Shogun dead. As soon as word of that reached Kyoto, Kato's force would kidnap the Emperor. Meanwhile, the Tokugawa strongholds of Shizuoka and Kunozan would have fallen to his own tough brigade, and he would be ready to march in either direction, as the situation dictated. He would use the arsenal at Kunozan to equip the men who would flock to him. There was everywhere hatred for these Tokugawas, he was sure of it. A spark, and it would explode. He and his men, five thousand tough and daring men, would strike that spark.

It was a plot of incredible daring, and the odds were sharply against success. That fact he dismissed. The only thing that mattered was that success was possible, and that life on any other terms was unacceptable. All his life he had been driving towards this point. There could be no turning back.

He had been born in Yui, the village they had just passed through, forty-six years ago. His father had been a dyer, and the shop was still there, run by a brother who was somehow content with that life. His father had been more than just a village dyer. He had been dyer to Hideyoshi. He had dyed kimono materials in patterns complex and elegant, and he had dyed the great man's battle flags, and screens for his encampments. It was only after Hideyoshi was dead, and his followers scattered, that the dyer had settled in Yui and taken a wife.

The father wanted something better for his first son than his own trade. He wanted him to be a priest. He sent him to the village temple, where it was agreed that he showed promise, and where they arranged a transfer to the great temple of Rinzaiji in Shizuoka. He was a brilliant boy but an intractable acolyte. From the beginning he showed far more interest in the arts of war than in the practice of Zen Buddhism. For that reason, he was delighted to be at Rinzaiji. Sessai had been abbot there, as well as at Seikenji. Within Rinzaiji's cloistered walls, that great abbot-general had tutored Ieyasu and planned Yoshimoto's campaigns, and his library of military treatises was still intact. The boy struck up a friendship with a masterless samurai, a *ronin*, living nearby, and whenever he could get away from the temple they would talk together of battles and the men who had fought them. It was this out-of-work warrior, remembering better days, who filled him with tales of Hideyoshi, just as his father had done while he worked among the dye pots at home. The story of the man who had risen from son of a foot soldier to Lord of the Empire was heady stuff for an ambitious boy. He came to think that there was not much difference between Hideyoshi's beginnings and his own.

But when he asked who was the greatest military figure in the nation's history, the *ronin* unhesitatingly went back three centuries to Kusunoki Masashige. Kusunoki was part of the dark and complicated struggles which swirled around two rival emperors. In the endless campaigns he shone for generalship, and in the endless intrigue, for loyalty and integrity.

One day the boy chose a new name for himself: Yui Tachibana Shosetsu Mimbunosuke. Yui because he had been born there,

Tachibana because Kusunoki had been descended from that illustrious family, Shosetsu in deference to Sessai ("setsu" and "ses" are written with the same character, meaning "snow"), and Mimbunosuke because it suggested a relationship with a man who had once been lord of Yui and had lived in a castle atop a pointed hill. His new name, he felt, was appropriate to his abilities. It certainly reflected his ambitions. He is remembered as Yui Shosetsu.

When he was twelve his father died, breathing a last request that the boy enter the priesthood before the week was out. And that would have been the story of his life, except that three days later he suddenly became deaf, dumb, and mad. He was taken to all the doctors thereabouts, but he only became more violent, and finally he was shipped off to his uncle, a blacksmith in the neighboring village of Kambara. There he was quieter, but since he was little help around the shop, his uncle was not unhappy when he took to disappearing daily from morning till night.

Five years later he startled the blacksmith by speaking to him in a perfectly natural voice. He confessed that deafness, dumbness, and madness had all been

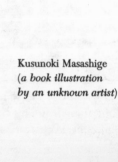

Kusunoki Masashige
(*a book illustration
by an unknown artist*)

feigned to escape the priesthood. He had been using his days to study military treatises and learn swordsmanship, he said, and now he was ready to face the world. He was about to take off on a long pilgrimage as a solitary man-at-arms. His startled uncle bade him good-bye and good luck.

Shosetsu traveled first to the ancestral lands of Kusunoki. After soaking up local atmosphere he went to the local shrine, and there at the foot of a great pine tree he buried a sturdy box. In it were two items of his own manufacture, a banner like those Kusunoki had used, and the old warrior's family tree, compiled by Shosetsu when he was still a boy at Rinzaiji.

For the next five years he roamed the country, one of those dashing, sardonic, lone warriors now so indispensable to Japanese movies, suddenly there with flashing sword when all seems hopeless, disappearing into the mist after dispatching a villainous band.

Whenever he found a master swordsman he took lessons, and he never lost a chance to pit his skill against the best. Wherever he went he found adventurers like himself, for the strong arm of the Tokugawa Shogunate had ruthlessly punished its enemies, and many a daimyo who once lorded it over great territories was reduced to nothing, and his retainers cut adrift. There were four hundred thousand of these *ronin* in the country. A few of them settled down, as Mochizuki had done when Shingen was crushed, but many of them took to the highways, sometimes alone, sometimes in bands; sometimes pursuing a vendetta they had sworn themselves to, sometimes just looking for trouble because that was all they were trained for. They were Shosetsu's kind, but he could outfight them, he could outthink them, and he was a born leader. When they parted it was always with a vow that they would meet again, and he would hint at great adventure and great glory.

At last he decided he was ready, and he went to Edo. There he set about to attach himself to one of the popular professors of military science. He chose one who was a descendant of Kusunoki, and though unable to offer the usual surety, he not only talked himself into the school, but swiftly made himself the master's right-hand man. It even began to be noised about that Shosetsu was the abler of the two.

After that it was not difficult to take over completely. There was a young fellow who was betrothed to the old man's daughter: a few poisoned words made him think that he had fallen out of favor and was to be killed as the surest way to break the bargain. There was a rendezvous with that enraged young man at a lonely spot when Shosetsu, the master's only companion, was momentarily out of action adjusting a sandal. The first murder was followed closely by a second, as Shosetsu made himself a hero by cutting down his master's assassin.

Of course Shosetsu was chosen as the new head of the school. Lest anyone doubt that he was entitled to this eminence by blood as well as ability, he confided a strange dream to several students. Kusunoki had appeared to him, he said, and stated, "You are my lineal descendant, and if you require proof of this, dig at the foot of the great pine tree at the shrine by my native place!" Shosetsu added that he certainly intended to do no such thing because he put no stock in dreams, but some of the students set out at once, and of course they found the box with the banner and the family record. This was regarded as nothing short of a miracle, and his fame mushroomed.

He was doing very well now, for his lectures on tactics and strategy were not only eloquent but refreshingly practical, and he took his examples from modern campaigns instead of those of misty antiquity. His was unquestionably the most popular school in the city.

Then the word went out, and soon hundreds of tough, lawless men were drifting into Edo from the provinces. Shosetsu received them all, and though he could not harbor them without exciting suspicion, he managed to place them with the daimyo who flocked to his school. The new arrivals were "instructors," he said, "the very best available," and, with that, some novel characters entered the teaching profession.

Moreover, he expanded the activities of his school to establish a number of shops where he made and sold weapons and armor. This gave employment to many, including his blacksmith uncle from Kambara. It also provided Shosetsu with a tidy income, and it permitted him to build up an arsenal. His plot began to take form.

He had two chief lieutenants. Marubashi said he was a son of a deposed and executed daimyo, and swore to avenge his father by annihilating the Tokugawas. Kato was one of the followers Shosetsu had picked up on his travels. Both were brave, personable, strong, and brilliant swordsmen, but they recognized Shosetsu's genius and they were completely loyal.

As Shosetsu lay in the inn at Okitsu that stormy night, he once more assessed the strengths and weaknesses of these two men, and once more he cursed the luck that had upset their first attempt.

The third Shogun, the grandson of Ieyasu, had died on the fourth of June, and a boy of ten had succeeded him. Seizing the opportunity provided by the change-over, Shosetsu had placed the plot in motion the next day, and Kato and his men had set out for Kyoto, slipping out of Edo in twos and threes so as not to arouse suspicion.

At this crucial moment, Marubashi had fallen seriously ill. Everything had had to be postponed, and, in the meantime, the tension of waiting in Kyoto had so unnerved Kato's chief aide that he had squandered most of their money on women and wine, and then been so ashamed that he had disappeared.

More than three months had slipped away, but now they were ready again. The government powder-magazine had been mined, could be blown up on signal. Gunpowder was set all over Edo, ready to be exploded when the magazine went. The city was a tangle of wooden houses with thatch and shingle roofs. Whipped by strong winds, flames would quickly engulf it, and in the panic, Marubashi and three hundred men bearing the Tokugawas' own insignia would dash into the palace and kill the Shogun. It was that simple.

What Shosetsu did not know, as he lay in the Minaguchi-ya, while wind and rain lashed the inn, was that Marubashi also had wasted funds entrusted to him, and had borrowed more. The notes were overdue because of the forced postponement, and that same evening he was frantically trying to stall one man who had loaned him money and to borrow more from another. Both were more than reluctant. Marubashi pleaded for just a few days' grace, and he promised tenfold repayment. His answer was incredulous smiles, and finally to convince his skeptical creditors, he gave away the plot.

At that, both men agreed to help, but instead they hurried to the authorities. And as Shosetsu lay in the dark, the government finally learned the secret he had kept so well. Under the noses of the authorities he had built up a force of five thousand men, he had accumulated an arsenal, he had amassed a small fortune. For years he had deceived the secret police. But now they knew.

Towards dawn the wind began to quiet, and Shosetsu drifted into sleep. At almost the same moment, "hot-foot relay couriers" were dispatched to Shizuoka and Kyoto, and a strong force of police set out to capture Marubashi. They cried "Fire!" in front of his house. When he dashed out with only one short sword, they took him.

As Shosetsu left the Minaguchi-ya on the last leg of his journey to Shizuoka, the grilling of Marubashi had already begun, and the dispatches were well on their way down the Tokaido. That evening, as he entered the city, he heard behind him the bell of a courier, and, like other passers-by, he stepped aside. The runner dashed by. His almost naked body glistened with sweat, his muscles bulged with strain, but his legs pumped on. Over his shoulder he carried a stick, and at the end of it, a packet with the government's seal. Shosetsu's death warrant had caught up with him.

Unknowing, Shosetsu walked on. He passed the moated walls of the castle he meant to storm two nights later, and he gave the gates a practiced scrutiny. In the busiest street of the city, he came upon Umeya Kambei's inn, the city's best. This was rendezvous and headquarters. He entered.

He was expected, the innkeeper told him, the others of his party had already arrived.

Now there were nine of them, including a priest called Kakunen,

A courier dashing through the night
passes a man carrying a lantern
(*detail from a print
by Hiroshige*)

who would attempt to align the gods on their side. They settled
down for the last crucial hours. They checked their forces and reviewed their plans, and they waited.

The authorities had this description of Shosetsu: "Short in stature,
pale in complexion, with thick hair, sharp eyes, narrow forehead,
and broad lips, looking impudent . . . reported never to have shaved
. . ." With precious little more than this jaundiced sketch to go on,
they started screening the city.

The secret police went to work. Part of a great network of spies,
these men had reports on the goings and comings to and from every
province. They were acutely sensitive to the pulse and flow of traffic on the Tokaido, and as they scanned the lists of customers at

every inn, something about Shosetsu's group did not ring true. They checked, and then gave their orders. On the night of September 9, a hundred and fifty police slipped into position around the inn of Umeya Kambei. They had orders to take their men alive. What the government wanted most of all were confessions and a list of conspirators.

On this, the last night before their attack, Shosetsu and his men had little to do but wait. Two of them played *go*, and the sharp click of their markers on the wooden board cut through the low hum of talk and the occasional grunts of the swarthy one who watched them. In a corner, a man sprawled on the mats, trading amatory triumphs with another who leaned with his back against the wall. The young fellow sat by them, listening, wetting his lips; it was clear that their recital was for his benefit. One man sat alone, fingering his chin for bristles and jerking them out with tweezers.

Go players
(*a book illustration
by Jichosai*)

The inn becomes involved in a rebellion

In the inner room, behind paper doors, Shosetsu sat before a low stand, reading. In a corner was the priest, impassive. Steam purred from an iron kettle on the charcoal brazier, and tea things were at his side, should Shosetsu pause and glance his way.

From the hallway there was a sound of slippered feet, and the voice of a maid close to the door. "Please excuse me." The door slid open, and dropping to her knees inside the room, she bowed low. "Sorry to trouble you. There is a man in the entry. He requests to see the master."

The swarthy one who was watching the game stabbed through the silence. "His name?"

"He said—he appears to be from the police."

The door to the inner room was suddenly open and Shosetsu stood there, sword in hand. His eyes flicked to the swarthy one. That man rose, adjusted his kimono, and moved deliberately out of the room, along the twisting corridor, and down the stairs.

There was no word while he was gone but every man's hand was on his sword. They heard him returning, still deliberate. Then he was in the room. "It is the police."

They leapt to their feet, their swords out. Shosetsu's hand stopped them. The one who had gone to the entrance continued, "He says a hundred and fifty men surround us. He orders us to go to the castle."

"Tell him we will come but we must dress," Shosetsu ordered. "Hold him off!" The man left again.

They wanted to die fighting. If they had to be killed, they wanted to kill first. But Shosetsu would not permit it. The best that could happen would be a few dead police. The worst would be capture, and torture, and names given out in pain too much to bear. "We knew that this could happen. We must die here, by our own hands."

They burned their papers and their plans. Shosetsu took from his kimono a last message, ready against this chance. He opened it, inked a brush, and at the end he wrote his final words, a farewell poem.

They sat then, all but the priest, in two facing rows, with Shosetsu at their head, and they pulled their kimonos open till their bellies were bare. They took their short swords, for this was the moment they carried them against, and each man wrapped the upper blade in paper so he could grasp the steel closer to its gleaming point. The swarthy one returned, nodded, and quickly took his position among them. Shosetsu bowed, and they bowed, in a last salute. Only the priest sat apart, palming his beads, praying.

Some were pale, some sweaty. One clenched a towel between his teeth, one murmured a prayer. Each man picked up his sword, grasped it in both his hands, pointed it straight.

Shosetsu looked at them. Each of these men was alone now, his world turned in upon himself. He looked at his own blade, gripped it hard, and he, too, was alone. One last frantic thought raced through his brain: "O myriad gods and Buddhas, this is a bad dream. Let me wake up!" He doubled over the blade and plunged. A scream caught in his throat, and then, with a last violent thrust, he ripped the blade across his belly.

The captain of police burst open the door and stepped into blood. Eight men lay sprawled in a lake of blood, convulsed in agony. The priest was still praying, his robe flecked with carmine. There were shouts and turmoil, and police thundering through the inn. In the midst of it all, the priest slipped away.

When they got around to reading Shosetsu's deposition, it told them little. He had been misjudged, it said. Treason was the furthest thing from his mind. He had only tried to restore morality to government.

The government was not convinced. It executed his aides in Edo and Kyoto, with all their families, and it trussed his body to a scaffold in the river bottom, to hang as carrion warning against his kind of ambition. And it closed the inn of Umeya Kambei.

The police gave Mochizuki some bad days, too. They traced Shosetsu's movements and they established that he had slept at the Minaguchi-ya the night before he reached Shizuoka. They grilled Mochizuki time and again, trying to gain an admission that he knew Shosetsu and was confederate to his plot. Night after night most of the inn's guests were police spies, trying to catch Mochizuki off guard, or get some damaging statement from a servant. But in the end they gave up. They cleared Mochizuki and the Minaguchi-ya remained open.

Strangely, the government was frightened. Massive, absolute, without a single major enemy who dared to raise his voice, nevertheless the government was frightened. It was fear that led some wild-eyed men of Edo to a truly preposterous judgment. They declared that Shosetsu was a Christian and his plot a Christian plot.

For the government was afraid of *ronin*, and it was afraid of Christians, and it had a pathological dread that these two might somehow combine. They had once, at Shimabara, and men in Edo still shuddered when they thought of it.

Shimabara had come with melodramatic timing. The Japanese had been poised to carry out an old scheme, the conquest of the Philippines. Had they succeeded, and there was little to stop them, history since then would have been very different.

Hideyoshi had coveted the Philippines, and might have added them to his crown had he not bogged down in Korea. Ever since, the idea had kept popping up, and about 1635 the Dutch chose to revive it. To the Hollanders it meant putting their old enemies, the Spaniards, out of business. To the Japanese it meant destroying the great base for Christianity in the Far East.

Late in 1637 the government decided to go ahead. A force of ten thousand men was picked. The Dutch would furnish half a dozen ships to escort the transports.

Then came Shimabara. Mochizuki of Okitsu heard the news on the night of December 16, 1637, from couriers who reached Edo the next day. On a neck of land near Nagasaki, a group of farmers had revolted. They had reason enough. Their daimyo, one of the evilest in the country, had seized so much of their crops for taxes that they were near starvation, and he had reinforced his demands by such barbaric tricks as binding a man's arms and then setting fire to his straw raincoat. But it happened that their neck of land, called Shimabara, was a spot where Christianity had taken root early and grown strong, and the fighting that had flared against hunger and oppression speedily became something else. It became a fight for a faith that had been savagely suppressed. The banners of the mutiny bore the hated cross.

At first the government did not take it seriously. It was a collection of rabble, farmers armed with sickles and scythes. But the samurai who were sent against them were annihilated. The rabble were thirty-seven thousand strong, and if they lacked leadership at the beginning, they soon gained it. Some two hundred *ronin*, smelling a good fight, flocked to join them. The rebels entrenched themselves in an old castle, and armed themselves with the weapons of the troops who had been sent against them. They were no longer a joke.

Important personages were sent down the Tokaido to crush the revolt. Mochizuki watched the first ones move confidently and leisurely, the later ones, swiftly and grimly. Finally, in the face of appalling losses, a new commander from Edo settled down to a seige. He had fifty thousand men and a strategy of starvation.

He also ordered the Dutch to send round a ship to bombard the rebels from the sea. The Dutch did as directed, but the hail of derision from inside the castle, the taunts about having to call on foreigners for help, got under the general's skin, and he dismissed the ship with thanks.

On the twelfth of April, it was judged that hunger had done its work. A general assault was begun, and two days later every man, woman, and child inside the fort had been massacred, with one exception, who had been a traitor to their cause.

Shimabara was the last flaming episode in the early history of Christianity in Japan. The government never ceased to fear the alien creed, the fury of persecution never let up, but after Shimabara it was hard to find victims.

And Shimabara wrote finish to the expedition against the Philippines. The government reasoned that if Japanese fighting men had so deteriorated that it took fifty thousand of them four months to crush an insurrection of rabble, there was no calculating how many would be needed against the Spaniards.

Men had changed in fifty years. Ieyasu, sitting before a map of the world while Will Adams talked geography, had seen Japan as a hub of trade with all nations, with a great Japanese fleet reaping profits from the seven seas. His grandson, sitting before those same maps, could see only how small was Japan compared with other nations, and how the Christian world was creeping up on her. Afraid to face the world, he tried to shut it out. The Spaniards were expelled, and then the Portuguese. Only the compliant Dutch and the cousin Chinese were allowed to remain, and they could bring their ships only to Nagasaki. The Japanese overseas fleet was destroyed. No Japanese ship could sail to foreign countries, and no Japanese who was abroad could return to his native land. Japan was to be a hermit country, trying to forget the world, hoping to be forgotten.

Within Japan, a vast net of police power settled over the country. In Ieyasu's day, daimyo had begun to spend part of their time in Edo to keep on good terms with the Shogunate. His grandson systematized the whole business. He decreed that each lord of the realm spend half his time in Edo, usually alternate years, and when he was home in his own territories his wife and children were to remain in Edo as hostages, to keep him from getting ideas.

Checkpoints were flung across the highways, like the one that blocked the Tokaido deep within the Hakone Mountains, gateway to Edo. They guarded especially against two things: guns being smuggled into Edo, and hostages being smuggled out.

The country was honeycombed with secret police, spying, probing, reporting. Shosetsu had defied these police, he had intrigued under their noses, but in the end he had been trapped by them.

He came thirteen years after Shimabara, but the memory of that rabble revolt still brought nightmares to the government in Edo. That was why frightened men saw Shosetsu as a Christian. It was a judgment that would not have pleased him. He had no religion but himself.

The story of Yui Shosetsu and his ill-starred plot is a tangled mixture of truth and legend, and where one begins and the other leaves off, no one knows.

This is not surprising, for if the government could have obliterated his memory completely, it would have. But Yui Shosetsu had to happen. Coming in the years that saw the land tamed to a cozy, introverted, and ironbound peace, he was the inevitable last gasp of the roaring, warring centuries when the right man could come from nothing to win the country. Because he was inevitable, it was inevitable that his story would live, passed from hand to hand in manuscripts illicit and full of errors.

Almost every statement about Shosetsu is disputed. It is not possible to say with certainty, for example, that Shosetsu studied at the temple of Rinkoji in Yui, or the great Rinzaiji in Shizuoka. No records exist, nor should one expect them. A temple does not keep registers of every boy who studied there, and if one of its boys turned out to be a traitor, it is certain that his record would disappear. Temples keep what is good for them, and destroy what is not.

There is even a story that he studied at Seikenji. I was tempted to use this version, for it ties Shosetsu to Okitsu, but it is not heard frequently, and it seemed to me that I would be cheating. Still, for all I know, it may be true. Seikenji also has its associations with Sessai, abbot and general, and certainly it is closer to Yui than Rinzaiji.

There is not even agreement that Yui was born in Yui. There is a very vocal group that puts his birth in Shizuoka, and many other places have been nominated, but there is no doubt that the popular fancy lights on Yui. The town itself is insistent. They may not be proud of him, but he is the nearest thing to a celebrity they have, and they do not mean to let him get away.

The inn becomes involved in a rebellion

They refer you to the Shosetsu Dye Shop. It is on the old high-way, and Yui must have passed it on his last trip to Shizuoka. As you enter, the left half of the house is the work place, filled with antique dye-encrusted pots. The right half is office and living quarters, its floor raised a couple of feet above the hard earth of the shop. There, on straw *tatami* mats, you sit and talk with the stocky, broad-faced man who is now the owner. If you met him on the street you could tell his trade, for his hands are indelibly stained with the deep blue vegetable color called *ai*, which, generation after generation, remains the favorite Japanese dye.

He sits there among his patterns and his samples. He brings out a length of silk dyed in nineteen sections, each showing a favorite Japanese motif, from lion and peony to waves and sea birds. He displays a sample book containing ninety-four intricate stencil patterns. The book is three hundred years old, he thinks, and he still has calls for these designs.

Years of defending his story have made him a little contentious, but he warms when he senses a sympathetic audience.

"My family is descended from Shosetsu's," he states. "This shop is where he was born. This is his father's house.

"At least," he corrects himself, "half of it is. The living quarters burned and were rebuilt two hundred and thirty years ago, but the dye shop is just as it was in his time.

"Of course I can't prove anything by the family records at the temple," he goes on. "If the record of his birth hadn't been destroyed, the whole family would have been wiped out, just as Marubashi's family was in Edo. In that case"—he spreads his hands—"I wouldn't be here.

"It was Priest Kakunen who saved us," he adds. "He escaped from Shizuoka and came here to alter the records. He also brought to the family some of the hair from Shosetsu's head. It was secretly buried in back of this house.

"There are really three graves of Shosetsu. There is our grave, and in Shizuoka there are two graves, one for his body and one for his head. The night after his body was exposed in the river bed of the Abekawa, someone of great courage rescued his head, the most precious part of the body, and took it to the temple called Bodaiji, where it was buried. There are many stories about who did this, but it must have been Priest Kakunen.

"All during the reign of the Tokugawas the grave here at our home was kept unmarked and secret. After the Tokugawas were overthrown, the grave was opened. More than eight feet down they found a strong box with stones above it. The head of the family was going to open the box, but since it would have been a difficult job and it had already grown dark, he decided to wait till the next morning. That night he was seized with a high fever and terrible chills, which he took as a warning that the box should not be opened. It never was. The next morning it was reinterred, unopened. Would you like to see the grave?"

He leads the way through the kitchen, whose earth floor is almost covered with freshly dug potatoes, out into the garden, and down a little embankment. There, in a grove is a gravestone and a small shrine. Below are the railroad tracks, and beyond them the sea.

On the way back to the house, the dyer points to a moss-covered well. "Wonderful water," he says. "In Shosetsu's time, the inn for daimyo was just across the street, and water for them was drawn from this well. Perhaps when he was a boy Shosetsu helped carry the buckets.

"Certainly he looked up to the family who lived there and ran the inn. They were the most important family of the village, descended from the lord of Yui. One of the names Shosetsu chose for himself, Mimbunosuke, was hereditary in their line."

You search out the temple of Rinkoji, where they say he first studied as a small boy. You find it in the quiet hills that hem the valley of Yui, and as you admire the view of the town and the sea, the priest is politely noncommittal. Yes, they say he studied here, but no, there are no records. Have you visited the dyer? And perhaps you would like to talk with the priest at the temple of Shohoji, very near the dye shop. He has made a study of Shosetsu.

The priest of Shohoji laughs as he welcomes you. "It's a good story the dyer tells," he says, "but there's no truth in it. I've probed this local legend, and I know how it got started, though there's not much I can say or write about it as long as I live in Yui.

"There was a man in this town who was involved in Shosetsu's rebellion. The last of his descendants, an old widow lady, died in 1873. The dyer's family had cared for her in her last years, and so they came into possession of the story that had been handed down in her family, and the relics that give it credence. Since Shosetsu was called Yui, and it's often said his father was a dyer, they announced themselves as his lineage. That's all there is to it."

Then he adds two names to the bewildering list of Shosetsu's birthplaces. "It was either in Hachioji, on the outskirts of Edo, or in Kamakura," he states. "Both of them have districts called Yui.

"The priest, Kakunen? Yes, there was such a man. I'll show you his grave in the cemetery of this temple. He died in 1786, a hundred and thirty-five years after Shosetsu."

The dyer's story is refuted point by point, and yet one curious fact remains, and even the skeptical priest affirms it. Shosetsu named himself Mimbunosuke to imply that he was descended from the lord of Yui. You wonder, if he was not born here, how he ever came to hear of this local squire, or why he tried to claim relationship.

Perhaps you go next to Shizuoka's temple of Bodaiji, where they say his head is buried. The temple is nowhere near where it was in Shosetsu's time. It has recently been moved to the outskirts of the city, and stands last in a row of relocated temples, all raw new wood on bare, flat land.

The temple's cemetery was moved with it, and they show you Shosetsu's grave. It is set apart, with an old but undistinguished monument.

The temple is prouder of a stone basin in which Shingen, who brought the first Mochizuki to Okitsu, is said to have washed his hands, but you get the priest to talk about Shosetsu.

"Someone threw the head into the temple garden," he says, "so of course the priest gave it a decent burial. It happened very early one morning, so early that the gates of all the other temples were still closed. Our temple got its nickname from that incident. People call it 'Hayaoki-zan,' the 'Get-up-early temple.'" You learn that Bodaiji is an offshoot of Rinzaiji, and you think that, perhaps, in a sense, Shosetsu came home here.

The last stop is the monument erected to his memory not so many years ago, where the Tokaido highway crosses the Abekawa, the Abe River, in the city of Shizuoka. Close by the bridge are the shops which make and sell Abekawa *mochi*, the bean-paste sweets which are famous all over Japan. It's a scrubby scene today, but you try to imagine it as it must have been when there were many shops, each with its pretty waitresses to entice customers off the road. Even without this lure, you enter one curtained doorway.

"Some of the other shops claim to be older," the owner admits. "This business is two hundred years old, and I'm the seventh in line. The shop burned during the war, but before that we had a very old house. Customers used to come and stare at the smoky rafters and sigh about how they were the same rafters the artist Hiroshige must have sat under. Nostalgia was part of my stock-in-trade.

"Abekawa *mochi* first became popular when word got around that it would bring good luck to any young man on his way to Edo to make his fortune," the man tells you, proving that public relations is not such a new art, after all. "It was originally made to offer to Ieyasu when he left the city on this road to inspect some of his gold mines. The distinctive Abekawa cake is covered with very sweet brown flour made from powdered beans. When Ieyasu asked about it, they told him it was gold dust, an answer which delighted him." This seems in character, for Ieyasu had great affection for gold.

"Yui Shosetsu? Ah, yes. His body was exposed in the river bed not far from here. It was the government's way of letting the people know what a traitor must expect. There's a new shop down the street that makes Shosetsu wafers. Of course that shop claims he was born in this city, but he was the son of a dyer in Yui."

He leads you over to the monument, a slab of rough stone carved with Yui's name and his farewell poem, his little September poem. The shopkeeper traces with his finger the difficult, cursive script, and reads the words aloud:

> "In this lonely time of autumn
> I go upon a long and lonely journey,
> Severing all ties."

Sixth and Seventh

Generations

Today and 1691

CHAPTER SIX

In which the inn shelters important and exotic guests

PRINCIPAL CHARACTERS
Today

Ito, *head of Matsuzakaya department stores*

and among the people of the inn:

Mochizuki, *twentieth master of the Minaguchi-ya*

1691

Ito, *merchant and patron of the Minaguchi-ya*
Denzaemon, *head of the post house at Okitsu station*
Ichikawa ⎰
Tezuka ⎱ *Headmen of Okitsu and owners of its honjin*
Englebert Kaempfer, M.D., *physician to the Dutch mission*

and among the people of the inn:

Mochizuki Hanzo, *sixth master of the Minaguchi-ya*

*The crest of
Matsuzakaya
department stores*

THE MASTER of the Minaguchi-ya today represents the twentieth generation of Mochizukis who have lived in Okitsu. I met him later than I did his wife, Isako, for while she acts as hostess and supervises service to the guests, he handles business affairs. But when he emerges from his office he becomes a gracious host.

I asked him one day about some of the Minaguchi-ya's notable guests over the years. He talked of Imperial uncles and aunts and cousins, of generals and admirals and statesmen, and then he added, "But I'm sure that the family who have been our patrons longest are the Itos. They are one of the great merchant houses of Japan, and if you don't know their name you certainly know the name of their chain of big department stores—Matsuzakaya.

"When I was a boy the Ito family came often to the inn, as they do today. My grandmother told me they had been regular customers as long as she could remember.

"They had a son about my age. We played together and became good friends. Years later, when we were both university students, I sometimes spent a holiday with him at their home in Nagoya.

"I shall never forget the old mansion which stood behind their modern home. It looked like a temple and was so dark and anti- quated that it was quite unlivable. When I crossed that threshold I felt that I was stepping back a century or two into another Japan.

"Inside was a great hall which held the altars and name-tablets of Ito ancestors. There were hundreds of them. Never a day passed that wasn't someone's anniversary. There was always incense burn- ing before at least one altar.

99

"I remember seeing the tablets of men who had been retainers to Nobunaga when that great lord was battling to unify the country. And I saw the tablet of the Ito who in 1611 abandoned his samurai status to become a merchant: he did voluntarily what fate had done to my own ancestor, that first Mochizuki of Okitsu, some three decades earlier.

"Behind the old house were ten huge storehouses, originally built to hold the silks and stuffs in which the family dealt, but long since filled with family treasures and family records. How I envied the Itos, for all written record of my own ancestors had been lost in fires that time and again swept Okitsu.

"I was so impressed that I suppose I learned as much Ito history as my friend Ito. I learned the date—1768—when they invaded Edo by buying out a store called Matsuzakaya, a name they adopted for all their stores. I learned the epochal date—1905—when Western-style counters were installed in their Nagoya store, so that for the first time clerks stood to serve customers instead of sitting with them on the matted floor while boys brought goods from storerooms.

"One holiday when I was staying with the Itos an old servant brought young Ito a worm-eaten little book from one of the storehouses and pointed out a certain passage. My friend read it, smiled, and handed the book to me. It was a travel diary written by the great-grandson of the founder of the Nagoya store. In it he described a trip he made to Edo in 1691. The marked page read: '8th day of the 3d month. Stopped tonight in Okitsu at the Minaguchi-ya, where we were most warmly received.'

"Neither my friend nor I had known that the association between our families was as old as that. And when I went home I found that, as far as my family knew, that diary was the oldest written reference to the Minaguchi-ya."

I asked Mr. Mochizuki if he thought it could be arranged for me to see the old diary. I explained that it would mean a great deal to me. He said that the Itos were coming to the Minaguchi-ya soon again and that he would ask them.

Next time I saw him he had the answer. The old mansion, the storehouses, and most of their contents had burned in bombing raids on Nagoya during the war. The diary had been among the records which were lost.

It was a spring day to remember. The sun was warm, the breeze fluttered promises on which small boys flew kites against a newly washed sky. In fields along the highway, farmers broke the ground and released the strong, sharp smell of earth. Ito had never felt so alive. He hiked briskly, reveling in the power of his legs and the thrust of his chest, and the rapture of being twenty-five and healthy.

He had walked all day, savoring the clean, sure working of his body, not willing to trade that buoyancy for jostled torpor in a palanquin. His companion had kept pace with him. Several times Ito had urged the older man to ride for a while, but each time he had firmly refused.

The man was a good traveling companion, Ito thought. He had been a little unhappy when his father had insisted that the firm's chief clerk come along. He himself would have chosen someone nearer his own age. But now he was pleased with the arrangement. The clerk had made this trip to Edo many times with Ito's father, now two years in retirement, and frequently along the way young Ito had been grateful for his companion's knowledge of special places to eat, or of ways to shake off undesirable fellow travelers, or of how to dismiss beggars with the least fuss and expense. And now that they were halfway to Edo, the young man was more than willing to admit that he was going to be glad to have the clerk's support when he moved among the shrewd merchants of the Shogun's capital. Since his father's retirement, young Ito had been head of Nagoya's most famous kimono and dry-goods house, but he was a little apprehensive about this first trip on his own. Their firm had no branch in Edo, but it was eying the prospects.

All along the highway, too, the chief clerk had displayed an astonishing fund of lore about each area they passed through. He could talk for hours on local legend or local history, but he could also be silent. Ito was thankful for both, and for the man's sure sense of when each was wanted.

It was now midafternoon or a little past, and they were approaching Okitsu, where they would spend the night at the Minaguchi-ya. Neither had spoken in some time, but as they topped a low hill and saw the village and the beach before them, the older man drew out of his memory a pensive quotation from a thirteenth-century travel diary: "When one passes through this village, smoke from the salt fires is faintly seen. There are small fishes drying in the fields, scattered pines, the shady color of the sea."

They passed Seikenji, looming above them on the mountainside. At the row of salve shops lining the road opposite the temple, young salespersons cried that he must try their special medicine. Glancing

The salt-making beach at Okitsu on a moonlit evening (*a print by Hiroshige*)

102

their way, young Ito flushed and quickened his pace. He threw a covert look at his chief clerk, found that man's face impassive.

Now they were in Okitsu station. Inns lined the road and waitresses hailed them to stop for the night. Just ahead, two girls hauled

Waitresses persuading travelers to lodge at their inn; another traveler, already inside, is washing his feet. On the signs inside the inn are given the names of the artist, engraver, printer, and publisher of the print
(*a print by Hiroshige*)

a traveler bodily into an inn. When Ito reached that open-fronted hostelry he saw the waylaid man with his feet already in a tub of water. One girl was washing travel grime from his legs while the other immobilized him in an embrace. "His howls are not convincing," said the chief clerk.

At the Minaguchi-ya they were greeted personally by Hanzo, the sixth generation of Mochizukis at Okitsu. Leading the way to the inn's finest suite, Hanzo assured Ito that the Minaguchi-ya was honored by his visit, representing as it did a new generation continuing an old association. He inquired after the elder Ito's health and complimented the younger on his vigor. After he retired, the service was most attentive.

The youngest of the maids caught Ito's eye at once. Her make-up was light and her skin glowed clear and clean. It was she who helped him out of his travel kimono and into a fresh one provided by the inn, and when she tied his sash in back he thought that her hands fluttered over his hips for one unnecessary instant. But when he turned, her face was demure.

He came back from his bath with body tingling. "There is nothing," he said to himself, "like a vigorous scrub and a hot tub after a good day's walk." As he draped his towel over a rack where the garden breeze would catch it, the young maid slid open the door to bring him tea. "Well, hardly anything," he mentally amended.

He sat on the cushion she laid for him in the place of honor, and she poured his tea. He liked her hands. She had the door open to leave when he thought of something else. "Will you please," he asked, "bring ink and a brush."

He watched her as she made his ink, pouring a few drops of clear water on the stone, rubbing the stick of ink through the pool until the liquid grew richly black. Her little frown of concentration made him smile and his eyes danced to the rhythm of her hand, her arm, her shoulder, her breast. A wisp of hair escaped from her elaborate coiffure and fell across her cheek. He reached forward to touch it. She was not startled, but with his hand still on her cheek she looked up and smiled back. She smiled a promise.

The chief clerk returned from the bath then, and after very audibly drinking his tea, fished out his diary and began meticulously to complete the day's accounts. He would not, Ito knew, be off one-tenth of a *mon* when they reached Edo.

Ito found his own diary. He did not have to bother with travel expenses but he made it a rule to set down a few notes every day. He took up his brush but sat without writing. The fresh green of the garden shimmered in the twilight, the air was kissed with the scent of pine from supper fires, and he had a long, delicious night to look forward to.

Finally he dipped his brush in the ink that the girl had made for him, set down the date, and wrote: "Stopped tonight in Okitsu at the Minaguchi-ya, where we were most warmly received . . ." At that moment there was a soft murmur from the corridor, and the maids brought in supper.

Next morning, for some reason, Ito was slow getting started, and it was well after dawn before he and his clerk were ready to leave the inn. Hanzo brought the bill and thanked them for their patronage. Ito assured him that they had enjoyed their stay. It had occurred to him, he remarked, that the comfort he had enjoyed at the Minaguchi-ya was a far cry from what his grandfather or great-grandfather had encountered when they had journeyed to Edo.

This was one of Hanzo's favorite topics. "Indeed things have changed," he cried. "In Ieyasu's time, your great-grandfather had to carry his food with him. The most he could have expected from the usual inn was a little hot water to soften his cooked, dried rice. And most inns were crude affairs where a fastidious traveler was thrown together with Lord knows what kind of riffraff, not to mention thieves and murderers.

"Of course, as you know, there are still thieves and murderers on the highway, but the government is doing its best to eradicate them. Why, only last week we received a circular about some vagabond who inveigled a traveler into sharing a room at an inn, and then robbed him. They caught the rogue and cut off his head and put it up on a stake near the scene of his crime, but there are many others —do be careful of overfriendly strangers."

In the inn's entry, Ito and his companion each thrust his sword into his sash. They were commoners, but even a commoner was permitted to wear a sword while on a journey. A traveler had no choice but to carry all the money required for his trip: this made him a tempting target, and no one denied him the right to be armed against the perils of the road.

As they replied to a chorus of farewells, Hanzo caught the lingering glance between Ito and the young maid. "Aha," he thought, "no wonder he was hard to rouse this morning." And he made a mental note that if Ito stopped at the Minaguchi-ya on his way home, which now seemed likely, the same maid must be assigned to him.

Hanzo had decided to walk with his guests a few minutes to speed them on their way. "I'm happy," he remarked, as they paced through the village, "that you'll be crossing Satta in broad daylight. There are still cutthroats up there, and I've heard of a brutish renegade priest who extorts money at sword's point. Of course he calls it an offering. A man is a fool to attempt the pass alone at night. Do you know the story of Heisaku?"

Ito and the clerk did not.

"It happened years ago, just how many I'm not sure. Heisaku was a young man of Okitsu. He went to Edo to work, and three years went by without his seeing his father. The thought that he was neglecting his filial duty preyed on his mind. He wanted to ease his father's last years, and so he quit his job, and taking his savings and a parting gift from his employer, he set out for home.

"He wasted no time on the highway and by sunset of the fifth day he reached Yui. He had an aunt living there and he stopped to call on her.

"The old lady was overjoyed to see him. She told him his father was hale and hearty, and prattled on about the family, as women will, until it was quite dark. She wanted him to spend the night but he insisted he could not stop so near home. She had heard of highwaymen attacking travelers on Satta and sometimes killing them, but he belittled her fears and set out on the last leg of his journey.

"His aunt spent a sleepless night, worrying about him, and early next morning she started for Okitsu to make certain that he had arrived safely.

"She found Heisaku's father, aged but stalwart, sitting alone in his house. At first he appeared not to understand her talk of Heisaku, but as she poured out her story his eyes wandered to some clothes hanging on the wall. Following his gaze, the woman saw the kimono that Heisaku had been wearing the day before. She almost wept with relief, thinking that Heisaku was safe at home after all, but his father grew pale and continued to stare distractedly at the clothes. Suddenly he began to scream, 'It was a mistake! It was a mistake!' and he dashed from the house.

"Later they found two bodies on the rocks at the foot of Satta, the bodies of Heisaku and his father. And if you look sharp along the path at the top of the mountain you'll see a monument to the memory of a traveler who was killed by his father, and a highwayman who killed his son, all unknowing."

With this cheerful tale Hanzo bid good-bye to his guests, wishing them a safe and profitable journey. Then he retraced his steps towards the Minaguchi-ya, accepting homage in the form of bows from lesser innkeepers whose establishments lined the road. When he reached the middle of town it occurred to him to stop for a chat at the post house, where his friend Denzaemon held forth.

The post house was the heart of any Tokaido station. In Okitsu it dominated the village, an imposing two-story building with white plaster walls, set back from the highway so that its clutter of men and horses would not block traffic.

In front was the square where government notices were posted. There were traffic regulations, injunctions to thrift and filial pity, and the standing ban on Christianity with its inducement of gold for a tip exposing a Christian. It had been a long time since anyone around Okitsu had been able to collect such a reward. Beside the post house was a courtyard where pack horses were stabled and loaded, and where hostlers and kago-carriers loitered until called for duty. The kago was the standard travel vehicle on the Tokaido, a light palanquin hung from a pole carried on bearers' shoulders.

Hanzo skirted the public notices, which he knew by heart, glanced into the courtyard, noisy as usual, and entered the post house. There he picked his way through a maze of clerks to the rear where Denzaemon was ensconced to oversee his empire. A boy quickly appeared with tea.

Like Mochizuki, Denzaemon was an important man in Okitsu. Otherwise he would not have been head of the post house. It and its counterparts in the other fifty-two stations were neither inns nor eating places but they were the backbone of the government's traffic system.

Their men and horses were available first, and without charge, to travelers on government business. Daimyo paid the official rate, which was set in Edo. If things were not too busy, Denzaemon could extend the same rate to samurai, to merchants who purveyed to the Shogun, and to those pampered darlings, the big-bellied *sumo* wrestlers. If things were slack, even a commoner could rest his blisters at a price set in spirited haggling, man to man.

In addition to kago-bearers and pack horses, Denzaemon had eight fleet-footed runners to relay the Shogun's letters and edicts. When runners from a neighboring village streaked in with such a message, secure in a black-lacquered box bearing the Tokugawa crest, Denzaemon's men were ready to speed it on its way. They ran in pairs,

Sumo wrestlers, having rounded Satta Mountain, ford the Okitsu River (*a print by Hiroshige*)

108

in case one should meet with an accident; and at the sound of their bell even great daimyo yielded the road. It had been runners like these who rushed Yui Shosetsu's death warrant to Shizuoka.

With a hundred horses and a hundred kago-bearers, the post house employed a large part of the village. But during the seasonal migration of daimyo to or from their enforced residence in Edo, this pool was not enough. Then Denzaemon had the power to levy more men and horses from the neighboring villages. It was one more tax and it hit the farmers hard because it came at their busy season. In some areas their anger flared into revolt, but Denzaemon's peasants seldom did more than complain, however bitterly. Either they trudged in with their horses or they sent him a penalty payment. He was just as happy with the latter, for then he hired roustabouts as substitutes, and pocketed the difference.

The men who lived by their labors on the highway were a special breed, rough, tough, and magnificently tatooed. In summer their tattoos and their loincloths were all they wore. In midwinter they might tolerate a kimono, but even then they would, in one observer's words, "for expedition's sake tack their gowns quite up to their belt exposing their back and privy parts naked to everybody's view, which they say, they have no reason at all to be ashamed of."

They could be instantly recognized by great calluses on their shoulders, from carrying kago, and signs of buboes in their groins, from consorting with wrong women. Their songs were ribald, and their jargon mystifying. They drank liquor from teacups, gambled with passion, and whored with vengeance.

They regulated their service by the amount of their tip, and they were not above increasing it by threats in some lonely spot. But if they made trouble for a stingy customer, they could be a great help to a generous one. If, for example, it seemed impossible to reach a checkpoint before closing hour, one of them might take a sliding door off the kago, and run ahead with it. When he came to the barrier, he would mark time and make a great show of shouting, "Go on! Go on!" as though he were carrying the whole load. The rule was that a palanquin which reached the gate before closing time could go

The men who lived by their labors on the highway were a special breed
(*a book illustration by Nangaku*)

through that night, and this act was enough to satisfy the requirement.

Even when their customer was a daimyo, the tip regulated the service. They couldn't threaten him, but they could regale him with a jolly song if they were pleased, or embarrass him with a sarcastic one if they were not.

Denzaemon's contingent of this lusty brotherhood lived in a rowdy encampment behind the post house. As boss and hands they were natural enemies, but they granted each other a kind of wary respect and managed to get along.

But Hanzo had not stopped at Denzaemon's to chat about kago-bearers. Both men were concerned over that recent directive from the travel commissioner which Hanzo had mentioned to young Ito. In addition to citing the case of the thief who had already lost his head, the circular went on to declare that there were too many such crimes, and it ordered local officials into action. All men who frequently stopped at inns, or stayed at them overlong, were to be investigated, and the suspicious ones reported without delay. Failure in this would bring down drastic punishment on station officials. Hanzo and Denzaemon considered this, and shuddered.

But they managed a grin as they read together the next portion of the directive. It cited reports that travelers were sometimes forced to pay excess charges at river crossings: coolies would go out of their way to wade through deep holes and then demand more money because they were wet "all the way up to here," or they would discover in midstream that their passenger was so heavy that only a healthy bonus would enable them to deliver him safely. These practices must cease, the commissioner thundered. River officials would see to it that charges were based strictly on the depth of water at the proper crossing, and they would insure that even minor travelers were protected from extortion.

Ichikawa and Tezuka were in charge of Okitsu's river crossings. Tezuka ran the upper crossing with seven assistants and a force of a hundred and seventy coolies. Ichikawa was in charge of the lower, with the same number of assistants and two hundred fifty laborers.

These two men were unquestionably the village's leading citizens. Hanzo and Denzaemon were obliged to defer to them, and while relations were cordial enough, there was secret pleasure in seeing superiors discomfited. And this circular was certain to do just that.

Ordinarily, a town's Headman ran the post house, but since in Okitsu that job was delegated to Denzaemon while Ichikawa and Tezuka took over the river crossings, it is evident that the river office was more important, or more profitable, which is the same thing.

The same two men also operated the town's two leading inns, which were called *honjin*. All up and down the Tokaido, *honjin* were designated for the exclusive use of daimyo and court nobility. Next in grade were *waki-honjin*, or side-*honjin*, which were ordinarily used by a daimyo's chief lieutenants but could be used by a daimyo if traffic piled up so that the *honjin* were already taken; if not busy with some daimyo, *waki-honjin* were free to take general travelers. The Minaguchi-ya was a *waki-honjin*. A *honjin* could never have accommodated a businessman like Ito, but the Minaguchi-ya could.

It was unfair, and they knew it, but Hanzo and Denzaemon shared a joke about the advantages of running both a *honjin* and the river crossing: if one were blessed with a well-paying guest, how simple to hold on to him by closing the river as being too dangerous to cross. There was not one whit of evidence that either Tezuka or Ichikawa ever succumbed to such unworthy thoughts, but it was a standing jest around Okitsu that whenever Tezuka, a close-fisted man, was blessed with a wealthy daimyo, he prayed for high water.

So Hanzo and Denzaemon sipped their tea and managed to raise each other's spirits, so recently dampened by the clear implication in the highway commissioner's circular that village elders were to be held responsible for any unfortunate incident in their town. Even with this threat hanging over their heads, it was difficult to be down-

River coolies would go out of their way to wade through deep holes (*a book illustration by Jichosai*)

hearted in the face of the burst of prosperity that was almost upon them. The very next evening not one but two daimyo would stay in Okitsu, appropriating both *honjin*, and, in addition, the Dutch from Nagasaki were scheduled to stop over on their yearly journey to Edo. The Dutch were given daimyo status for their trip and hence were entitled to *honjin* accommodations, but in every encounter with daimyo the Hollanders invariably found themselves outranked, as they were on this date in Okitsu: they would therefore be installed at the Minaguchi-ya. Hanzo was delighted, for they were the most exotic guests an innkeeper could look forward to.

The Japanese saw other foreigners from time to time. They saw Koreans and Ryukyuans and Chinese. But the only Europeans who were now tolerated in the island empire were the Dutch. They brought a breath of the strange and forbidden Western world. Their light coloring was fascinating in itself. The Japanese tagged them "Red-hairs."

The Dutch looked forward to their annual journey with even more excitement than did the Japanese who played host to them. This visit to Edo to pay their respects to the Shogun was their one chance a year to see something of Japan. The rest of the time they were confined to Nagasaki, and chiefly to a tiny islet in the harbor. Only rarely were they allowed to visit Nagasaki city, and then under offensively heavy escort, all of whom had to be treated to a very expensive dinner.

It was the same story on their trip to Edo. To escort, attend, and guard four Hollanders there were a hundred Japanese, all traveling at the expense of the Netherlands East-India Company. But this drain on the corporate purse was not enough to dampen the thrill of getting out of Nagasaki.

The first of their annual visits had come in 1642, when the third Shogun took occasion to lay down the law. The Dutch would make port at Nagasaki and nowhere else; they would instantly report any Christians entering Japan on any ship; and they would render to the Shogunate complete reports of what was going on in the rest of the world. Failure to comply would mean being kicked out as the Spanish and Portuguese had been, and so the Dutch undertook to please.

Every year they carried to the Shogun and his court a heavy load of gifts, carefully selected for their value. These, in effect, were their annual taxes, and the Dutch considered them reasonable enough, in view of the profits they made on their trade.

Their journey took about three months, a month going up, a month in Edo, and a month coming back. They went overland from Nagasaki to Kokura, by ship on the Inland Sea to Osaka, and then up the Tokaido to Edo. They were carefully routed around Kyoto, it having been made clear to them that the cloistered Emperor was only the country's head priest, too sacred to be disturbed: the Shogun wanted no doubts cast on his own right to govern. On the Tokaido their party increased to about a hundred and fifty, for the baggage sent ahead from Nagasaki to Osaka by boat now had to be carried on men's shoulders.

Reminded that his alien visitors were almost upon him, Hanzo took leave of his friend Denzaemon and returned to the Minaguchi-ya. There was work to be done.

It was unlikely that the Hollanders would notice any difference between Mochizuki's inn and a *honjin*. Just ten years earlier, fire had swept Okitsu station, destroying the Minaguchi-ya along with most of the rest of the town. Ichikawa, Tezuka, and Mochizuki had received government grants to put them back in business, and the whole town had helped them rebuild, for *honjin* and *waki-honjin* were, after all, public utilities of a sort. Using the government's money, Hanzo had blandly defied its regulations and built an inn exactly like a *honjin*. (There had been some sputtering over his presumption, but Hanzo had a way with him and the sputtering had died away.) This meant that, unlike common inns whose front was hospitably open to the street, the Minaguchi-ya boasted an imposing gate and entrance which gave it a striking resemblance to a temple.

Hanzo was particularly proud of the gate and of the tile dolphins which sported at each end of its massive tile roof. He had commissioned these dolphins especially, and he maintained that each flipped his tail with unique grace.

Behind the gate stretched a long areaway, paved with white sand, leading to the second feature supposedly reserved to *honjin*, the big entry. This was the size of a small house, almost twenty-five feet square, with an elaborately gabled roof, an alcove for spears and halberds, and a berth for the chief guest's palanquin.

Adjoining the gate was a large storeroom for luggage and kago. In front of this was a pit to make loading easier, overhung by deep eaves for protection in rainy weather. Past the storeroom was the entrance to the family's living quarters, which occupied a modest corner of the property. Through this doorway Hanzo bustled now, mentally listing things to be done.

Playing host to the Dutch presented special problems. Chief among them was that the inn had to be converted into a kind of jail. The Hollanders traveled under close surveillance and on no account were they allowed to wander alone. Hanzo had received strict instructions to seal any doors and windows opening their apartment to the outside. They would be allowed to walk in the garden, but there must be no possibility of their seeing over the wall. Hanzo knew that Dutchmen were very tall, and he prudently ordered his carpenter to add masking which would raise the wall to ten feet. There was nothing to be seen over the top except Suruga Bay and Miho, but rules were rules.

It was past noon the next day before Hanzo decided that the Minaguchi-ya was at last ready for the Red-hairs. Then he retired to dress. His wife shaved his forehead and his crown, carefully combed his heavily pomaded hair which grew long at the sides and back of his head, and trimmed it where it lay forward in a thick lock over his shaved pate. She brought out a fine dark kimono of figured silk, whose only decoration, high in the middle of the back, was a small embroidered crest. She helped him into *hakama*, skirt-like trousers which enveloped his kimono up to the waist, and adjusted his wide flaring shoulder pieces of starched silk, which, like the kimono, bore his crest.

He was now in the full dress called *kamishimo,* and the only thing to distinguish him from a samurai was that he slipped under his sash not two swords but one.

His chief clerk, similarly dressed but swordless, joined him, and with a servant they set out for Seikenji, where they would meet their guests. They were early. It would have been unthinkable to be late.

Seeing them approach, the owner of Seikenji's big medicine shop called Fuji-no-maru invited them to wait in his shop. Hanzo sent his servant up the highway to speed back word as soon as the Dutch were sighted, and then he and his chief clerk sat on cushions placed at the front of the shop's platform floor, sipped the inevitable tea, and chatted happily with Fuji-no-maru's owner about the busy and profitable night that each looked forward to. The shrill cries of the salve-sellers, which had so disconcerted young Ito, seemed to bother Hanzo not at all.

The Dutch, now nearing Okitsu, had been on the road since dawn. One of their number, each time they made the trip to Edo, was their own physician, for the cautious Hollanders did not propose to deliver themselves into the hands of Japanese doctors. In this year of 1691 he was Englebert Kaempfer, M.D., who busied himself throughout the journey by taking copious notes, and whose observations have come down to us in his fat and fascinating *History of Japan.* A stranger's eyes are often sharper than a native's, so it is not surprising that we owe to Dr. Kaempfer many of the best descriptions of the Tokaido and the bustle of life upon it.

The Tokaido, he wrote, was a highway "so broad and large, that two companies, tho' never so great, can conveniently and without hindrance, pass by one another." It was built of sand and stone, banked up in the middle for good drainage, and, since wheeled vehicles were taboo, it was not cut by ruts.

"Every where upon Tokaido," Kaempfer went on, "between the towns and villages there is a streight row of firrs planted on each side of the road, which by their agreeable shade make the journey both pleasant and convenient. . . . The neighbouring villages must jointly keep [the roads] in repair, and take care, that they be swept and clean'd every day. . . . The inspectors . . . are at no great trouble to get people to clean them; for whatever makes the roads dirty and nasty, is of some use to the neighbouring country people, so that they rather strive, who should first carry it away. The pinenuts, branches and leaves, which fall down daily from the firrs, are gather'd for fewel. . . . Nor doth horses dung lie long upon the ground but it is soon taken up by poor country children and serves to manure the fields. For the same reason care is taken, that the filth of travellers be not lost, and there are in several places, near country people's houses, or in their fields, houses of office built for them to do their needs."

Kaempfer noted difficulties, too: "hills and mountains, which are sometimes so steep and high, that travellers are necessitated to get themselves carried over in kago, because they cannot without great difficulty and danger pass them on horseback"; rivers which "run with so impetuous a rapidity towards the sea, that they will bear no bridge or boat"; and those man-made impediments, the barrier-gates flung across the highway as checkpoints. The barrier in the Hakone Mountains was a mere nuisance for the Dutch, who traveled with an official escort, but it was a dreaded ordeal for many Japanese. It was snugly situated in the heart of the mountains, where the highway bordered the lake, and there was no easy way to bypass it. Traffic was often congested there, and it was frustrating to reach it after it had closed for the night, but it took a hardy soul to risk going around. If he was caught, the penalty was crucifixion.

Women, especially, were given a bad time, for the Shogunate was vigilant against the escape of its hostages, and the higher the class, the worse the ordeal. Every woman had to carry an official certificate which authorized her travel and carefully identified her. First, she was classified, whether nun, priestess, pilgrim, widow, wife, young girl, or prostitute. Then she was described: if pregnant, injured, blind or demented; if marked by tumors, wounds, or cautery; if distinguished by a bald spot or thinning hair.

When she approached the barrier-gate, she first produced her certificate for a quick check of its validity. Then she was obliged to pay a handsome tip to a teahouse woman who had established herself in the lucrative position of a go-between, after which she was ushered in to the officials. Lord help her at this point if her pass was smudged or the writing hard to read.

If she was traveling from Edo, and looked to be of high station, she was turned over to female examiners. Young women had to submit to examination in a special smock, and this meant a big fee to a special concessionaire who rented them.

If any discrepancies were discovered, the unfortunate woman was taken into custody until the whole thing could be cleared up with the authority who had issued her certificate, a matter of several days at least; but if everything was unquestionably in order, the necessary stamps were affixed, and she was on her way at last.

This was the Tokaido, with its conveniences and its obstacles. It was the world's busiest highway, linking what were probably the world's largest cities: lusty young Edo, seat of government if not the capital; proud old Kyoto, still the capital even if it had no power to govern; and hustling, money-loving, shrewd Osaka, the commercial (without qualification) capital of the country. Between these cities, on this highway, under its firs, across its rivers, and through its barrier-gates, surged a motley traffic.

There were businessmen. There were great merchants like Ito, with their eye on the market that was Edo; their goods moved by sea but they went by land—it was far more fun. There were peddlers: patent-medicine men, sellers of almanacs and charms, of ink and utensils.

There were religious pilgrims, a happy crew mostly, singing and clapping their way on a light-hearted jaunt to some famous shrine or temple.

There were great daimyo, swashbuckling their way with massive entourage from home fief to Edo or back again. They were the reason for *honjin* and *waki-honjin*. They were the greatest boost to business since peace, for most of them had to use the Tokaido, and a lord of any importance could hardly keep face with a parade of less than two or three thousand men.

Kaempfer saw many of their processions, processions like the two that were converging on Okitsu that same day. And he probably got a better look at them than did the ordinary people of Japan, who, if they found themselves near such a cortege, were obliged to kneel with their faces in the roadway. Listen as the doctor catalogs the paraphernalia of pomp displayed by a daimyo of middling grade:

"1. Numerous troops of fore-runners, harbingers, clerks, cooks, and other inferior officers, begin the march, they being to provide lodgings, victuals and other necessary things, for the entertainment of their prince and master, and his court. They are follow'd by,

"2. The prince's heavy baggage . . . with his coat of arms . . . carried upon horses, each with a banner . . . or upon men's shoulders, with multitudes of inspectors to look after them.

"3. Great numbers of smaller retinues, belonging to the chief

An ink peddler
(*a book illustration
by Jichosai*)

officers and noblemen attending the prince . . . some in . . . palanquins, others on horseback.

"4. The prince's own numerous train, marching in an admirable and curious order, and divided into several troops, each headed by a proper commanding officer: As

"1. Five, more or less, fine led-horses, led each by two grooms, one on each side, two footmen walking behind.

"2. Five, or six, and sometimes more porters, richly clad walking one by one, and carrying . . . lacker'd chests, and japan'd neat trunks and baskets upon their shoulders, wherein are kept the gowns, cloaths, wearing apparel, and other necessaries for the daily use of the prince; each porter is attended by two footmen, who take up his charge by turns.

"3. Ten, or more fellows walking again one by one, and carrying rich scymeters, pikes of state . . . and other weapons in lacker'd wooden cases, as also quivers with bows and arrows. . . .

"4. Two, three, or more men, who carry the pikes of state, as badges of the prince's power and authority, adorn'd at the upper end with bunches of cockfeathers . . . or other particular ornaments. . . .

"5. A gentleman carrying the prince's hat, which he wears to shelter himself from the heat of the sun, and which is cover'd with black velvet. He is attended likewise by two footmen.

"6. A gentleman carrying the prince's sombreiro or umbrello, which is cover'd in like manner with black velvet, attended by two footmen.

"7. Some more . . . trunks, with the prince's coat of arms upon them, each with two men to take care of it.

"8. Sixteen, more or less, of the prince's pages, and gentlemen of his bed-chamber, richly clad, walking two by two before his palanquin. They are taken out from among the first quality of his court.

"9. The prince himself sitting in a stately . . . palanquin, carried by six or eight men, clad in rich liveries, with several others walking at the palanquin's sides, to take it up by turns. Two or three gentlemen of the prince's bed-chamber walk at the palanquin's side, to give him what he wants and asks for, and to assist and support him in going in or out of the palanquin.

"10. Two, or three horses of state, the saddles cover'd with black. One of these horses carries a large elbow-chair, which is sometimes cover'd with black velvet. . . . These horses are attended each by several grooms and footmen in liveries, and some are led by the prince's own pages.

"11. Two pike-bearers.

"12. Ten or more people, carrying each two baskets of a monstrous large size, fix'd to the ends of a pole, which they lay on their shoulders in such a manner, that one basket hangs down before, another behind them. These baskets are more for state, than for any use. . . . In this order marches the prince's own train, which is follow'd by

"5. Six to twelve led-horses, with their leaders, grooms, and footmen, all in liveries.

"6. A multitude of the prince's domesticks, and other officers of his court, with their own very numerous trains and attendants, pike-bearers, chest-bearers, and footmen in liveries . . . the whole troop is headed by the prince's high-steward carried in a palanquin. . . .

"It is a sight exceedingly curious and worthy of admiration, to see all the persons, who compose the numerous train of a great prince . . . marching in an elegant order, with a decent becoming gravity, and keeping so profound a silence, that not the least noise is to be heard, save what must necessarily arise from the motion and rushing of their habits, and the trampling of the horses and men."

The Tokaido's travelers were certainly intriguing, even spectacular. But it is not difficult to understand why Dr. Kaempfer was equally fascinated by the weird and wonderful types who made the highway their home and their life.

At any time of day there might be a mountain priest, long-haired, black-hatted, ponderous rosary looped over rough hemp uniform, pacing beside the Dutchman's horse, thumping the ground with a great staff, rattling its iron rings, and flinging out a windy speech

A mountain priest
(*a book illustration
by Hakuyu*)

capped by a "frightful noise" blown upon a "trumpet made of a large shell."

Incantations and prayers were the business of his kind, austerities in the mountains the key to their powers. They were able to command both native Shinto and imported Buddhist gods, "to conjure and drive out evil spirits, . . . to recover stolen goods, and to discover the thieves, to fortel future events, to explain dreams, to cure desperate distempers, to find out the guilt, or innocence, of persons accused of crimes and misdemeanors." In pursuing the last they would likely require that the accused walk over burning coals: no innocent man, they asserted, would char.

Kaempfer was cool to these zealots, but he warmed to the *bikuni*, begging nuns. When one of them singled him out, approached him, and sang him "a rural song," he dug into his pockets, for if a gentleman "proves very liberal and charitable, she will keep him company and divert him for some hours," and they were "much the handsomest girls we saw in Japan."

Once these *bikuni* had used song to propagate Buddhism among housewives, but they had slipped from ancient standards. Now they seldom bothered with housewives and their songs seemed little concerned with Buddhism. They painted their faces and wore attractive kimonos. True, they shaved their heads, but they took care to cover them with comely hoods of silk. Their manners were delightful, said Kaempfer, and "seemingly modest. However not to extol their modesty beyond what it deserves, it must be observ'd, that they make nothing of laying their bosoms quite bare to the view of charitable travellers, all the while they keep them company, under pretence of its being customary in the country, and . . . for ought I know, they may be, tho' never so religiously shav'd, full as impudent and lascivious, as any whore in a publick bawdy-house."

Kaempfer was not far off in his surmise, if surmise it was. Assault on a nun was considered one of the five heinous crimes, but *bikuni* invited a certain amount of assault and seldom complained about it afterward.

Children there were, too, sometimes the offspring of mountain priests, who brought them along to help in begging. "These little bastards are exceedingly troublesome. . . . In some places they and their fathers accost travellers in company with a troop of *bikuni* and with their rattling, singing, trumpeting, chattering, and crying, make such a horrid, frightful noise, as would make one mad or deaf. . . .

"There are many more beggars . . . some sick, some stout and lusty enough, who get people's charity by praying, singing, playing upon fiddles, guitars, and other musical instruments, or performing some juggler's tricks . . . [some] sit upon the road all day long upon a small coarse mat. They have a flat bell . . . lying before them, and . . . with a lamentable singing-tune . . . address the God Amida, as the patron and advocate of departed souls. Mean while they beat almost continually with a small wooden hammer upon the aforesaid bell, and this they say, in order to be the sooner heard by Amida, and I am apt to think, . . . by passengers too. . . .

"The crowd and throng upon the roads in this country is not a little encreas'd by numberless small retail-merchants and children of country people, who run about from morning to night, following travellers, and offering them . . . their poor . . . merchandise; such as for instance several cakes and sweetmeats, wherein the quantity of sugar is so inconsiderable, that it is scarce perceptible . . . or else all sorts of roots boil'd in water and salt, road-books, straw-shoes for horses and men, ropes, strings, tooth-pickers, and a multitude of other trifles. . . ."

At the edge of Okitsu, Dr. Kaempfer kept right on taking notes: "This town being situate not far from the sea, the inhabitants make very good salt out of the sand on the coasts, after they have pour'd sea-water upon it at repeated times."

The Dutchmen's train had reached the town, and now it halted. Hanzo was kneeling before them, bidding them welcome. Wrote Kaempfer: "The landlord observes the same customs upon our arrival, which he doth upon the arrival of the princes and lords of the empire . . . he addresses every one of us, making his compliments with a low bow, which before the palanquins of the chief Japanese, and our resident, is so low, that he touches the ground with his hands, and almost with his forehead." Hanzo rose, dusted his knees, and fell in at the head of the troop to lead it into town.

On his way from Seikenji to the Minaguchi-ya, Kaempfer, having lost his begging nun at the edge of Okitsu, now turned his eye to the painted females in front of each general inn. "Walk in, walk in," they cried, "walk right in, gentlemen. You'll find warm welcome here." "They make," the doctor remarked, "no inconsiderable noise. . . ."

There was noise, too, in front of the Minaguchi-ya, where a curious crowd had gathered to stare at the Red-hairs. Urchins made faces and screamed, "Koreans!"—an epithet that exhausted their concept of foreigners.

It was a brief show. The Dutch dismounted quickly and, screened by their Japanese escort, passed through the dolphin-topped gate into the raked-sand areaway. Hanzo repeated his welcome, his compliments, and his low bows. The guests removed their boots and stepped up onto the matted floor.

The Minaguchi-ya had four rows of rooms but at the moment all their sliding doors were opened and the handsomely painted landscapes which they bore had given way to the cool green vista of the garden, seen straight through the building. The innermost quarters were the finest, and there the Dutch were led, as rows of doors closed shut behind them. They were penned for the night, and it irked them, but it was a pleasant prison. The garden lay before them and swept round on the left, as intimate with their room as sea to ship. Behind the wall on their right was a privy (immaculately fresh and fragrant with flowers), a dressing room, and a bath. There a big tub of satin-smooth, sweet-scented pine, brimming with steamy water, faced the open doors of its own small garden.

Not all the party, of course, could stay at the Minaguchi-ya. The four Hollanders and the chief Japanese were installed there. Hanzo had made arrangements for forty lesser Japanese to stay in general inns, and his friend Denzaemon had assisted by nominating several farmhouses to sleep the porters. With daimyo and Dutch, Okitsu bulged that night.

Now it was time for Hanzo's brief moment with his exotic guests. "As soon as we have taken possession of our apartment," Kaempfer recorded, "in comes the landlord with some of his chief male domesticks, each with a dish of tea in his hand, which they present to every one of us with a low bow, according to his rank and dignity. . . . This done, the necessary apparatus for smoaking is brought in, consisting of a board of wood or brass, . . . upon which are plac'd a small fire pan with coals, a pot to spit in, a small box fill'd with tobacco cut small, and some long pipes with small brass heads; as also another japan'd board or dish, with . . . something to eat, as for instance, several sorts of fruits, figs, nuts, several sorts of cakes . . . and other trumperies of this kind." Had he and his associates been Japanese, Kaempfer noted enviously, other necessaries would have been served by the maids of the establishment. "These wenches also lay the cloth, and wait at table, taking this opportunity to engage their guests to farther favors. But 'tis quite otherwise with us. For the landlords themselves, and their . . . domesticks, after they have presented us with a dish of tea, as abovesaid, are not suffer'd, upon any account whatever, to approach or to enter our appartments, but whatever we want, 'tis the sole business of our own servants to provide us with the same." Hanzo had had his last look at the Dutchmen until they were to leave.

He was, however, kept busy. The Japanese in the party demanded service, and the kitchen had to be looked after. The Dutch, throughout their journey, insisted on "dishes dress'd after the European manner" and so they brought their own cooks from Nagasaki. Hanzo's cooks had to prepare supper for the Japanese escort, and the innkeeper did not have to be told that two sets of artists in one kitchen was an invitation to riot. He intervened several times to smooth ruffled temperament.

While two culinary cliques made Hanzo's kitchen a danger spot, two daimyo's trains were doing as much for the whole town. One was already installed at Tezuka's *honjin*, the other was at the moment strutting slowly towards Ichikawa's.

Dr. Kaempfer, corked up in the Minaguchi-ya, did not see this approach, but he had seen many on the road. The palanquins of the daimyo and his chief officers were raised high in the air, "whilst the bearers by their short deliberate steps and stiff knees, affect a ridiculous fear and circumspection." And all the while, pages, pike-bearers, umbrella- and hat-bearers, chest-bearers and footmen in livery performed that strange dance reserved for great towns, their meetings with another lord, or, as now, their approach to a post station where they would pass the night. "Every step they make they draw up their foot quite to their back, in the mean time stretching out the arm on the opposite side as far as they can, and putting themselves in such a posture, as if they had a mind to swim through the air. Mean while the pikes, hats, umbrellos, chests, boxes, baskets, and whatever else they carry, are danced and toss'd about in a very singular manner, answering the motion of their bodies."

Thus they came to Ichikawa's *honjin*, its entrance screened with curtains blazoning their lord's crest. That worthy disappeared into the interior, the noisy work of posting guards and unloading the baggage went forward, and the village elders, looking harassed, checked the fire watch and uttered little prayers that there would be no clashes tonight between rival groups.

At the Minaguchi-ya, dinner was served. The Dutch had brought their own serving ware, chairs, even a dining table. On that table appeared foods carried from Nagasaki, including European wines foggy from being jogged up the Tokaido. Hanzo added odds and ends: one pheasant, one halibut, one sea bass, twenty-three eggs (most of these disappeared at breakfast), tangerines, and hot saké. It would seem that the Dutch were fair trenchermen, but Dr. Kaempfer insisted that their Japanese escort exhibited far greater capacity. Dinner for the Japanese that night was supplemented by rice cooked with red

Daimyo entering a Tokaido *honjin* draped with curtains bearing his crest, while the *honjin*-keeper and town dignitaries bow respectfully; in the foreground are attendants, pike-bearers, and chest-bearers (*a print by Hiroshige*)

beans, that ceremonial dish having been ordered for them by the Dutch as a pretty compliment.

Dinner in the Japanese apartment was lively: ". . . They sit after meals drinking and singing some songs to make one another merry, or else they propose some riddles round, or play at some other game, and he that cannot explain the riddle, or loses the game, is oblig'd to drink a glass. 'Tis again quite otherwise with us in this respect for we sit at table and eat our victuals very quietly."

Four sober-sided Dutchmen stowing away pheasant, halibut, and sea bass (*a print by Kawakami*)

Okitsu went on a binge that night. Gambling was wide open and frenzied. Inns rocked with songs and drunken laughter and women's squeals. The Minaguchi-ya reverberated to the Japanese party and its raucous game of forfeits. And in the midst of it all, four sober-sided Dutchmen faced each other across their table and stolidly stowed away pheasant, halibut, and sea bass.

The inn shelters important and exotic guests

The Minaguchi-ya finally quieted down but the town sizzled until dawn set all three cavalcades in motion again. By arrangement never put into words, the lesser daimyo stayed in his *honjin* until the greater had passed, and thus avoided a dignity-bruising encounter. By then, the Dutch had consumed the last of Hanzo's twenty-three eggs.

"When everything is ready for us to set out again," wrote Kaempfer, diagramming Hanzo's second appearance before his guests, "the landlord is call'd, and our resident, in presence of the two interpreters, pays him the reckoning in gold, laid upon a small board. He draws near in a creeping posture, kneeling, holding his hands down to the floor, and when he takes the table which the money is laid upon, he bows down his forehead almost quite to the ground, in token of submission and gratitude, uttering with a deep voice the word, ah, ah, ah! whereby in this country inferiors shew their deference and respect to their superiors." Hanzo was, however, registering more than deference and respect. It was with genuine pleasure that he laid hands on some gold. Many Japanese officials traveled at government expense, which meant troublesome requisitions and almost endless red tape before payment appeared. The fact that the Dutch paid cash did not lessen their popularity with innkeepers.

"It is a custom in this country, which we likewise observe," Kaempfer adds, "that guests before they quit the inn, order their servants to sweep the room they lodged in, not to leave any dirt or ungrateful dust behind them."

Hanzo escorted his guests out of Okitsu as he had escorted them in, basking in glory as he strode along the highway. At the edge of the station he bowed them on their way, wishing mightily that he might continue with them right into Edo.

The last of the great guests gone, and without a single untoward incident, the town relaxed, sprawling lazily in the spring sunshine. Hanzo, Ichikawa, Tezuka—all were pleased with the night's business. Daimyo, like the Dutch, paid cash, and there had been generous tips all around, plus what their men had dropped in individual pursuit of pleasure. From the owners of Seikenji's salve shops to the river-crossing coolies, Okitsu's townsmen jingled coins and smiled.

Not that it was all profit, as old Tezuka would have been the first to tell you. A *honjin* or *waki-honjin* had the same problem that has plagued innkeepers since the first inn. "Most annoying of all is to lose things—tableware, candlesticks, smoking sets, etc. If fifty smoking pipes are offered, scarcely ten are returned. Tea cups and other small things are carried away under clothing. All this occurs because there are so many people milling around, including the daily-hire bearers, and everything is hustle and bustle. Some throw away their straw sandles and demand new ones. When it rains, straw mats are taken away as raincoats. Many of the things we lose were hired for the occasion from other places." But the people of Okitsu had heard this speech before.

The Dutch went on to Edo. There they lodged in an inn appropri-

A daimyo's attendants preparing for an early start from a Tokaido *honjin* (*a print by Hiroshige*)

ately named Nagasaki-ya. Lodged is perhaps not the right word, for again they were closely confined. In the teeming city, but not able to roam it, their greatest thrills came from watching the "flowers of Edo," the fires that almost nightly scarred the city before its intrepid firemen put them out.

It was astonishing, though, how many kinsmen their innkeeper suddenly acquired, all of whom found it imperative to call on him while the Dutch were in his house. It was even more astonishing how many of these were noted scholars and great daimyo. True to character, the scholars sought information about medicine, physics, botany, and astronomy, while the lords of the empire wanted to talk politics, geography, history, and the art of war. The innkeeper applied himself to study of the stars and world affairs.

After more than two weeks of this, the day arrived for the Dutch to make their trip to Edo Castle. Their gifts were formally laid out in the audience chamber, and they waited, interminably it seemed, in various anterooms until finally the resident-director was summoned. He crawled on hands and knees to a designated spot in front of the Shogun, bowed his forehead to the floor, and retreated, crablike, in the same position.

Once, that had been all there was to it. But in Kaempfer's day the Dutchmen were not let off so easily. All four of them were led deeper into the palace. In an inner chamber the Shogun's ladies and his several offspring were secreted behind a bamboo screen. Before this audience, which could see without being seen, Dr. Kaempfer and the two secretaries were required to perform: ". . . To walk, to stand still, to compliment each other, to dance, to jump, to play the drunkard, to speak broken Japanese, to read Dutch, to paint, to sing, to put our cloaks on and off . . . [and to] kiss one another, like man and wife, which the ladies particularly shew'd by their laughter to be well pleas'd with. . . . I joined to my dance a love-song in high German. In this manner, and with innumerable such apish tricks, we must suffer ourselves to contribute to the court's diversion." Only the director, by looking exceedingly solemn, managed to escape performing.

On their journey back to Nagasaki, the ordeal at court behind them, their guards were a little more lenient. It was on their return visit to the Minaguchi-ya that Hanzo managed to smuggle in a few visitors. Physicians, particularly, were eager to learn the latest European methods. Dr. Kaempfer's evenings were usually busy with clandestine visitors, and eighty-five years later another Dutch physician, C. P. Thunberg, introduced the mercury treatment for syphilis. Along the Tokaido, medicine and surgery profited from these visits of the Dutch.

And many Japanese journeyed to Nagasaki to study there, perhaps to earn a certificate of proficiency from the Red-hairs. Some of them wrote treatises based on what they had learned, like the early one called *Komo Geka* ("Red-hair Surgery"). All over Japan men were learning Dutch as the one remaining avenue to the achievements of Western science. There was even a poem written about it:

> Dutch letters
> Running sideways
> Are like a line of wild geese
> Flying in the sky.

The 1690s

CHAPTER SEVEN

*Which explores the pleasures offered by a Tokaido
post town, and some of the troubles and compen-
sations which come the way of an innkeeper*

PRINCIPAL CHARACTERS

A samurai from Satsuma, *who falls ill at the inn*
A mendicant priest, *who tries to cure the samurai*
Terao, *disfigured officer escorting the Shogun's tea, whose
posthumous name is Kashin*
Basho, *poet and wanderer*

and among the people of the inn:

Mochizuki Hanzo, *sixth master of the Minaguchi-ya*

*The two characters
reading "Basho,"
as they would be carved
on a seal*

IT IS too bad, really, that Englebert Kaempfer never had a chance to sample the pleasures of Tokaido post towns. Had he been able to escape from his Japanese guardians and the stuffy resident-director, he would have had a whale of a time.

Each of the fifty-three stations had its own personality, but they were alike in catering to the whims of the traveler. Each had everything to cheer him—inns, restaurants, teahouses, souvenir shops; barbers, masseurs and masseuses, all kinds of amenable ladies.

As with so many little luxuries, the popularity of the Tokaido's girls can best be judged by the Shogunate's strictures against them. In 1659, prostitutes were banned at highway inns. Obviously this prohibition had little effect, for three years later all fifty-three stations received another circular saying the same thing. And so it went, edict piling on flaunted edict, until in 1718 the government sighed and gave up. Each inn could keep two "waitresses," it said, and then it resigned itself to a violation of that limitation by setting a scale of fines which were simply a tax on each additional girl. Prostitutes were almost indispensable to a successful general inn. Mysteriously, five of the fifty-three stations managed without them, but Okitsu was not one of these.

In Okitsu, however, one would not have seen a magnificently dressed courtesan of the highest class, attended by footmen and maids, parading through the streets to a *honjin* and a rendezvous with some daimyo. The nearest place for a spectacle like that was two stations away in Shizuoka. Shizuoka had a licensed quarter which had been authorized by Ieyasu, and which was said to be the model for Edo's famed nightless city, the district called Yoshiwara. However, the city of Shizuoka had dropped in importance since Ieyasu's day, when it was the country's unofficial capital, and

A massage (*a book illustration by Bunpo*)

its bordellos were forced to offer bargains which Yoshiwara never stooped to. For instance, a man might invite a friend to join him, and this "parasite" might play without extra charge provided he left by nine o'clock in the evening.

Hanzo was just as pleased that great courtesans were not available to his customers, for he had no desire to be host to those haughty, temperamental creatures. He was, in fact, comfortably above the whole problem: since the Minaguchi-ya was a *wakihonjin* it did not have to compete for the favor of general travelers, and it never kept prostitutes. There were times when its attractive maids proved vulnerable, but these were extracurricular lapses. Hanzo was philosophical about them.

Thankful to be above the roughest kind of competition, Hanzo sympathized with those who had to engage in it. The general inn-keepers of Okitsu had some particularly difficult years when they struggled in vain to come up with an attraction to equal that of the next station, Shimizu. There the celebrated sister team of Wakasa and Wakamatsu shed glamour on the whole town and particularly on the inn called Funaki-ya.

These girls were the talk of the Tokaido. Travelers, hostlers, and kago-carriers traded gossip about them up and down the highway. Their charms were legendary, their price fantastic. Bewitched travelers would simulate illness to stay over at the Funaki-ya day after day, waiting their turn. (They could truthfully claim they were running a fever.)

Countless travel diaries paid tribute to these sisters, based mostly on hearsay, and the celebrated novelist Saikaku wrote a story about them. Wakasa, he said, slept on his hero's left and Wakamatsu on his right. Saikaku, who tended to make his heroes irresistible, went on to report that his man had so enthralled the girls that they followed him when he left, supporting his travels with their earnings until they decided to shave their heads and become nuns. Okitsu inn-keepers would have been delighted had this been true. As it was, they had to content themselves with the knowledge that only a small fraction of Tokaido travelers could crowd into the Funaki-ya.

Hanzo and his friend Denzaemon at the post house often traded talk about each other's problems. "An innkeeper's troubles," Hanzo was fond of saying, "can be classified under two headings: competition and customers. And," he invariably added, "it all boils down to customers: either there aren't enough of them, or there are too many of the wrong kind."

Hanzo cheerfully admitted that the Minaguchi-ya was seldom troubled by lack of customers, but he maintained that no general innkeeper suffered as he did from difficult patrons. "Oh yes, a common innkeeper gets some low types," he would cry, "but they can't be compared with some of my supposedly high-class guests. You see," he would explain, "an ordinary inn's problem customers are *nobodies,* and can be dealt with as such. But mine are *somebodies,* and they must be handled with care."

There was substance to Hanzo's argument, as Denzaemon well knew. Take, for example, the problem if a traveler fell ill or died along the highway. This was an exigency that town elders often cudgeled their brains over. They were put to considerable trouble and expense when someone inconsiderately expired in their streets or, even worse, in one of their inns.

Some towns, which shall here be nameless, made a practice of thrusting a sick traveler into a kago and hustling him on to the next station. There the officials were likely to repeat the process until the poor man died of exposure or exhaustion, if nothing else.

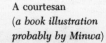

Partly to combat such heartlessness, there was a growing habit among travelers to carry a paper which said in effect: "If I should die along the way, I shall be grateful if my remains are disposed of according to the custom of the place. There is no need to go to the trouble of notifying my next of kin."

This was a thoughtful gesture, for it absolved townspeople along the way of any responsibility save that for decent burial. But it applied only to commoners. No one could be so cavalier with a member of the upper classes. That was Hanzo's point, which was aptly illustrated by the case of Satsuma samurai.

It began with the arrival at the Minaguchi-ya of three samurai in the service of the Lord of Satsuma. One had looked drawn and weary, and

A courtesan
(*a book illustration
probably by Minwa*)

next morning he was not able to continue the journey. His companions, explaining that their business was too urgent to permit delay, continued on their way to Edo, adjuring Hanzo to give the sick man the best of care.

At first the samurai's condition did not appear serious. He professed to believe that a few days' rest would make him right, and he refused to let Hanzo call a physician. Neither man, however, was able to cope with Hanzo's mother, a lady of iron will and theories of her own whenever someone fell ill. Overriding all objections, she appeared in the sick-chamber followed by an ancient servant bearing the inn's kit of patent medicines.

After analyzing the man's ailments, she prescribed a large dose of a bitter physic in which she had great confidence, and thwarting the samurai's plan to pour it into the garden, she stayed to see that it was swallowed.

Confounding her expectations, the patient became steadily worse, and by evening objected hardly at all when Hanzo summoned a physician. That gentleman questioned, poked, stroked his chin, and prescribed moxa, the old oriental remedy in which little cones of dried vegetable fiber are burned on the skin. Dr. Kaempfer, who was of course interested in Japanese medicine, explained to his readers that: "The chief intention of burning is, to draw out the humours and vapours, which lying concealed in the body, prove the cause of the sickness." In this case, the physician directed that six cones of moxa be burned on a spot about five inches above the man's navel. This was done.

Despite the treatment, the samurai had a very bad night and by next morning was desperately ill, with acute spasms of pain in the belly. Hanzo now was genuinely worried, and called a whole concourse of physicians. There was almost but not quite unanimous agreement on acupuncture, and accordingly a slender gold needle was thrust into the patient's abdomen at nine specified points. There was immediate relief, but some hours later the pain recurred with even greater severity.

It would not be fair to deride Japanese medicine of that day. Dr.

Kaempfer did not, and he was in an excellent position to compare Japanese and Western methods. Indeed, when he spoke of moxa and acupuncture he found much in their favor in comparison with the "barbarous apparatus of our European surgery . . . red hot irons, and that variety of cutting knives and other instruments requisite for our operations, a sight so terrible to behold to the patient, and so shocking even to the assistants, if they be not altogether destitute of all sense of humanity and mercy. . . ." He testified that he had seen acupuncture relieve pain "almost in an instant," and as for moxa, "Even the Dutch in the Indies have lately experienced, what a good effect may be expected from burning with the moxa in arthritick, gouty, and rheumatick distempers." But the fact remains that neither moxa nor acupuncture had done anything towards making the samurai well.

Hanzo, tense and worried over his guest's condition, fretted in his office at the front of the inn, harassing the servants with repeated demands for the latest word from the sickroom. Their reports were not encouraging, and the innkeeper continued to stare moodily at the office brazier, its glowing charcoal, and the softly hissing teakettle. As dusk crept down the street and the room darkened, he became aware of a new note in the sounds of evening traffic. There was distant trumpeting, a mournful bawling that pierced his consciousness, to announce the progress of an itinerant priest making his way down the street, blowing on a conch shell, soliciting alms. Hanzo bit his lip and dispatched a clerk to call him in. It was a last desperate measure.

The mendicant appeared, and the innkeeper was aware of harsh angular features and blazing eyes. As he led the way through dim corridors, Hanzo felt those eyes boring into his back, and when the ascetic kneeled over the sick man, Hanzo had a giddy sensation of seeing demon pitted against demon, the demon in the samurai's body against this strange demon from the mountains and the streets.

At Hanzo's insistence the priest retired to an anteroom to cast his spell. There, almost vanishing in clouds of incense, he wrote cabalistic signs on a paper and began occult rites over it. Later the paper was to be torn into strips and rolled into pills which the patient was to drink with a draught of river water ritually drawn in the darkness just before dawn. This was as it was to have been done, but at the moment the priest's incantations reached their height, the samurai died.

The samurai's death may have ended his troubles, but it only started Hanzo's. There had to be an autopsy, at which he and the other town elders had to testify, and a series of reports to the central highway administration in Edo, and painful explanations and more reports to the samurai's companions when they returned from Edo, and further reports and explanations to the Lord of Satsuma, directed both to Edo and to clan headquarters in far-off Kyushu. Priests called in to exorcise the apartment insisted that it be completely torn down and rebuilt, and even that several feet of earth underneath be changed. Hanzo was quick to admit, however, that the Lord of Satsuma had expressed his appreciation very handsomely when he next passed through Okitsu, and had left a gratifying gift of money to cover expenses. He could clearly see that Hanzo had done everything possible for the stricken man.

All in all, Hanzo decided, in reviewing the incident, the dead and dying were less trouble than some guests who were very much alive.

He had especially in mind those representatives of His Sacred Majesty, the Emperor. For centuries the Emperor had sent an annual messenger to the shrine of the Sun Goddess at Ise, for the Sun Goddess was, as everybody knew, his first ancestor. Now that Ieyasu had been enshrined as deity of the new, Tokugawa, Japan, it seemed sensible as well as discreet to make another annual pilgrimage, to his mausoleum at Nikko.

The Emperor's envoys were picked from among the highest nobility of the old court, but it was a nobility which had gone to seed. Most of its members had grown incompetent from idleness and avaricious from penury. Teeth blackened, faces rouged, they hit the road for a spree of freedom and high living.

From Kyoto to Edo, they traveled the Tokaido, and from Edo to Nikko, the Nikko highway. On this latter stage of their journey the country people treated them with awestruck reverence, not because they were nobility but because they bore the Emperor's offering. People fought for garbage from their tables in the belief that eating it would cure any ailment; their bath water was treasured to be drunk in case of illness; and mothers brought children to crawl under their palanquins because this would insure the youngsters a long and happy life. To the envoys, veneration like this was almost too good to be true, and they lost no chance to convert it into saké, entertainment, and hard cash. Their favorite trick was to fabricate an accident, like falling out of a palanquin, and then to demand compensation from local officials. In more than one instance, harassed station officials were forced to truss some august emissary firmly in his palanquin and hustle him on to the next station while

A nobleman
of the Imperial court
and an attendant
(*a book illustration
probably by Ariwara*)

he screamed vituperation. It is no wonder that the envoys, once they had delivered the Emperor's offering at Nikko, and thus relinquished that which had made them so awesome, often found it expedient to return to Edo by a different route.

The people along the Tokaido were too sophisticated to be such easy marks, but they still had to be on their guard. Hanzo, along with Ichikawa and Tezuka, never derived any robust pleasure from entertaining one of these patricians, nor did they feel greatly rewarded when they were paid, not with money but with their distinguished visitor's finely brushed autograph. It was easy for the guest to pretend that his calligraphy was of great value, but the market was glutted.

Nevertheless Hanzo and Denzaemon agreed that nothing was as nerve-racking to all officials along the highway as passage of the Shogun's property. At the top of the list was tea from Uji, an area near Kyoto which then as now was considered to produce the finest tea in all Japan.

Every spring three high officials left Edo with a retinue of about two hundred men. In their care were the Shogun's three precious tea canisters, pots number one, two, and three, each carefully packed in a large box, plus about forty less exalted vessels for less exalted tea. Each now was empty. It was the officials' mission to refill them and bring them back.

The first and finest crop of tea was harvested in April or May. Then the thirteen most honored tea-growing families of Uji carefully selected their choicest leaves for dedication to the Shogun.

When the party arrived from Edo, they went into full-dress session with the two families of Uji celebrated as the nation's greatest tea experts. Each man, after carefully cleansing his mouth, tested the tea by tasting a sip of brew. Satisfied, they packed the tea in the jars that they had brought, left two or three in Kyoto as a gift to the Emperor, and set out for Edo, accompanied by a patrol of guards.

With the tea in their possession, they outranked every other traveler on the road. There was no daimyo so powerful, no Imperial messenger so illustrious, but that he had to give way to the Shogun's tea.

The roads and towns were cleaned as for no other occasion. Farmers were forbidden to work in their fields, and burning of rubbish was unthinkable. Well in advance of the procession, anything dirty or

A Tokaido inn: some guests bathe and others enjoy a massage as they relax after the day's travel (*detail from a print by Hiroshige*)

doubtful—including most people—was forbidden to use the road, and as the tea approached, the highway was completely cleared. All remaining travelers retreated to a safe distance, and if they were still visible from the road, went to their knees and bowed their faces to the ground. At each town along the way, every official, after scrupulously bathing, had to be present in full dress, lined up with his co-officers along the highway, his forehead almost touching it.

Thus it happened that Hanzo was witness to a moment of searing melodrama. The year was 1694, the occasion was a rest stop for the party bearing the Shogun's tea to Edo, the place was the highway before Seikenji. Hanzo had been lined up, along with Ichikawa, Tezuka, Denzaemon, and others, their noses in the dust, when the escort and the precious canisters arrived. Now he was doing his part in offering refreshments.

That year one of the three chief officers of the tea mission was a man named Terao, whose face was disfigured by an appalling skin disease. Throughout the journey, one of his fellow officers had jeered at Terao unmercifully. Here at Seikenji, in front of all the town officials, he again leveled his barbs at the unfortunate man. But Terao had reached the breaking point. With a scream like that of some wounded animal, he sprang at his traducer. His sword flashed, and flashed again, and again. The jeerer crumpled in the dirt.

No one moved. Terao stood over the body, his sword aimed at

A Tokaido inn: dinner is served to a man lolling in his room, another man returns from his bath, and country geisha make up for the evening (*detail from a print by Hiroshige*)

145

the throat, as if daring it to stir. Slowly he stepped back. He reached for the hem of his kimono, drew his sword through folded fabric to wipe blood from steel, slid blade into scabbard.

Hanzo stood directly before him, frozen like every other spectator at the scene. For a long moment he felt that Terao was struggling to speak. Then a harsh voice came from that cankered mask. "The Nichiren temple," it said.

The words cut through Hanzo's terror. The man was asking for the temple of his own sect. Hanzo bowed, turned, and moved down the highway. Terao followed.

The Nichiren temple of Yokaiji was across the highway from the Minaguchi-ya. The five-minute walk there was the longest in Hanzo's life, an interminable march through a deserted street with a killer at his back. Finally he reached Yokaiji's gate. Again he bowed and Terao strode into the temple compound.

The abbot received him and Terao confessed. His crime was enormous, not so much for the killing as to have done it while entrusted with so grave a mission. The whole cause of the trouble was the disease that had disfigured him, and he vowed to the priest that if an altar were erected to his memory, he would cure the illnesses of those who prayed there. And then he disemboweled himself.

The altar was established, with Hanzo as one of the contributors. It was dedicated in Terao's posthumous Buddhist name of Kashin, and speedily became a Mecca for the sick. A service held on the twenty-first of every month attracted great crowds, so that it gave rise to a fair, with stalls lining the lane to the temple. On the twenty-first of May, the anniversary of his death, the crush was terrific. In later years, when tea had been transplanted from Uji and was being grown around Okitsu, the tea-picking girls made it their special festival.

Kashin's altar still exists. The priests of Yokaiji read a sutra there every morning, and on a stone base in front of the altar they fill a number of cups with fresh water. Even today an elderly worshiper sometimes comes to the altar, prays for better health, and either drinks a cup of water or pours it on some ailing spot.

It is traditional that when a person is cured he paints his name on a red and white lantern and presents it to the altar. The ceiling is crowded with lanterns, many old, some new.

Kashin's ashes are inside the altar. His tombstone is beneath it, within a latticework enclosure. For the children who romp in the temple courtyard, this is a favorite place of concealment when the game is hide-and-seek. Kashin's face frightened children when he was alive, and probably he is happy now to have them play so near.

It was not only the Shogun's tea that traveled with great ostentation. There were other products, too, like matting for the floors of Edo Castle, and magnificent handmade papers for the Shogun's letters. Okitsu had its own favorite product. There was a famous old plum tree by the side of the highway in front of Seikenji. At New Year's time, flowering branches were cut from this tree and carried to Edo to provide a setting for the year's first recitation of Noh texts, an event always held on the third day of the year. During their trip up the Tokaido, the white plum blossoms of Seikenji held the rank of major daimyo.

And there was the special occasion of the elephant. It was a gift to the Shogun from Cochin China. There had been a pair, but the female took sick and died in Nagasaki, leaving the male to hike alone to Edo. The first elephant ever seen in Japan, he was a sensation, and the Shogunate was determined that he reach them without mishap. Earthen bridges were built across each river where no shallow ford was available, cattle were banished from his vicinity because it was alleged that he disliked them, and there were strict orders to maintain quiet at night so he could get a good sleep. Apparently all went well, for the ponderous creature reached Edo and lived there twenty years.

The Minaguchi-ya did not have to house the elephant. It was one instance, as Hanzo remarked, when he escaped big trouble. But with all the travelers who were worrisome, there were many who were a real delight. Hanzo's proudest memory was of such a one. It was of the evening that he and other members of the Okitsu Poetry Club shared with Basho, the greatest poet of their age.

Basho was a wanderer. He was one of those poet-priests whose urge to see the full moon here, the sea and pines there, or the mountain crags at another celebrated place, kept them moving over the face of their land, leaving poems and prose sketches which would in turn impel later generations to the same restless search for beauty in nature.

One of these men set down the rules by which he traveled, and lived:

> Be prepared to die at any time. Don't think of tomorrow: tomorrow will take care of itself. Life is vanity.
>
> Put away carnal desires, as well as hope for honors and luxuries.
>
> Observe the five commandments of Buddhism, which forbid killing, stealing, fornication, drinking, and idle talk. (However, there can be exceptions for drink and a little idle talk.)
>
> Give everything down to the skin if you meet with highwaymen. Be ready to give up your life if they want to kill you, and never fight back.
>
> Don't higgle over ferry and inn charges, and tip as one should.
>
> Give alms to beggars and medicine to the sick when you meet them on the way.
>
> Never refuse a request for calligraphy, but never offer it unless requested. Plagiarism is taboo.
>
> Never ride a horse or kago, except in places where it is very difficult to go by foot.
>
> And when you feel inclined to break these rules, stop your journey and go home.

When one of these great and gentle artists passed through a town like Okitsu it was a major event, especially if he could be persuaded to meet with local poets for an evening of composing impromptu short verses. Hanzo was one of Okitsu's amateur poets, struggling valiantly and occasionally effectively with the seventeen-syllable form. On the evening that Basho joined their group, Hanzo proudly played host. They met in the Minaguchi-ya's best suite, and there each man strove to compose verses of point and sensibility on a common theme. One of Hanzo's efforts had been extravagantly praised when the

Basho (*detail from a print by Hiroshige*)

master had called it "very apt, very fresh and apt," and for days Hanzo had moved in a rosy cloud. The only thing that could have added to his joy would have been for Basho to have accepted his invitation to spend the night at the Minaguchi-ya. However, the poet chose to stay up on the mountain side at the old temple of Seikenji, where, in truth, the view was better and the literary associations richer. When their meeting broke up, the poetry club had walked with Basho through a moonlit night to Seikenji's gate. After they had said good night they lingered, hating to end an evening so glorious, going over again the verses that they and the master had put together. It seems a pity that none of those poems have come down to us.

Basho wrote little about the Tokaido, which was much too common for his taste, but memories of his passing through and of the night he stopped there lingered in Okitsu, and a couple of generations later the poetry club of that day put up a monument by the side of the highway, and on it they engraved one of Basho's poems. No one today knows why they chose the poem they did. Perhaps it had some association with Okitsu which has now been lost. It can be translated:

> When the autumn wind is blowing
> It is lonely everywhere.

Shortly after the monument went up, the town was caught by a depression, and it was not long before most of the townspeople decided that their bad luck was caused by the melancholy poem. They took down the stone and were all for throwing it into the sea, but the abbot at Seikenji persuaded them to let him take it for the temple's garden, and he laid it face down over the pond to form a bridge.

Later the town recovered its prosperity, and people began to think they had been silly to be so superstitious about a poem, so they retrieved the stone and set it up in its former place. But soon business was bad again, and the monument was promptly returned to Seikenji.

It is still there, its poem reflecting in the still water of the pool.

The 1690s

CHAPTER EIGHT

*Which investigates the medicine shops of Seikenji,
and their special attractions*

PRINCIPAL CHARACTERS

Yakushi Nyorai, *the Buddha of medicine*
Maru-ichi, *the "founding house" of the salve shops*
Fuji-no-maru, *the "main house" of the salve shops*
Kamakuni, *a court attendant traveling the Tokaido*
Kakuhei, *his servant, who shares his master's tastes*
Sentaro, *boy salesman of Fuji-no-maru*
Juzo, *who killed Sentaro's father*

The calligraphy of
Ike no Taiga
on Maru-ichi's sign

WHEN I FIRST visited the Minaguchi-ya, the inn was essentially the same as it had been for sixty-five years, a sprawling complex built after a great fire had almost leveled the town in 1879. I was given to understand, however, that from the street the inn presented quite a different appearance than it had in the old days, for when the highway through Okitsu was widened and paved, it had been necessary to slice off the front of the Minaguchi-ya and its impressive gate. To compensate in some degree, a much smaller gate had been installed in the areaway leading to the entrance. This lesser gate had originally belonged to that medicine shop and sometime inn called Fuji-no-maru, which faced Seikenji—the same shop at which Hanzo had waited for the Dutch party including Dr. Kaempfer. Fuji-no-maru was going to have to sacrifice this gate to the widened highway, and since it was small enough to fit in the Minaguchi-ya's newly restricted entryway, the head of Fuji-no-maru had offered it to the Mochizuki of that day. It was one way to preserve a little of the flavor of the old road.

Fuji-no-maru was in its day a rather special inn. Technically it was not an inn at all. Inns were authorized only at the fifty-three stations, and Fuji-no-maru, at Seikenji, lay outside the station limits, though within the town of Okitsu. It was therefore classified as a "halfway house," and it was not supposed to accept overnight guests—another of the Shogunate's restrictions which was as often broken as obeyed. But legal or not, its innkeeping was only a sideline. A more important activity at Fuji-no-maru was manufacture and sale of a medicinal salve. This salve was Okitsu's most celebrated local product.

As one reads old guidebooks, it sometimes seems that the Tokaido must have been lined with shops from one end to the other, each hawking a local specialty. Some of these products, like Shizuoka's Abekawa *mochi*, became very famous indeed, and it took strong character to report to the folks at home that one had passed through Shizuoka without sampling this celebrated sweet. But even lesser wares were faithfully catalogued in the guidebooks, and a knowledgeable traveler could recite his way from one end of the highway to the other by naming the local specialties instead of the towns and villages.

Yui, for instance, was famous for its abalone. After crossing Satta Pass into Okitsu, one encountered, in swift succession, stalls vending tasty seaweed, Dragon King tobacco, and chopped clams and vegetables baked in the shells.

But, indisputably, Okitsu's best-known product was *koyaku*, the all-purpose salve of Seikenji. Fifteen houses, lined up opposite the temple, made and sold *koyaku*, and thousands of straw-sandaled feet collecting blisters on the highway made it a profitable business. A soothing, healing balm was an almost irresistible buy.

In the row of shops, the two biggest were the ones on the ends. Fuji-no-maru anchored one end, Maru-ichi the other.

The old shops are gone today, but in the buildings which have replaced them the family establishments are carried on under the same names. Following a suggestion from the Minaguchi-ya, I began my inquiry into the *koyaku* shops of Okitsu with a call on the house of Maru-ichi, easy to spot for its bold trademark, a circle (*maru*) with a single (*ichi*) horizontal line through the middle.

Maru-ichi called itself the "founding house," and thereby preempted slightly more authority when it spoke of the medicine's miraculous discovery. It all went back, they said, to a five-story pagoda which had once been a part of Seikenji. Pagodas are by their nature sadly attractive to lightning and Seikenji's must have lasted scarcely a century, but while it stood it was a noble structure.

It had been dedicated to Yakushi Nyorai, the Buddha of medicine, a benevolent deity who heals all diseases, physical and spiritual, including even that nagging complaint of half the population, the infirmity of being born a woman. (One of Yakushi Nyorai's twelve vows was that in the next rebirth all women will be transformed into men.)

Going back again to the time when Shingen thrashed Yoshimoto, the defeat caused several of Yoshimoto's retainers to weary of the temporal world, and, shaving their heads, they retired to the temple of Seikenji. If the religious life was not as gay as the one they were used to, it at least offered more security. It was to one of these reformed courtiers that Yakushi Nyorai appeared in a dream, with a commandment to create a cure-all medicine, and detailed instructions as to how to go about it. Upon awakening, the priest sent children of the village into the woods and fields to gather the ingredients, and then he showed them how to make the salve according to the Buddha's explicit directions. The idea seems to have been that the children would make the medicine and give it to those who needed it, but their elders were quick to see the folly of this, and they promptly appropriated the formula. They packaged it in clam shells or wrapped it in bamboo sheaths, and they were in business.

Today the house of Maru-ichi no longer makes medicine. The present head of the family grows tangerines in sunny fields above the temple. "But they still made salve in my mother's time," he says, "and she left me a box with the formula, samples of the ingredients, and all the necessary instructions. Told me that if I ever wanted to go into business again, I'd find everything I'd need in the box, even the wood block from which we struck off prints we gave as souvenirs, a view of Seikenji as it loomed across the street.

"And, do you know, we still get inquiries about our medicine, especially from inland farmers. In wintertime their hands get terribly chapped. No modern, drug-store medicines seem to help, and then they remember that their parents and grandparents used this wonderful salve from Okitsu, and I suppose they rummage around the house till they find an old wrapper, or maybe the old folks search their memories till they remember our name, and then they write to us. I hate to tell them we've gone out of business.

"Those farmers were among our best customers. On their way home from visiting Kyoto or the great shrines of Ise, they'd stop here and stock up. Not only for themselves. Our salve was one of the prized gifts they could take back to friends and relatives.

"It was good for everything—chapped hands, blistered feet, sore shoulders. To apply it, you'd put a dab of salve on a piece of paper and spread it thin with hot brass chopsticks used to tend charcoal. Then you'd clap the medicated paper on the sore spot.

"Of course, I must admit you'd get a powerful stink when the hot chopsticks touched the salve. It was made from pine resin, sulphur, and something else, some secret substance, and it was black as tar.

"They made it by boiling the ingredients together for about a week in an iron pot. Two pots, actually. It was cooked for a while in one, and then strained through silk into the other, and cooked some more. I still have the pots.

"Making the medicine was so simple that most of the houses had another business too. Ours sold noodles, so a customer could have lunch here as well as buy the Tokaido's most famous remedy."

One of Maru-ichi's biggest attractions was its sign, which hung under the deep eaves. In bold and beautiful letters, carved deep into a handsome plank set inside a modish frame, it proclaimed "Banno-ko" (*banno*, all-purpose, and *ko*, salve). Travelers—even daimyo with their retinue—used to stop just to admire this sign, for its calligraphy was the work of one of Japan's most famous artists, Ike no Taiga. Just how Taiga, who was born in 1723 and died in a year easy for Americans to remember, 1776, came to make this sign is a lost story. Perhaps in his own Tokaido travels he developed a blister, and having discovered for himself the efficacy of Maru-ichi's salve, he became a willing propagandist. Perhaps it was an ordinary commercial arrangement. If so, the mind falters at the thought of how many go-betweens must have been involved in the delicate transactions. Anyway, for one reason or another, Taiga took brush in hand, dipped it in rich, black India ink, and freely, confidently, painted the flowing letters. The sign no longer hangs under the eaves. It is treasured inside the house, a token of a livelier day.

Since Maru-ichi had appropriated the dignity of the "founding house," Fuji-no-maru at the other end of the row, had to be content with proclaiming itself the "main house," and probably it was the biggest of all.

With no single sign which could compare in prestige with Taiga's splendid effort for Maru-ichi, Fuji-no-maru hung three under its eaves. The biggest was gilt and black lacquer, like Maru-ichi's. It read "Main House," and bore the crest of the *ronin*-priest to whom Buddha Yakushi Nyorai passed the original instructions. This handsome insignia consisted of a circled wisteria blossom and leaf, and it was from this that the house won its name, for "wisteria" is "fuji" in Japanese. There was also a pair of vertical signs which must have been hung together. One blazoned "the salve conveyed through a dream," and the other told the traveler, in case he was befogged, that he was at Seikenji.

Like Maru-ichi, Fuji-no-maru has its box with samples of the ingredients. There is a lump of pine resin, some sulphur, and a little bag of the mysterious "something else"—the "powdered bones of a snake."

Fuji-no-maru, salve shop and inn, was no doubt a profitable enterprise, for from it came the comfortable fortune which, through a bit of luck, survived World War II. Most of the wealth around Okitsu was tied up in adjacent farmlands. It would have been difficult to think of a safer or more attractive investment—until General MacArthur and his crusading Americans came along with land reform. Then the holdings of the landowners were redistributed to the farmers who actually tilled the soil. Fuji-no-maru's wealth was also in land, but in upcountry timberland rather than farms, and therefore not seized. The rich stands of cedar and boxwood have yearly grown more valuable, and the present owner is reputed to be one of the richest men in Okitsu. It all started with a redolent black salve.

So far I had learned of a salve shop which was also a noodle restaurant, and a salve shop which was also an inn, but I was far from hearing the whole story. It was not the salve business, even coupled with a tendency to accept overnight guests, that made every general innkeeper of Okitsu jealous of these shops. And it was not a desire to lay in a supply of ointment that impelled so many of the Minaguchi-ya's customers to sally towards Seikenji in the evening after dinner.

Let me call in our old friend Englebert Kaempfer for a first-hand report. On one of his trips to Edo, the Dutch stopped for the night one station short of Okitsu, at Shimizu. Dr. Kaempfer wrote: "On Saturday, March 10, we set out before sunrise.... An hour and a half from Shimizu, we came to Seikenji, a small town of about two hundred houses, lying at the foot of a mountain, on which grew plenty of firs. At Seikenji they make a famous plaister, the principal ingredient of which is the rosin of the firs growing on the abovesaid mountain. They sell it in small pieces, wrapt up in barks of trees, or leaves of reed. A stair-case of stone leads from the town up the mountain to a temple called Seikenji, famous for several fabulous stories said to have happen'd thereabouts, but much more to be admir'd for its beautiful situation.

"I cannot forbear taking notice, before I proceed any further, that on the chief street of this town, thro' which we pass'd, were built nine or ten neat houses, or booths, before each of which sate one, two, or three young boys, of ten or twelve years of age, well dress'd, with their faces painted, and feminine gestures, kept by their lew'd and cruel masters for the secret pleasure and entertainment of rich travelers, the Japanese being very much addicted to this vice. However, to save the outward appearances, and lest the virtuous should be scandaliz'd, or the ignorant and poor presume to engage with them, they sit there, as it were, to sell the abovesaid plaister to travelers. Our bugio, or commander in chief of our train, whose affected gravity never permitted him to quit his palanquin, till we came to our inns, could not forbear to step out at this place, and to spend half an hour in company with these boys, mean while we took the opportunity of walking about the town, and observing what else remarkable occur'd to us."

As Kaempfer noted, love between men was neither new nor uncommon in Japan, and, in the period which he observed, it was generally taken for granted. Centuries before, it had flourished in the quickly spreading Buddhist temples and monasteries, whose members were forbidden the love of women. (It was no accident that the boys of Seikenji were situated directly opposite the temple.) Then it had spread to the warrior class, among whom it was frequently proclaimed that love for a woman was an effeminate failing. In both cloister and barracks, the love of man for man was more than mere sensual gratification. Ideally, at least, it was based on a lasting relationship of loyalty and devotion.

However, as has frequently been chronicled, sex does not always live up to the ideal. The world's oldest profession had its male as well as its female practitioners, and the all-male Kabuki theatre was, for a time, chiefly a showcase for the charms of pretty young men.

These, of course, were the snares of city life, flourishing in the glittering pleasure districts of Edo, Kyoto, and Osaka. Among the fifty-three stations there were few which did not offer women of easy virtue, but there was only one which offered boys as well. This distinction belonged to Okitsu. To the ardent pederast, it was an oasis of pleasure. To the harried innkeepers of the town, it was one more headache: they faced competition not only from the sister-team of Wakasa and Wakamatsu at the next station but from the boys of Seikenji in their own town.

It is generally agreed that all the medicine shops had their boys, many of whom, as they grew older, took to the road as traveling salesmen. Then they forsook the feminine kimonos they had worn in the shops, and dressed in the foppish style of an exquisite young dandy. They were frequently found at the fairs which were held monthly in the compound of almost every Shinto shrine and Buddhist temple. There they energetically peddled their salve, and discreetly offered themselves. Someone around 1707 took the trouble to record one young man's harangue, which went something like this:

"Folks, I hail from Seikenji in Suruga Province, a place, as you know, of peerless scenic beauty, famed in poetry and song.

"Now the ware I offer you is a cure-all salve called Shi-kin-ko, manufactured in front of the temple according to a miraculous prescription handed down from generation to generation.

"Why, you ask, is it called Shi-kin-ko? Why, because 'shi' stands for purple and 'kin' means gold. Take a bit of this precious salve, spread it thin as I do now, and it presents the color of glittering gold. The opening of your cut is purple, and hence the name. Shi-kin-ko! Purple-gold salve!

"There are many famous salves in Japan, but throughout the length and breadth of this land, throughout the sixty provinces and around the eight great bays, no salve is more cherished than the salve of Seikenji.

"Daimyo buy it! Borne in their palanquins on their way home from Edo, they trade their gold and silver coins for the famous red-seal salve, the miraculous-cure salve of Seikenji.

"Now I don't have to tell you good people what this medicine can do. You know, I'm sure, but just to remind you, quickly, this salve is good for boils and bruises, scrofula, whitlow, and bites by serpents and centipedes. It cures cramps and sprains, burns, ulcers of the skin, scabies, neuralgia, beriberi, and pains in the arms of young maids. Heart disease!—that dreaded malady that can strike down a man before he's forty! If you suffer from heart disease, plaster this salve on your sore spots. The pain will disappear, and it will not recur in your lifetime!

"Because of this salve's miraculous effects there has been no end to the demand for it, from generation to generation. Now, instead of your having to go to Seikenji, I bring it to you, the same, the genuine, salve of Fuji-no-maru!

"When I am traveling, the regular price of this salve is twenty *mon*, but because I want everybody to share its benefits, I am offering you half a shell-full for only six *mon*, which is dirt cheap, and make no mistake about it. Now step right up and make your purchase!"

The boys of Seikenji quickly crept into the popular literature of their day. There is, for instance, a hilarious satire on the ever-popu-

lar travel diary. Most often such a diary is a lugubrious story of
exile or an exalted one of religious pilgrimage, but in this case the
heroes are court attendant Kamakuni, "a famous sodomite," and
his servant, Kakuhei, who shares his master's tastes. Their journey
up the Tokaido is an epic of frustration. Typical is the night they
stop at an inn in Samegai. Kamakuni's heart is set on a massage,
but when he hunts for a masseur, he can find only a "thickly painted
woman, coquettishly revealing her red silk undergarment, while
smoking a silvered pipe and spitting all the while." As Kamakuni's
two greatest aversions are women and tobacco, he is "sick at heart,"
and that night, massage-less, he sleeps very badly.

Imagine his joy, then, when he reaches Seikenji. Swept along
exuberantly from one shop to another, Kamakuni and Kakuhei sample the wares in each, "with sliced abalone fresh from the sea as a
side dish." When they finally stagger from the town, they are so
burdened with salve that Kakuhei has to carry a huge bundle of it
on his shoulders.

The famous novelist Saikaku, who had already turned his shrewd
eye on Wakasa and Wakamatsu, drew on Seikenji as background
for this tale of vengeance:

In the red-light district of Shizuoka, two samurai, lifelong friends
but at the moment addled by drink, fall to quarreling, and when
they draw swords, one kills the other. In a panic, the killer flees,
setting off a long quest for vengeance by the victim's wife, son, and
brother. Since these three have been disgraced by the murdered
man's brawling in a brothel, they are evicted from their lord's
mansion, and they settle down in Okitsu.

There the mother takes her son's toys away from him, and starts
to teach him to use a sword. Unluckily, her brother-in-law develops
a passion for her, and before long she finds it necessary to dispatch
him with a dagger and then to take her own life in atonement.

This leaves the boy Sentaro alone in the world at the age of nine,
but since Okitsu was one place where a boy of nine was ready for
a career, he is soon installed in a salve-seller's house, "to learn about
the world." He is apprenticed to the house of Fuji-no-maru, and

because he is a very good-looking boy, a great many travelers stop there to buy salve. So he passes the years until he reaches thirteen, at which age he judges himself old enough to seek vengeance for his father's death.

By this time, the murderer, Juzo by name, has come to repent his unmanly flight, and hearing that Sentaro, true son of a samurai, is resolved to find him, he sets out to meet the boy and place himself at his disposal. But when he arrives in Okitsu, he learns that he and the boy must have passed on the highway, so he hurries back home. When he gets there he finds that Sentaro has gone on to the north. When he comes to the northern provinces, the boy has moved to the west, and when he arrives in the west, Sentaro is hunting him in the south.

They chase each other for over a year, until Juzo, quite exhausted, comes back to Okitsu, and puts up a notice-board by the Okitsu River. On it, he informs Sentaro that he will be waiting for him at home, and there he goes. Unfortunately, his travels have given him

. . . they are so burdened with salve that Kakuhei has to carry a huge bundle of it on his shoulders (*a book illustration by Jichosai*)

lumbago, and realizing that his end is near, he gives this message to the abbot of the local temple: "As I have told you, my life is in default to young Sentaro. If I die now I cannot pay my debt to him, but my death is inevitable. When I give up the ghost, thrust my body into the ground just as I am standing now, and when Sentaro comes, dig me out of the ground, even if I am only a skeleton, and let him revenge himself." Soon after, Juzo dies, and the abbot faithfully follows his request.

After his long and futile search, Sentaro comes back at last to Okitsu, and he finds the notice-board. At once he sets out on the last leg of his pilgrimage.

When he arrives, the priest tells him the story, and Sentaro begs that the body be disinterred. When it is, they are amazed to see that, despite its long burial, it is not wasted at all. The face looks like that of a sleeping man.

Seizing his sword, Sentaro cries out, "I am the son of Senzaemon. You are the murderer of my father, and I am here to revenge him!" Whereupon the corpse opens its eyes, and with a smile on its face, stretches out its head for the blade.

This valiant gesture wipes out Sentaro's rancor. He helps to return the body to the earth, and joins in the funeral service. Then he shaves his head, becomes a disciple of the abbot, and spends the rest of his life at the temple, praying for the souls of all concerned.

Saikaku's tale was popular in Okitsu because of its local setting. Hanzo was one of the first to buy the little paper-bound book, which quickly became well thumbed from being passed among the clerks in the office, about the only members of the inn's staff who could read. Most of Okitsu's population indulged in that guessing game which is always popular in the wake of a book about one's own district—trying to identify the fictional characters with townspeople. Hanzo's wife was heard to insist that Sentaro's mother had worked as a maid at the Minaguchi-ya, and as time went on she developed convincing details of that unfortunate woman's ill-starred affair with her brother-in-law.

But although today few but literary scholars know Saikaku's story or the travesty on a travel diary, the boys of Okitsu live in another tale so familiar that scarcely anyone can remember how and when he first heard it, a tale imbedded in Japanese culture through the classic theatre of Noh. The drama, called *Miidera*, contains no reference to salve-sellers, but the relationship is obvious.

A beautiful boy from Seikenji is kidnapped by a priest from the great temple of Miidera, on Lake Biwa near the city of Otsu. The boy's mother sets out to search for him, but her grief and the strain of her long quest unbalance her mind. At last she wanders to Kyoto's Kiyomizu Temple, where she has a dream which is interpreted by a soothsayer to mean that she must go to Miidera on the night of a full moon. She does, and hiding there she hears a priest murmuring to a companion as they view the moon together. When the companion replies, the mother hears the voice of a boy speaking in the accent of Seikenji, and she knows that she has found her son. Rushing to the temple bell, she rings it as the bell of Seikenji is rung. At the sound of the bell she recovers her reason, and the boy, recognizing the manner of ringing, runs to her, and they are reunited.

The boy salesmen of Seikenji were at the height of their popularity during the pleasure-loving decades around 1700. Sometime during the last half of the eighteenth century they disappeared, and from then on, the salve was on its own. It persisted until the coming of the railroad.

"When people stopped traveling by foot," says the heir of the founding house, "the old trade was doomed. You can't sell salve to people who whisk through town on a train. Our house was the last to make it, as we were the first, but the day came when we stopped gathering resin, put away the pots, and ended the history of medicine-making in Okitsu."

Today the salve shops, noodle shops, and inns of Seikenji have disappeared, like most of the old Tokaido landmarks. For a time Fuji-no-maru's gate, transferred to the Minaguchi-ya, provided a link with those lively establishments. Now even that gate is gone, but the Minaguchi-ya remains and flourishes.

The 1690s

CHAPTER NINE

Which concerns the light-hearted pilgrims of the Tokaido

PRINCIPAL CHARACTERS

Among the people of the inn:

Mochizuki Hanzo, *sixth master of the Minaguchi-ya*
Mochizuki Hanshiro, *his son, seventh master of the Minaguchi-ya*
Hanshiro's bride
The chief clerk of the Minaguchi-ya

*Torii gate of
a Shinto shrine*

IT WAS at supper that Hanzo first broached the question. As he finished a serving of rice he glanced at his son Hanshiro, and then, handing his empty bowl to Hanshiro's young bride, who sat respectfully outside the family circle, he remarked that the coming spring might be the best time for Hanshiro to make his pilgrimage to Ise.

Two hearts leaped up. Hanshiro for months had been praying for this word. His bride, keeping her eyes on the rice bucket as she re-filled her father-in-law's dish, felt a flush creep over her face, betraying a wild hope that she might be allowed to go along. No one appeared to notice. Every eye was on Hanshiro, every tongue wagged over his luck. She continued to serve supper. She would eat when all the others had finished.

The time was ripe to think of Ise. New Year's festivities were over, and one's thoughts turned naturally to spring, to the earth's warm stirring and the wanderlust that came with it. But more than that, Hanshiro knew, his father's announcement implied a decision to retire soon. Hanshiro's pilgrimage should come first, for once the burden of operating the Minaguchi-ya fell on his shoulders, it would be difficult for him to get away.

Certainly he must some day go to Ise. The Shinto shrines there, sacred to the Sun Goddess, represent the cradle of the Imperial lineage. Long ago it had been forbidden for any but the Imperial family to worship at those shrines, but an ancient taboo had been twisted into a latter-day compulsion, and by Hanzo's and Hanshiro's time it was generally accepted that a man ought to visit Ise every year. This was manifestly out of the question, but it was agreed that he could not expect prosperity in business or any of the other blessings at the disposal of the gods if he did not make the pilgrimage at least once in his lifetime.

The Shogun sent his representatives, daimyo followed suit, and the common people fell into line. Most of the travelers on the Tokaido were religious pilgrims. But let it be noted that they were joyous pilgrims. As one acute historian has put it, a pilgrimage was an excuse for a journey and a journey was an excuse for a spree.

Hanshiro was neither so antisocial nor so spendthrift as to want to travel alone. Like his father and grandfather before him, he had joined the Ise Club of Okitsu. There were some two hundred members. Every month each of them contributed about a penny to the club treasury, and when spring rolled around, the members gathered for a spine-tingling lottery. Of the two hundred names, six were drawn. Those were the lucky individuals who that year would make the trip, and the entire club treasury was turned over to them. The club president went along at club expense. That was his reward for managing the society, and besides he was guide and mentor, primed with paternal discourse on the wonders along the way.

It was not seriously expected that Hanshiro's name would be drawn that spring, and his plans were not based on that unlikely contingency. He would pay his own way. Like any other member of the club he was welcome to join the group on that basis, and that was the way to travel congenially and economically.

Despite his bride's frantic little hope, it was never suggested that she go along. She never dared ask Hanshiro, and he never mentioned it to his father. Had such a suggestion come from his father, Hanshiro would have acquiesced, but without enthusiasm. He was quite certain he would have a better time without her.

It was not that he was unhappy about his bride. He saw in her nothing whatever to object to, though of course he didn't know her very well. They had been married only four months. He knew that his father and mother had selected her very carefully and he was sure that she would prove to be a good wife and mother. She was a daughter of the owner of a *waki-honjin* in Shimizu, so she was very well trained for her responsibilities at the Minaguchi-ya. And she was certainly hard-working. As befitted a bride's position in any household, she was first to rise in the morning, last to go to bed at night, and busy every hour between.

Nor was she in any way repulsive to look upon. The clerks in the office considered Hanshiro a very lucky fellow and, when the chief clerk was out of earshot, frequently speculated on the fancied delights of a chance encounter with her in some secluded spot.

Hanshiro might have been surprised at their quips. He did not find his bride exciting. She seemed shy and unresponsive, and even on their wedding night he had found himself thinking of the vixen whose charms were for sale in a certain house down the street. Whether she was gay or cross, that miss was a girl who could make his pulse pound.

In short, Hanshiro was not in love with his young wife, and it never occurred to him that he ought to be. There is an old Japanese saying that if you love your wife you spoil your mother's servant, and Hanshiro had no wish to do that.

His father and mother briefly discussed the possibility of sending the young couple off together, but they rejected it. There was a custom in Okitsu that a girl should make her pilgrimage to Ise before her marriage, and while it might have been unreasonable to expect an out-of-town girl to have complied with Okitsu custom, Hanshiro's mother considered that the Mochizukis would be put upon if they now sent her. Besides, she was most useful around the Minaguchi-ya.

Hanzo did consider the possibility of sending his young chief clerk. That young man was in his middle twenties, a few years older than Hanshiro, and the two got on very well together. It was unusual to have a chief clerk so young, but the position had become hereditary. The young man's great-grandfather had held the job, and so had his grandfather, and his father. When the father had died three years earlier, it had seemed to Hanzo natural and inevitable that the son, though young, should take over. He was smart, he was personable, and he knew the Minaguchi-ya inside out. Hanzo thought of him almost as a son. Years earlier he had been the only boy around the inn, for Hanzo's wife was then producing a discouraging succession of daughters, and Hanzo had seriously considered that if he were given no son he would adopt this winning youngster. But then Hanshiro had been born, and the chief clerk's boy had lost his chance of some day becoming master of the Minaguchi-ya.

Just now he lost his chance of a pilgrimage to Ise, for when Hanshiro reported that two of his young friends were going along, Hanzo decided that they would be company enough.

As expected, Hanshiro's name was not drawn in the lottery but he promptly announced to the club president his intention of joining the group at his own expense. His two friends did likewise. Later additions were the wife of a man who had been chosen in the lottery, and four unmarried girls, so that all together there were fourteen in their little band, nine men and five women.

When they set out, wearing the wide reed hats that marked them pilgrims, they were given a gala send-off by the rest of their club and a horde of friends and relatives. Hanshiro was surprised to realize that the face he sought out among all others was his wife's. He was quieter than the others as they left Okitsu but he soon cheered up. After all, this was a party. He was determined to have the time of his life.

It was true that the priests of Ise struggled to maintain an aura of piety around these expeditions. Kaempfer heard all about this, and wrote that "it is requir'd . . . that the pilgrim . . . should abstain religiously, from what will make a man impure, as amongst other things from whoring, nay lying with his own wife." At Hamamatsu the good doctor was "very confidently told of a strange accident, which happened to an Ise pilgrim, who then lay at a monk's house at that place. He had obtained leave of the prince, in whose service he was, to go thither in pilgrimage, but being not an over scrupulous observer of that purity and abstinence requisite to perform this holy act, he very impudently had to do with a whore in his journey thither, which so incens'd the gods, that in punishment for their wickedness, the lewd couple could not by any force, or art, disengage themselves from their sinful embraces. They would make us farther believe that they had lain in the condition then already a fortnight, and had been view'd by their relations and thousands of other spectators." Somebody had set up a sure-fire side show.

Young Hanshiro and his friends were not worried. They knew their gods better than Kaempfer did, and saw no reason to believe that those easygoing Shinto spirits would be offended by a little fun. The pilgrims from Okitsu sang and clapped their way along the highway, and at night, when they stopped at one of the inns their club used year after year, there was revelry as long as they could keep their eyes open. Of course they always did the lively Ise dance. Everyone agreed that Hanshiro was the best dancer among them.

Ise itself was a joy. The countryside was covered with a cloud of cherry blossoms, glowing faintly pink against the darker hills. The little group from Okitsu was caught in a river of people, flowing under a canopy of blossoms, chanting the Ise song.

The town was the most prosperous and solid-looking that Hanshiro had ever seen, its streets lined with huge inns and teahouses. That night he and his two friends slipped away from their group at the inn to visit one of those bright, noisy houses. They simply had to see the Ise dance danced at Ise by Ise girls, and they were a lot less worried about the anger of the gods than about missing this once-in-a-lifetime chance. The girls were terribly appealing, and utterly delightful in all sorts of ways, all night, but at dawn the young men were back at their inn ready for the goal of their pilgrimage.

Hanshiro never forgot marching along the clean gravel path under the great natural nave of towering cedars, through the torii gateways, up the broad stone steps to the white-curtained gate of the outer shrine. There he laid down his staff, removed his travel cloak, added his coin to the growing, clinking pile on the mat before the gate, clasped his hands, and bowed his head in prayer. His heart

The Ise dance (*a print by Hiroshige*)

pounded and his eyes filled with tears. Then he turned away, gathered up his staff and cloak, and went back down the stone steps.

The Japanese know better than most how difficult it is to sustain a lofty mood, and invariably provide relief. It came now. The two- or three-mile path to the inner shrine was lined with attractive girls, beautifully kimonoed, singing and playing the samisen to beguile the pilgrims, and receiving a generous reward of coins in return. It was just what was needed to lift the spirits.

Then came the river where one washed hands and mouth, another torii gate, another cedar-lined path, and another moment of worship, this before the even more sacred inner shrine. Hanshiro wrapped in oil paper the talisman that he had bought, tied it under his reed hat, and with the rest of his group was ready for the return journey.

The trip home was inevitably anticlimactic. The others appeared to be having a good time but to Hanshiro it was warmed-over fun. The days dragged and the road seemed endless. True, there were impressive sights and lovely vistas but he gazed upon them with a singularly empty feeling. If only his wife were there to share them! She would feel about them as he did, he was sure of that. She would appreciate the sentiments he uttered now to unheeding ears. He composed a few poems, but slipped them into his purse without reading them to his friends. They were for her.

Their re-entry into Okitsu was a triumph. The town had kept a careful check of their whereabouts and halfway from Shimizu they were met by a holiday crowd. Their dusty kimonos were covered with gay jackets, they were garlanded with flowers, they were hoisted onto ribbon-bedecked horses. They were swept into town by a wave of cheering, singing friends.

Hanshiro had little time at the Minaguchi-ya. He distributed souvenirs to his family and servants—face powder and seaweed, dried fish and cakes, reed hats and flutes, and a special piece of silk for his wife. Then it was time to dress for the club banquet. His wife helped him. She seemed very silent, but then he rattled on so that she had

The path to the inner shrine was lined with attractive girls singing and playing the samisen (*a book illustration by Kangetsu*)

little chance to speak. He thought she was pale, but no matter, he'd bring blood to her cheeks tonight.

The banquet was long and noisy. Hanshiro had thought that its purpose was to let the members hear all about this year's trip, but every time he tried to tell some amusing experience a garrulous oldster would interrupt with interminable reminiscence about his own pilgrimage years before. Still there was saké and song and everyone demanded that he do the Ise dance, and when he finished, the applause was tremendous.

He came back to the Minaguchi-ya late, through cool sobering air under a skyful of stars. An old servant locked the gate behind him and handed him a light to guide the way to his room. His heart raced as he followed the corridors. She would be there, sitting drowsy by the lamp, waiting for him. But the room was empty.

After a stunned moment he saw her letter. She had sinned while he was away, it read, and she could no longer face him as his wife. She had run away with the chief clerk. She begged forgiveness.

The runaways were caught in a cheap inn at Shizuoka. Hanshiro refused to see them, and so his father Hanzo went to identify them and to recover the money the chief clerk had taken. He heard their story: their first accidental encounter when she was working late at night alone in the cavernous kitchen; their subsequent meetings under the lash of guilt and passion; their decision to run away.

They were trussed back to back on a horse, placarded as adulterers and thieves, and led away to the execution ground. Hanzo watched stonily as they were paraded through the streets. Then he returned to Okitsu. There were many who believed that the stroke which killed him a month later was the direct result of the scandal.

Hanshiro's Ise talisman lay before the family shrine but he never glanced at it without bitterness. Supposedly effectual for only a year, it was banished even sooner. A family could scarcely be without such a charm but thereafter some member of the household—never he—bought one each New Year's season from a peddler-priest who made them his specialty, along with almanacs which catalogued the good and bad days for every human activity from marrying to planting morning-glory seeds. Hanshiro also regarded these almanacs with distrust: his own wedding day had been labeled most auspicious. He married again, of course, but he never made another pilgrimage.

Other pilgrims passed the Minaguchi-ya, all kinds of people with all kinds of motives. Many a man made an Ise pilgrimage to escape a nagging wife or to skip out of town just ahead of his creditors. But not every man eluded his troubles. Dr. Kaempfer, when he entered Okitsu, saw something besides salt-making: "In a wood, before we came to this place, we found a small board hung up by the road to notify to passengers, that hard by, in a place rail'd in, there lay the dead body of a person, who, upon his return from Ise, had hang'd himself, and that anybody, that knew, or lost him, might reclaim and fetch him away."

Small tragedies like this did not check the flow of pilgrims. Even dogs journeyed to Ise; no doubt they went in the company of boys, but many received credit for doing it by themselves, and lived to a pampered old age on the glory they achieved. Restless shop apprentices slipped off to Ise, knowing their master would find it difficult to do anything but praise them when they returned. Lovers eloped to Ise, hoping by this act of piety to gain sanction for a union otherwise forbidden; they were never granted lodging at the Minaguchi-ya.

Frequently these secret pilgrims left with little preparation and less money and made their way by begging. Sometimes those who had money saved it by making a secret pilgrimage, for a "secret pilgrim," one who left town without a fanfare of farewell from a host of friends, was not obliged to bring back souvenirs for all of them.

The well-to-do knew that pilgrimages were too much fun to be left to the poor. City businessmen formed their own societies for journeys to noted shrines and temples, where they advertised their visit by pasting their club card on pillars, walls, and even ceilings.

To reach high places, they carried telescoping sticks. A number of these associations nominated the Minaguchi-ya as a regular stopping place, and Hanshiro was always delighted to welcome them. They paid well.

There was yet another kind of Ise pilgrimage. About every sixty years some witchery would sweep the country. Then hundreds of thousands of men, women, and children would drop what they were doing and take to the road. One of these spells was cast in Hanshiro's time, in 1705. Listen to these excerpts from various accounts of that day.

"The fact was," one man wrote, "that around the 20th day of the third month the youths in my neighborhood suddenly became restless. It was as if they sensed an apocalypse. Within three or four days almost the entire population of the city set out on the pilgrimage to Ise. . . ."

"It started," another set down, "on the 19th day when the pupils of a private school of calligraphy at Number 8 Tea Street were possessed with a desire to go to Ise. They set out on the morning of the 20th. . . ."

"My own children were no exception. They secretly set out before dawn on the 24th. Under other circumstances they might have been blamed for leaving home without telling their parents, but the way things were I took it for the will of God, and I followed in the afternoon. Fortunately I found them safe and we continued the journey together. . . ."

"In this town there are many blacksmiths, each with a number of apprentices. The apprentices were crazy to make the pilgrimage. In some cases the masters were left alone in the shop, and unable to do business without help they closed up and set out themselves. . . ."

"Even geisha and minor prostitutes like bath-house girls begged their masters for permission to go to Ise. Since they were so restless and threatened to run off at any moment, their masters often set out themselves, taking their families and all the prostitutes in their employ, even if it meant leaving an empty house behind. That way they could give both family and employees an outing, and it was far cheaper than losing an expensive property like a prostitute. . . ."

"In Sakai, seventy per cent of the entire population went on the pilgrimage. In many houses no one was left. There was only a note on the door, 'Gone to pay thanks at Ise.' So many houses were left empty that local officials issued orders that at least one member of every family must stay at home. . . ."

It always started with some mysterious sign from heaven. Perhaps a sacred sword would fall from the sky, or there would be a shower of paper talismans or even of silver coins wrapped in paper. As soon as it was reported in one place it was bound to happen in others.

"Rumors were that talismans fell," wrote one cynic, "and there was so much fuss about it that the mere sight of odds and ends caught up in strong winds set people to clamoring the advent of divine blessing. I checked with officials and was told it was the mischief of mountebanks."

"Most of these happenings," muttered another man darkly, "are hoaxes of the fox, and I did not try to learn much about them."

Whether caused by foxes, divine intervention, or mass hypnosis, the crowds were real. The official count for fifty days from April 9 to May 29, 1705, was 3,620,000. Even allowing for an excited tally, a tremendous number of people pushed into Ise. More than one observer compared them to an endless line of ants.

It started in the city, spread to the country. It started with children, spread to adults. Thousands of children ran away from home with neither money nor suitable clothing.

"By five o'clock this morning," wrote a Kyoto man, "3,603 children have been counted leaving the city. There is no telling what the total will be by dawn. Some people along the road give them petty cash. Two shops near Sanjo Bridge have been kind enough to give each child a reed hat and to write his name and address on it. In some places local officials have mobilized night watchmen to see that children do not sleep in the open or go hungry. Many of them are only five, six, or seven years old."

The light-hearted pilgrims of the Tokaido

The inns were jammed. At first Hanshiro resisted. He wanted to accept only a reasonable number of guests so that he could take care of them properly, in a manner befitting the Minaguchi-ya. But he could not bear to see people sleeping under eaves or in fields. He opened the gate, and every night almost two hundred people squeezed in. They lay shoulder to shoulder in the rooms, even sprawled in the corridors.

Fortunately, the fishermen of Okitsu brought in full catches day after day and the local governor authorized the sale of rice from government reserves. Hanshiro was able to feed his guests adequately, in spite of his cook's threatening a nervous breakdown. But it became impossible to buy saké even at the wildest black-market prices, and every evening he felt obliged to make abject apologies. Never before had such a thing happened at the Minaguchi-ya.

A group of pilgrims followed by priests (*detail from a print by Hiroshige*)

In some areas, flooded with pilgrims, a fever of charity broke out and raged as hot as the fever of pilgrimage.

Some gave free food and a bath to those who sought shelter under their eaves. Others opened up their homes to offer free lodging. Finally there was a rush to rent houses and throw them open as charity inns.

Even those tough-bitten characters the kago-bearers caught the spirit and gave free rides to travel-worn children and old people.

In cities, the thoroughfares were lined with booths where pilgrims were offered rice balls, dumplings, bean paste, seaweed, headgear, towels, walking sticks, straw sandals, medicine. Some wealthy merchants had a tradition of charity whenever one of these mass pilgrimages occurred. "They set up tables by the side of the road," explained one diarist, "and pile cash on it. They give a silver or gold coin to every pilgrim who passes by, saying 'Sorry to bother you, but would you please take this with you?' Thus they give away all their money—preposterous!" But at least one of these lavish givers was rewarded by having tablets of divine blessing fall on the roof of his house, or so it was said.

Oh, there were exceptions to this glowing picture of good will. There was one town whose resolution faltered. Its citizens began nobly by giving every pilgrim a cupful of parched beans. This was a drain on the bean supply, so they planted more, but while the crop was still in the fields they dropped their project and joined the parade themselves. "It was," a report ran, "as if they had been bewitched by foxes."

Despite all the charity inns, there were many who could not find lodging. Some walked through the night and slept in wayside shade during the day. And despite all the charity there were rumors of profiteering. It was said that in some localities the price of straw sandals rocketed so high that the poor had to go barefoot. (There were also those who joined the pilgrimage only to make money by collecting charity along the way.) With hundreds of teen-agers setting out by themselves, some of them were bound to be victimized. Inevitably there were rape and robbery and killing.

Still the general impression was that a whole section of the country had gone on a happy bender. "The crowds are gay," said one reporter, "even hilarious, singing and clapping their hands. On both banks of the Minato River, huts have been built and geisha girls with samisen reproduce the high jinks between the inner and outer shrines. As fast as people give money to the pilgrims, nuns beg it away. Pilgrims, geisha, and nuns are all mixed up.

"There are bands of elegant youths who have joined the pilgrimage only out of curiosity, traveling by kago, gaily dressed, in full make-up, singing popular songs. Recently I came across a group of some fifty girls from sixteen to eighteen years old, all in cotton kimono of the same design and chorusing the Ise song.

"The crowds are so thick that groups carry banners to keep together. At first these banners bore a picture of a pilgrim and the name of their native place, but now the designs have become comic and even indecent. In large groups everyone holds to a long rope to keep from going astray.

"At Ise they have set up a Missing Persons Office. Groups who have lost members and members who have lost their groups register there and the office tries to reunite them. At night, men go through the streets calling out the names of the missing."

And so the crowds pressed on. They came in great waves. First there were two or three thousand visitors a day. The number suddenly swelled to a hundred thousand, fell again to forty thousand. The fever spread to other areas. The lines of ants grew longer, the crush more frenzied, until one day two hundred thirty thousand men, women, children tried to push to the shrine gates. There had never been such a day at Ise. That was the peak. The fever broke. Farmers found it was time for spring planting, blacksmiths rekindled their forges, schoolchildren went back to their lessons. No more swords fell from the sky, no more talismans fluttered to earth.

The priests at Ise tallied up the offerings and recovered their decorum. Hanshiro sighed and ordered new straw mats to replace the scuffed ones.

He was happy that it was over. The Minaguchi-ya was a *waki-honjin*, not a common inn, and he liked to choose his guests. He was delighted to go back to serving a few people of importance. He continued to bar eloping lovers.

1701–1703

CHAPTER TEN

In which the master of the Minaguchi-ya observes the course of a vendetta that stirs all Japan

PRINCIPAL CHARACTERS

Ichikawa, *master of the Ichikawa* honjin
Denzaemon, *head of the post house at Okitsu station*
Asano Naganori, *a daimyo, Lord of Ako*
Kira Yoshinaka, *direct retainer to the Shogun and master of ceremonies at the Shogun's court*
Oishi Kuranosuke, *chief steward to Asano*
Chikara, *his son*
Sampei Shigezane, *samurai retainer to Asano, once his page*

and among the people of the inn:

Mochizuki Hanshiro, *seventh master of the Minaguchi-ya*

The crest of
Asano Naganori

IT WAS the middle of a warm spring day, the fifteenth day of the third month of the year 1701. The calendar was a little askew in those days, so that the cherry blossoms were more than a month gone, and the mountains which backed Okitsu were now, where the pines were not too dense, freckled with the dusty pink of wild azaleas. Lunch was finished and Hanshiro sat in his office at the front of the Minaguchi-ya, half drowsing, half wondering if it were worthwhile to move to the family quarters for a nap.

The sounds were enough to put a man to sleep: the drone of a fly, the soft hum of maids' voices from the kitchen, the dimmed shuffle of noonday traffic from the highway beyond the wall. While these sounds continued, Hanshiro dozed. When they changed he felt it first in the back of his neck, and he was awake.

There was distant shouting. Something was happening at the post station.

The chief clerk was in the doorway.

"What is it?" asked Hanshiro.

"Emergency couriers," said the clerk. "Emergency couriers are coming through. The station is mobilizing runners for the next lap."

"Now?"

"Right away. Some say," the clerk added, "that the messengers are Lord Asano's from Edo to Ako."

Hanshiro rose to his feet. Asano's men were old customers. If some were passing through, he should be at the station to pay his respects. He called for street kimono, thought a moment, and summoned the cook. While his wife helped him into other clothes, he

185

ordered soup and a light lunch prepared at once and brought to the station. He strode out of the inn and up the road. A runner sped past him, on his way to alert the next station, Shimizu.

Hanshiro felt there was something ominous about these unheralded messengers. Couriers were usually scheduled a day in advance so that each station could ready its runners and selected inns could prepare food and restorative drinks. These men came with no warning. They must have started in great haste.

In front of the station house, the kago-bearers were already warming up. Stripped to their loincloths, they jogged slowly back and forth, loosening hard muscles.

There were twelve of them, four to carry each of the two light kago, four alternates who would run ahead to clear the road. Couriers traveled in pairs. If accident or illness stopped one, the other went on. A message dispatched by swift relay runners was faster, but the sender's own men could carry secret oral reports which no one would trust to a letter.

They went straight through, with only brief stops for food and rest. Their small, light kago were carried at a dead run, jolting and heaving through day and night. The passenger girdled his middle in yards of cotton cloth, wrapped another length around his splitting head. He looped a strap of cloth through the roof, and to this he clung. He could not relax his grip—he dared not fall asleep—or he would tumble out.

If these were Asano's men, as rumored, they would be rushing from Edo to their home castle at Ako, far past Osaka, a total distance of more than four hundred miles. At Okitsu they were not quite a quarter of the way. Hanshiro shuddered. It was a killing mission.

There was shouting down the highway. The kago were at the river. Ichikawa appeared. Hanshiro and the *honjin* owner bowed quickly and turned to face the road. The bearers speeded their warming-up. Space was cleared in front of the station.

Children swarmed around. "They're coming, they're coming!"

The kago burst from the narrow highway into the station plaza, set down with a jolt. The lead runner took two more steps and sprawled flat, his fingers digging into gravel. Others hung for a second to the pole over their shoulders, then fell away, staggering. No one minded them. The fresh runners of Okitsu moved into position, ready to go.

Instinctively Ichikawa moved to the first kago, Mochizuki to the second. Kneeling, Hanshiro saw a young man, once Asano's page. His smooth face was gray.

"Will you rest, sir?"

"No time!" He blurted it.

Hanshiro's chief clerk was beside him, holding a tray with a hot towel and a big cup of strong tea. The young man took the tea, drank, spat, and drank again.

"Will you take food?"

The reply was a wave of the hand, no. Hanshiro opened the towel and held it out. The young man took it, buried his face in it, let out a little moan.

There was a shout from up ahead. The bearers stooped under the ridge pole. The man thrust back the towel, grabbed his hanging strap as his kago jerked into the air. He looked once more to Hanshiro. His eyes held terror.

Terror at the ordeal still ahead, thought Hanshiro. And terror at the message that he bears. Another shout. They were gone.

Hanshiro and Ichikawa watched as the two kago disappeared, then turned towards the station office. Just as they entered, servants from the Minaguchi-ya panted up with soup and lunch boxes. Hanshiro waved them back.

A few grim facts had moved along the Tokaido with the couriers. Hanshiro and Ichikawa and station master Denzaemon pieced the story together. Lord Asano had attacked Lord Kira with his sword inside the Shogun's palace. Kira was wounded but not dead. Asano was under arrest.

Everyone knew it was forbidden to draw a sword within the precincts of Edo Castle. Things looked bad for Asano. His men were rushing home with the first word. The attack had occurred yesterday morning. Already the men had been on the road about twenty-six hours.

Ichikawa and Mochizuki knew both Asano and Kira. Both made Ichikawa's *honjin* a regular stop, and at these times some of their chief retainers lodged at the Minaguchi-ya. The lords themselves had on occasion stayed with the Mochizukis.

Asano was a daimyo of middling grade, Lord of Ako Castle. Kira was a direct retainer of the Shogun, and as such, though he held no fief and his rated income was a small fraction of Asano's, he had great personal prestige. Moreover, his family was one of those hereditarily in charge of ceremonies at the Shogun's court, and he himself was master of ceremonies.

The two innkeepers recalled the last times they had served these men. Asano had come through almost a year before, on his way to Edo for a year of attendance. Kira had not been seen in more than two years, for as a court official he spent most of his time in Edo. Ichikawa had a good memory for certain details even two years ago. "That was the time Lord Kira praised the rice cakes," he mused, "and ordered them sent to all his men, including those at the Minaguchi-ya."

"I remember." Hanshiro was irked. The rice cakes at the Minaguchi-ya had been at least as good as those sent over from the *honjin*. On second thought, the Minaguchi-ya's were better.

With innkeepers' insight they spoke of the men themselves. Asano: a provincial daimyo, spoiled and immature; not very wise in the ways of the world, guessed Ichikawa, and perhaps something of a prig, added Mochizuki.

Kira: they shrugged; as a direct retainer he was arrogant, for they all were, and he took bribes, for they all lived less on their stipends than on the graft which seemed to flow to them naturally because of their position. But as a guest he was princely, trying to outshine any daimyo in generosity.

The afternoon sped with talk of the two men and speculation on their fate. Word was received that another team of messengers was on the road. Mochizuki and Ichikawa made arrangements to wait on them. They arrived about nine in the evening and stayed no longer than the first two.

They carried confirmation of tragedy. On the previous afternoon, only hours after the incident at court, Asano had been sentenced to commit suicide. He had died before nightfall.

We must go back to the beginning. Every year on the second day of January, the Shogun's deputy-governor of Kyoto repaired to the Imperial palace to present the Shogun's felicitations of the season to the Emperor.

And every spring, at the time of blossoms, the Emperor sent his emissaries to Edo to make a return call on the Shogun. This was a ceremonial event of enormous importance in the Shogun's calendar, for it reaffirmed to all the country the cordial ties between Kyoto and Edo.

Each year the Shogun appointed two daimyo to receive the Imperial guests. In 1701 those named were Asano and Daté. Daté was doubly junior, still in his teens and with a fief half as important as Asano's.

Asano first tried to decline the honor, protesting that he knew nothing of court etiquette, but he was assured that he was no more ignorant of these things than any other daimyo and that Lord Kira, master of ceremonies, would coach him in all details.

This was the sort of occasion Kira reveled in. It not only made him the center of things, but it invariably brought forth a windfall of gifts from daimyo anxious to make a good appearance.

Daté's retainers took no chances as far as their young charge was concerned. Their gifts to Kira were lavish, gold and costly silks. Kira gloated. With this from Daté, what might be expected from Asano? Asano's fief was assessed at twice Daté's, and everybody knew that salt-making had increased his income far above what it was rated.

There are those who say that Asano's retainers bungled in not bribing Kira according to protocol. There are others who maintain that Asano himself, filled with priggish Confucian ethics, vetoed all efforts to pay Kira to do what, after all, was only his duty. At any rate, when Asano called on Kira for instruction he brought with him only the usual token gifts between friends, featuring one dried bonito.

Now, when a man is expecting a windfall it is difficult to think of any gift better calculated to infuriate him than a desiccated fish. Kira was outraged.

From then on life was hell for Asano. He could learn nothing about the ceremonies he was obliged to conduct. The only advice he could get from Kira was the curt suggestion, "Above all, be generous in your gifts to the envoys: generosity covers a multitude of faults, my lord." The hint was lost on Asano.

The ceremonies lasted three days. Asano managed to get through the first two by following the lead of his assistant, Daté, who was re-markably well trained. At eight o'clock in the morning of the final day, when the corridors near the audience chamber buzzed with last-minute preparations, Asano was still struggling. Humiliation and misery showed in his eyes, bloodshot from sleepless nights.

It was at this point that he ventured to ask Kira whether he should receive the envoys at top or bottom of a set of steps.

Kira snorted. "Fancy asking such a question at this time! You should have found out for yourself long ago, Lord Asano. Excuse me, I am busy."

As he turned to go, an attendant to the Shogun's mother ap-proached Asano and asked to be advised as soon as the audience was over, for his mistress had a message for the Imperial represen-tatives. Asano had just promised when Kira interrupted in a loud voice. "What is the problem? If it is anything concerning the en-voys you had better tell me. There is no trusting a bungler like Lord Asano."

It was the last straw. Asano's sword was out. "Remember!" he shouted, and he lunged at Kira. He slashed twice before strong arms pinioned him.

The court was thrown into uproar. The Shogun, advised in his morning bath, furiously ordered Asano's arrest. Another daimyo was appointed in his stead and the scene of the audience changed. As soon as the ceremonies were concluded, the Shogun met with his council. Overriding their suggestions for a full investigation and a cooling-off period, he announced his decision. For Kira, sympathy and the hope that he would recover quickly and resume his duties as before. For Asano, suicide by nightfall and confiscation of his fief.

The hapless daimyo was placed in a prisoner's palanquin, roped with a net like a common criminal, and carried to the nearby mansion of another lord, where his sentence was read to him. In final humiliation he was forced to commit suicide not in the house but in the garden, and there, at dusk, he ended his life.

The first messengers had left for Ako immediately after the attack. The second started that evening as soon they knew their master was dead.

Four and a half days on the road brought them half crazed to their home castle. The chief steward, Oishi, listened as they gasped their story, then summoned all three hundred retainers, now masterless *ronin*. Their conference continued for three days, but it was early apparent that they were divided into two camps.

All were agreed on seeking restoration of the fief and continuation of the family under Asano's younger brother and heir. But they disagreed on immediate tactics. The business manager of the clan insisted that they must surrender the castle quietly, for anything else would bring down further wrath. Oishi argued that such conduct would be spineless and would only indicate to the authorities that they could do as they pleased without fear of consequences.

It was Oishi's strong stand that won out, and at the end of the conference two representatives were dispatched to Edo with a message for the Shogun's representatives who had been appointed to take over the castle: the message acknowledged Asano's guilt but insisted that to save the clan's good name his retainers must die in the castle. It was a politely worded warning of a fight.

Shortly after the messengers left Ako it became clear that the Shogunate intended to take the castle by force if necessary. All daimyo of adjacent fiefs were ordered to mobilize their troops. In the face of this, Oishi called a second conference. The purpose, he announced, was to confirm the pledge to fight and die in the castle.

Of the three hundred retainers only sixty-one appeared. Missing were the cautious business manager, all his followers, and dozens of others. It was apparent, as one elder remarked, that many had fallen suddenly ill.

Oishi led those present through a solemn vow to fight to the end. When every man had signed and sealed in blood, he swore them all to secrecy and then revealed his true object. His insistence on fighting for the castle had only been a ruse to weed out the faint-hearted, he said. Only two things mattered: first, they must try to restore the clan under Asano's young brother, and second—he paused—they must take vengeance on Kira. There was a great cheer. Their vendetta was born.

To understand what it meant it is necessary to look at the age they lived in. It is true that vendetta was sanctioned by the law of the land. There was an established procedure: an application to the local authorities, who forwarded it to the central government, who registered it, and issued an authorization. But in the first place, revenge was considered the duty of the nearest relative, not of a man's retainers, and in the second place it was a soft age, more inclined to give lip service to martial virtues than to put them into practice.

It had been almost a century since there had been any warfare. Martial toughness had withered in luxurious living.

Pleasure-seeking and dissipation were in vogue. Licensed prostitution was at its romantic heyday, and sodomy, one of the few habits surviving from the age of wars, was common. Popular taste was reflected in soggy dramas of love suicide and the sexy stories of Saikaku.

Over this hedonistic scene there were dark shadows. The warrior class was facing bankruptcy, and most daimyo had a hard time making ends meet. (Asano's grandfather, who developed Ako's salt industry, was one of the wise ones.) Money was the new god, and money moved inevitably into the pockets of the despised merchant class. This was the birth of the crisis that would eventually bring

Courtesy of the Metropolitan Museum of Art, Fletcher Fund, 1929

Oishi Kuranosuke (*a print by Kuniyoshi*)

down the Shogunate, but at the moment the national goal was easy living and the national mood was gay.

It was against this background that the Ako *ronin* pledged themselves to redeem the honor of their lord.

When the clan emissaries left Ako bearing that first conference's decision to fight, Oishi ordered them to get to Edo before the Shogun's confiscating officers left. But the Shogunate dispatched its men sooner than Oishi had expected, and so it happened that on the second of April, when the men of Ako passed inconspicuously through Okitsu, the Shogun's officers were also there, taking lunch and a midday rest, some at Ichikawa's *honjin* and some at the Minaguchi-ya. Apparently no one saw the Ako party pass through, which is understandable since the town was buzzing over the presence of the Shogun's officers.

Hanshiro overheard a conversation between two minor members of the Shogun's mission, who, having gorged themselves, sprawled comfortably near his office, waiting for the call to move on. A lanky young man had heard the rumor that was sweeping up the Tokaido. "They say the Ako *ronin* mean to fight for their castle," he confided. "What do you think?"

The pudgy older man belched. "It's nothing to us," he answered. "If they want to fight, the neighboring daimyo will take care of them."

As the Shogun's officers moved leisurely down the Tokaido, the clan's representatives sped towards Edo. Two days after they passed through Okitsu they reached the city and learned that they were too late. At a loss, they consulted the clan's Edo steward, who took them to Asano's cousin, a daimyo, and finally to Asano's young brother. The two messengers were promptly turned around and hurried back to Ako.

They reached Okitsu the next day and stopped for lunch at the Minaguchi-ya. They were too impressed with their own importance to be discreet, and Hanshiro could not help but learn the gist of the orders that they bore. Steward, cousin, and brother—all had been appalled at the plan to fight. Their letters directed peaceful surrender.

Since the Shogun's officers were dawdling along in dignity, the Ako messengers soon passed them up and reached the castle a full week before them. Though Oishi professed to be chagrined, the letters that they bore were exactly what he had been hoping for. They gave him the excuse he needed to surrender the castle and get on with the vendetta.

He called a third conference, and this time, with the threat of fighting gone, all three hundred were back. Their final week in the castle was a busy one: roads and bridges had to be cleaned and repaired, a complete inventory taken, and the clan's paper money redeemed (they managed to issue silver at the rate of sixty to one hundred, which was considered excellent in those days of shaky finances). From the remaining cash in the treasury, they made a donation to the family temple so that religious services for the Asano ancestors would be continued, and they returned the widow's dowry to her family. Then Oishi set aside a sizable sum to be used in "restoring the family," and the remainder was distributed as final payment to the retainers. The business manager took his and disappeared before the evacuation.

On the eighteenth of April, 1701, the Shogun's officers arrived, and Oishi courteously rode out to meet them. He escorted them into the castle, and in Lord Asano's old room, which had been kept just as he left it, he entered a plea for help in restoring the family under Asano's brother. The officers, deeply impressed by their reception and the condition of the castle, agreed to do what they could.

Relieved of his responsibilities, Oishi moved to Kyoto. He bought a house in the village of Yamashina, just outside the city, and went through all the motions of settling into retirement there with his wife and children.

Yamashina suited his purposes. It was quiet but near Kyoto, and it was on the Tokaido highway for easy communication. He rebuilt the house and began to garden and to farm. His handling of affairs at Ako had been so exemplary that several daimyo offered him employment, but he declined them all. His only ambition, it appeared, was to live out his life as a country gentleman.

He did not register the vendetta. He was certain that a formal warning would make success impossible. Kira was already jittery. He had been tenderly handled by the Shogun, but the obvious disapproval of his peers had forced him to give up his position at court. His wife, who came from a strong and martial clan, advised suicide, but he was not the type, and instead he devoted himself to gaining the protection of her relatives, making his mansion in Edo as secure as possible, and spying on Oishi. Yamashina crawled with his spies. They appeared as workmen remodeling the house, as gardeners, as peddlers. They dogged Oishi's footsteps.

Oishi could not forget that his first responsibility was to try to restore the clan under Asano's young brother. No matter how his men burned for vengeance, they must not do anything which would jeopardize that goal. His greatest problem was keeping the hotheads under control. The group in Edo was especially troublesome and in September he found it necessary to dispatch one of his confidants to pacify them. Early in October he sent two more men, and finally on the twentieth of October he set out himself.

In Okitsu, Hanshiro heard rumors that the Ako *ronin* were moving towards Edo, though no one in the town had spotted the first or second group. But on the night of the twenty-eighth, Oishi himself stayed at the Minaguchi-ya. It was the first time Hanshiro had seen him, for Oishi had been home steward and had seldom left Ako. Hanshiro felt deeply honored and tried to show it. He personally supervised the broiling of the fish despite the intense annoyance of the cook, who still managed to produce an excellent dinner.

Shortly after Oishi's arrival, Hanshiro was plagued by the wailing flute of an unusually persistent begging priest. He had been paid off, but he stayed around. A peep at the fellow, his head encased in a basket-mask, convinced Hanshiro that he was not a priest but a spy, and this led to the discovery of two or three other questionable characters loitering about. Hanshiro revealed his suspicions to one of Oishi's men, who cheerfully confirmed them. Their group had grown quite used to these shadows, he said. They were ready for trouble but doubted that there would be any. Nevertheless, Hanshiro stayed up all night and posted most of the menservants as guards around the walls of the inn.

After he had shown his guests off the next morning, Hanshiro thought things over. He sensed that these men of Ako were plotting revenge, and yet, he decided, there would be no vendetta in the near future. Oishi was traveling too openly. He was not ready to strike.

Arriving in Edo early in November after thirteen days on the road, Oishi did all the things expected of him. He visited Asano's grave at the temple of Sengakuji (it is interesting how Asano came to lie there: the temple had been built by Ieyasu to honor Yoshimoto and his clan, whose hostage he had been as a boy and whose conqueror as a man; when the original structure had burned in 1639, Asano's grandfather had been appointed to help rebuild it and as a reward had been made a parishioner). He called on Asano's widow, who, following the conventions of the day, had became a nun. And he met with several officials to press the case for restoring the family.

Then, on the tenth of November, he held a secret conference with the Edo intemperates. He was confronted with vehement determination to strike at Kira next March, on the first anniversary of Asano's death. Even those he had sent from Kyoto had been converted, and Oishi was forced to consent to a March date. That was the way things stood when he left Edo.

Back at Yamashina, Oishi embarked on the course that was to bring so much joy to scores of dramatists who would later tackle the story, and so much anguish to hero worshipers. He began a life of sensational dissipation.

He divorced his wife and sent her back to her father with the three youngest children. (His eldest son, Chikara, stayed, for he was a sworn member of the vendetta league—its youngest member, barely fourteen.)

Free of his spouse, Oishi ran riot. The lavish gay quarters of Kyoto were not enough: he ranged as far as Nara and Osaka. The charms of women were not enough: he enjoyed a blazing affair with a prominent Kabuki actor.

To decorate his hearth he brought home a delectable courtesan, but her well-publicized allure failed to limit his wanderings. He never drew a sober breath if he could help it. He squandered money with fine careless rapture.

No doubt in divorcing his wife he hoped to save her from implication in the vendetta. No doubt he calculated that his depravity would induce Kira to relax his guard. But it is nonsense to picture his pleasure hunt as onerous self-sacrifice. "The path of duty is ever steep and thorny," intones one commentator, but no man ever enjoyed the thorns more than Oishi. He was a man of his times. He was having a last fling and it was a beauty.

His conduct was not without unhappy consequences. If he succeeded in duping Kira he also disgusted some of his intimates and lost them to the cause. And the young ex-page who had been one of the first messengers from Edo to Ako, the one in whose face Hanshiro had read tragedy—he was deceived too.

His name was Sampei. He was living with his father in a village thirty miles from Yamashina and he had often visited Oishi to talk about the vendetta. In that winter when Oishi turned to debauchery, Sampei lost all faith in him.

He asked his father for permission to go to Edo to find new employment, and his father, realizing that he meant to attempt single-handed revenge, refused. He begged his father to release him by disowning him, and again his father refused. Then he committed suicide. His father was afraid that if his death became known it would reveal the plot, and so he buried Sampei secretly on a lonely hillside.

New Year's came, ushering in 1702. In Edo, members of the league learned that Kira had retired, passing the headship of his family to his son. There were rumors that he would seek refuge with his wife's family at their castle deep in the central mountains, and it was clear that if he managed to do this, a vendetta would become terribly difficult if not impossible. Two men rushed to Yamashina with the news.

They interrupted Oishi's prolonged New Year's festivities. He gave them little satisfaction, but they worried him. He was now genuinely concerned that he might be held to a March attack before a decision was handed down about restoration of the fief under Asano's young brother, and he called on a trusted elder of the clan to pacify the Edo radicals. After insisting on a conference to assure himself that the Kyoto members of the league agreed with Oishi about postponing the vendetta, the old man went to Edo. There he succeeded in doing what Oishi himself had been unable to: he obtained agreement to withhold action until a decision was announced concerning the brother, even if it took three years.

They did not have to wait so long. On July 18 of that year of 1702, the Shogunate announced that the fief would not be restored and it placed the brother in permanent custody. All hopes were dashed. The Asano clan of Ako was wiped off the books.

The Edo group dispatched emergency couriers with the news. Again grim-faced men rocketed down the Tokaido clinging to the cotton straps of their heaving palanquins. Hanshiro noted them, and decided that this was the signal for action.

Oishi felt the same way. He had done all he could to restore the family. Now he could get on with revenge. In a general conference on the twenty-eighth of July he announced that he would go to Edo in October.

As the men in Yamashina raised their cups to success, Asano's young brother was leaving Edo for permanent exile in what is today called Hiroshima. A few nights later his glum little procession stopped at Okitsu and put up at the Minaguchi-ya. Hanshiro met them at the river and the next morning escorted them on their way far past Seikenji. In between, he did his best as host but there was no disguising the fact that this was a sad journey. Hanshiro himself wept.

Oishi made no effort to see the exile when he passed through Yamashina. A meeting might attract too much attention and revive Kira's fears. With the vendetta actually in motion, it was no time to be indiscreet.

Meanwhile there was much to be done. He made arrangements

to have his family cared for, that his children might grow up in honor. He set about to raise badly needed money, selling most of what he owned, mortgaging the Yamashina house.

Most important, he undertook to weed out the lukewarm members of the league. One hundred and twenty-five ex-retainers had by this time pledged themselves, and he wrote to each: "Now that the inevitable has occurred, and it is useless to make any more attempts to restore the Asano clan, I am returning your signed pledge, releasing you from any further embroilment in this matter. As for myself, I am thinking of going into the country with my wife and children to pass the rest of my days in peaceful retirement. You will perhaps follow my example or you are free to act in any way you choose."

Of the hundred and twenty-five, about half took the opportunity to drop out. Half returned their pledges with fresh declarations of loyalty.

Late in September, Oishi's son Chikara started for Edo with a couple of older members. On the seventh of October, Oishi set out up the Tokaido.

There were ten in his group, plus bearers hired to carry two long chests marked, "In the service of the Hino family." The Hinos were Imperial court nobility on close terms with the Shogunate; under that name the party was not likely to be interfered with.

They passed through Okitsu late in the afternoon eleven days later. They did not stop. Having stayed at the Minaguchi-ya only a few months before under his own name, Oishi was not such a fool as to check in again under an alias.

But the highway in front of the inn was the scene of one of those chance encounters which Oishi was powerless to avoid. Hanshiro spent little time watching traffic, but at that particular hour on that particular day he stood idly in his gateway. He saw the little procession approaching, noticed with interest that it belonged to the Hino family, and was about to make a respectful bow when he found himself looking straight into the face of Oishi. He recognized him at once and started to greet him warmly when something in

Oishi's frozen expression stopped the words. He caught himself, made his bow, and kept his head low while he composed himself. The procession passed by.

He thought about the encounter all evening. He could have been mistaken, of course, but he knew that he was not. On the other hand, Oishi might truly have entered the service of the Hinos, but in that case there would have been no reason for nonrecognition when their eyes met. One thing he resolved: if Oishi wished to go incognito to Edo, he, Hanshiro, would do nothing to spoil his plan. And he mentioned the incident to no one.

The encounter was on Oishi's mind, too, that evening as he rested in the *honjin* at Yui. He finally decided that there was nothing to do but hope that Hanshiro would say nothing, and with that he fell asleep.

A couple of days later his party reached the Hakone Mountains. Oishi was ready for trouble at the barrier-gate, but the Hino name and his carefully forged papers got them through without difficulty. A mile beyond he stopped to pray at a monument to the famous Soga brothers, who five centuries before had revenged their father's murder after eighteen years of effort. Finishing his prayer, he scraped a bit of moss from the stone and put it in his wallet as a talisman. Later, in Edo, he shared it with his son.

Moving cautiously as he neared Edo, he stopped first for three days at Kamakura, thirty miles short of the city. There he was met and guided to Kawasaki, about twenty miles closer, where he stayed at the home of a man who had formerly supplied fodder to the Asano clan. Aften ten days he finally moved into the heart of the city, checking in at the same inn which was headquarters for the Dutch on their annual visits.

His son Chikara was already at this inn, registered as a young merchant come to Edo for a lawsuit. Oishi posed as the young man's uncle-guardian, and the rest of the group, as employees of the family.

It was now about one week into November. All the members of the league were in Edo, scattered through the city under assumed names, spying on Kira, ferreting out information as servants, tradesmen, artisans, physicians, and priests. It seems certain that with its tight police system, the Shogunate must have known they were there. Oishi himself was convinced that the Shogun's council was aware of their activities but feigned ignorance.

One of their number, disguised as a rich merchant of Kyoto, was taking lessons in the tea ceremony from a certain master who also tutored Kira. He learned that there was to be a tea ceremony at Kira's early in the morning on December 6, and so, confident that Kira would be at home on the night before, the league scheduled the attack for the night of the fifth.

On the second they met for last instructions. A month before there had been fifty-five of them. Now there were forty-eight. They signed their final pledge, vowing that they would act as a team, each to perform his assigned part in the plan.

Then came news that Kira's party had been postponed till the afternoon of the fourteenth. The fourteenth was the monthly anniversary of their lord's death, and so they rescheduled their attack for that night.

On the fourteenth, in the midst of one of Edo's rare snowstorms, the senior members of the group met at the temple of Sengakuji. They paid homage at Asano's grave and then reviewed their tactics. They would split into two groups: one, under Oishi, would attack Kira's main entrance; the other, under the nominal command of Oishi's son Chikara, assisted by an elder, would attack the rear gate. They decided on passwords, agreed that Kira was their first and last target, and dispersed to meet again that night.

At their inns throughout the city, each of the men, announcing that he had to make an urgent visit to Kyoto, paid his bill and bid farewell to his landlord. Each of them stopped by the room of the eldest member of the league for a final cup of saké. Some of them took time for a leisurely supper of noodles.

At the rendezvous they dressed from the skin in new clothing, for they were undertaking not merely a battle but a rite. First, underwear of white padded silk, soft and warm; then a coat of mail, a padded kimono of black silk with the wearer's crest, trouser-like

The night attack on Kira's mansion (*a print by Kuniyoshi*)

hakama, leggings, gauntlets, helmet, and finally a mantle and hood of black and white. A few followed an ancient battlefield custom: each of these traditionalists burned incense in his helmet so that if the enemy took his head they would find it sweetly scented.

At two o'clock in the morning they set out, marching silently through deserted, snowy streets. There were only forty-seven now, for there had been one more defection. Of Asano's more than three hundred retainers, the burden of revenge fell on these forty-seven.

Near Kira's mansion they split, one group to the front, one to the rear. Slipping silently through the snow they overpowered the gatekeepers huddled over charcoal in their huts.

The main gate was strong. They made no attempt to force it but scaled it with ladders. The rear gate they battered open. They were inside.

Some screened the garden to prevent anyone's fleeing to seek help. The rest burst into the house.

As the attack began, Oishi dispatched runners to tell the neighbors what was happening. The masters of two of the nearby mansions were home in their fiefs; their caretakers chose to ignore the attack. In the third house the master was in residence; he ordered his men out, had lanterns lit in his garden, and, calling for a chair, sat there himself, ready to cut off any of Kira's men who might try to escape into his compound; he stationed one of his men at the top of the wall to shout the progress of the attack.

Some of Kira's men fought and died that night, but more, including Kira's son, dropped their swords and ran. The attackers slashed their way to Kira's room, found his bed warm but empty. As resistance died they scoured the huge house. An hour slipped away. They began to fear they had lost their quarry.

Then some of them broke into an old hut, used to store charcoal in the back yard. Two men came out fighting but were overcome. A spear thrust wounded a third. He came out wielding a short sword, was downed with another spear thrust. The body bore an old scar across the back. Asano's sword had put it there. Kira had been found.

Whistles sounded the signal. The man who had killed him severed the head and wrapped it in Kira's kimono. They assembled in the courtyard and by a roll call confirmed that none was missing. It was nearly dawn.

Before the main gate of the ravaged house they planted a declaration. It told how Asano had been driven to attack Kira; how he had been properly condemned; but how, since he had been prevented from killing his enemy, his retainers had been obliged to take up arms, "for it is impossible to live under the same heaven with enemy of lord or father."

Then they marched to a nearby temple, the fit helping the wounded. They were refused admittance but they waited at the gate, half-expecting an attack from Kira's relatives, half-expecting that some of Kira's family or retainers might wish to offer parting words to their lord. No one appeared. They moved to the river and boarded a ferry which took them along the bay to the pine-shrouded shore below the temple of Sengakuji.

At Sengakuji they carefully washed Kira's head and placed it before Asano's tomb. Then each man in turn knelt there, burned a pinch of incense, and bowed in prayer that his lord's spirit might now find peace. When their ceremony was finished the abbot called them into the main hall of the temple. He welcomed them and gave them a temple breakfast of rice gruel.

Two of the group were dispatched to report their vendetta to the Shogunate's inspector-general. That dignitary received them sympathetically, heard them out, and then hurried to advise the council.

The men waited that day at Sengakuji. At nightfall they were ordered to report next morning to the inspector-general. There, all next day, they were questioned, and finally told that pending a decision in their case they would be detained in the mansions of four daimyo. The Shogun, who had been so swift to dispatch their master, was now moving carefully.

Each of the daimyo went out of his way to show that he was honored. The lord to whom Oishi and sixteen others were assigned sent a palanquin for each man, and an escort of seven hundred and fifty samurai, including all of his principal retainers. And he greeted and praised each of his wards personally, though it was after two in the morning before they reached his house.

Later Oishi described their reception in a letter to Kyoto. He went on to tell how their host had begun immediate construction of special rooms for them, how he had provided new clothing, lavish food, saké, and tobacco.

Meanwhile the Shogunate was racking its brain. By the feudal code their action should have been praised, but it was obvious that this would encourage organized resort to force.

Every major official studied the question, every scholar at the government's disposal wrote a brief probing the moral issues at stake.

The debate raged all through January while the country held its breath.

The final solution was regarded as saving face for everybody. The forty-seven Ako *ronin* had conducted an unauthorized vendetta although their lord had received only due punishment for misconduct. They ought therefore to be punished as criminals. But in consideration of their loyal spirit they would be allowed to commit suicide.

The Shogun himself made one final effort to save the men. In a precedent-breaking act he consulted the Lord Abbot of the great Ueno Temple, an Imperial prince kept in Edo as a gilded hostage in case the Emperor became unruly. His Holiness only seconded the decision above, adding that the most merciful course was to let them die as martyrs, for if they were allowed to live some of them undoubtedly would commit unseemly acts which would tarnish their now spotless honor.

And so, on the night of February 3, just at bedtime, the *ronin* were told that in the morning their rooms would be decorated with flowers, for they would receive a messenger. They knew what that meant. The long ordeal was finished. They held a party.

The next morning an officer from the Shogunate delivered the sentence. They were served a gala breakfast with saké and sweets, and told to prepare themselves for their "happy departure."

Still there lurked a feeling that the sentence might be remanded. Such a rumor swept the city, and each custodian daimyo delayed as long as possible. At last it was evident that no second messenger was coming, and in the cold gray twilight of a February afternoon the sentence was carried out at each of the four mansions. All forty-seven were buried in a plot of ground next to their master's grave at Sengakuji.

The population was furious. Lampoons on the Shogun's justice were scribbled on walls and fences. Officials and daimyo were vilified. The "edification board" at the Bridge of Japan, Edo's busiest intersection, whose first precept admonished loyalty and filial piety, was torn down and thrown into the gutter. Replaced, it was torn down again and again, until its first advice was watered down to an innocuous injunction that "parents and children should love one another."

Twelve days after the members of the league died, the first dramatization hit an Edo stage. Of the more than one hundred and fifty different dramas since, the champion appeared in 1748. Oishi's debauchery was shown in titillating detail; young Sampei was transformed into an ill-starred lover called Kampei; and the grasping business manager at Ako reappeared as Kira's spy: it added up to a fifteen-hour marathon of revenge and sex. It was a smash hit—and it still is. It was considered the only Kabuki play fit for a samurai's family to see, and its name, *Chushingura,* has become the popular title for the whole story. It has been produced hundreds of times, and is today the only full-length Kabuki play to be presented regularly in anything like its entirety. It is revived at least once every year, and December, the anniversary month of the vendetta, would not be December without a production. Every year brings at least one new motion-picture version of the story.

Today the street in front of Sengakuji is usually lined with sightseeing buses. The smoke of incense rises in clouds over the tombs every day of the year.

Foreigners heard of the forty-seven a year after the vendetta when the Dutch "Kapitan" learned that Oishi had lived and plotted in the adjoining room of his Edo inn. He sat down and wrote a letter home to tell the story. Robert Louis Stevenson retold it, and Theodore Roosevelt said that he intervened as mediator in the Russo-Japanese War because when he was young he had read about the forty-seven loyal retainers of Ako.

Back in Okitsu in February, 1703, Hanshiro was stunned when word of the verdict and its execution sped down the Tokaido. He had been one of those who was sure that a way would be found to set the men free. He wept and was angry. All his life he remembered the mark of tragedy in young Sampei's face as he hurtled to Ako with the first grim news; he never forgot the spy-haunted night when Oishi slept at the Minaguchi-ya; and he had only to shut his eyes to see again Oishi's stern face denying recognition as he moved incognito to Edo.

For years Hanshiro talked of visiting the graves at Sengakuji, but he never made it. He could not overcome a distaste for pilgrimages.

Fifteenth and Sixteenth

Generations

1842

CHAPTER ELEVEN

*In which one of Japan's great artists visits
the Minaguchi-ya*

PRINCIPAL CHARACTERS

Hiroshige, *artist of woodblock prints, who immortalized the
     Tokaido highway*
Tohachi, *his friend*

and among the people of the inn:

Mochizuki Mohei, *fourteenth master of the Minaguchi-ya*
Mochizuki Genzaemon, *Mohei's nephew, fifteenth master of
     the Minaguchi-ya*
Nami, *his wife*
Mochizuki Raisuke, *Genzaemon's young brother, sixteenth
     master of the Minaguchi-ya*

*One of the seals
Hiroshige used
on his prints*

*"18th day . . . stopped to sketch as I neared the post town of Yui. Fine
scenery hereabouts."*

Most Tokaido travelers would as soon have set out on a journey
without money as without writing materials. Notebook and portable
brush-and-ink case were indispensable. A record of the journey, often
with sketches, was expected.

Very few of these diaries were intended for publication, nor was
that from which the above is taken, but when the traveler was
destined to become one of the best-loved artists in all the world, and
when much of his finest work centered on the Tokaido, the result is
inevitable. The writer's name was Hiroshige.

Perhaps the gods provided Hiroshige to picture the old Tokaido,
to picture old Japan, just before it was swept away. The road he
trod—and chronicled in woodblock prints—was essentially the same
road that Kaempfer had traveled a century and a half before. In
many respects time had stood still in Japan's secluded centuries. The
Tokaido had not altered much. It still stretched between Edo and
Kyoto, between Shogun and Emperor, and if tension had increased
between the two, there was little on the surface to show it. And so
Hiroshige has given us a record of the great highway when it still
belonged to men, before machines took over.

*"Had a rest and a smoke at Yui. Local products are abalone and
turbo—delicious! I bought some to take with me for dinner."*

He stopped as he began the climb to Satta Peak, at an old halfway house famous for food and a view. It would have been unlike
him to pass up either.

He moved through the inner room, hung with poetic tributes by noted men who had paused there, including himself, and sat on the rear balcony, jutting over Satta's lower cliffs. He faced the way he had come, towards Edo. Fuji loomed there, white-capped and lovely above the curving shore. There is an amiable fable, found in many old travel books, that in the other direction one can see the pine-clad hook of Miho, but I have stood on that balcony and I can certify that Miho is not possibly within the vision of anyone who cannot see straight through the bulk of Satta. Miho is there, of course, on the other side of the mountain, and given the slightest stimulation almost any Japanese can see it in his mind's eye, but Hiroshige was satisfied to gaze on Fuji.

He ate with great relish the specialties of the house, abalone sliced raw in vinegar, and turbo steamed in its own shell and juice. Over his right arm as it lay along the railing of the balcony, he watched the

A halfway house at the foot of Satta Pass in Yui: two travelers enjoy the view from its balcony (*a print by Hiroshige*)

212

almost naked women of Yui diving among the offshore rocks, gathering more of those tasty shellfish.

After he finished his lunch and before he resumed his climb up Satta, he took out his guidebook, a worn and familiar companion. A little book, only about three and a half by six inches, it consisted of one long sheet in accordion folds. Opened to its full length it stretched almost forty feet and gave a sketch map of the entire length of the Tokaido, but a traveler only opened to the fold he was currently interested in.

It was not only a bird's-eye view of the highway, it was a compendium of useful information and advice: rates for horse or kago at every station, charges at inns and teahouses, local specialties, and notes on every sight worth seeing. There were also practical hints: how to keep from getting seasick in a kago, the best foods to eat during hot weather, and how to stow one's valuables to foil sneak thieves at an inn.

Idly he glanced at its familiar eulogies of the view he was enjoying and the view from the peak he was about to climb. Hiroshige had made many trips along this road: he knew and loved it. Then, already looking forward to supper, he bought some abalone from the shopowner, and resumed his journey.

"Up the mountain path towards Okitsu; the view from the peak of Satta is unsurpassed. The landscape is rich along this part of the Tokaido. Made many sketches."

Hiroshige had already designed two popular prints of Satta. The first was in the series which made him a national favorite, the set called, "Fifty-three Stations of the Tokaido," consisting of a print for each station plus Edo and Kyoto. The print for the station of Yui shows Satta cliff and two travelers peering from its craggy ledge at the blue bay beneath them—dotted with fishing craft, set off by the white sails of cargo boats, sweeping towards the snow-covered cone of Fuji.

A few years after, for a series called, "Famous Places in Japan," he had chosen a point of view a little further down the mountain.

He showed a bit of the path and a few more travelers, but the same blue bay, the same white sails, the same snowy Fuji.

In years yet to come, not long before his death, he would design yet another Satta print, and he would stub his toe on it. He would picture the mountain from the perilous beach path, where travelers used to dash between the waves. Fuji would still dominate the background, but the foreground would be filled by a great crashing wave, a tortured coil of water after the manner of a man he never liked, his predecessor Hokusai. It would not be a happy print, but no artist is always as good as his best.

Today, climbing steadily, he paused to sketch, shifted his position, sketched again. He worked seriously, intently, fighting to catch the essence of a scene in a few quick strokes of black ink on white paper.

At the summit he stood quite still, until his stocky body seemed to merge with the mountain. He mused on the battles that had been fought there, for he had in mind a series of historical prints. They would be in tune with the times, a concession to official urging. The government, already besieged by domestic troubles, was beginning to be aware that foreign menace loomed across this wide blue ocean, and it was trying to rally the people by exalting the heroes of the past.

But thoughts of battles soon faded from Hiroshige's mind, and he was lost in the panorama that stretched before him. He saw it as it was then, in early springtime, with women diving for shellfish, but he could see it also as it was on a summer evening when fireflies staged luminous ballet, and in autumn when wild geese made it a port of call, and in winter when plovers wheeled and cried. At last a chill wind reminded him that the afternoon was nearly gone. He began his descent.

He stopped only when he reached the foot, at the little temple dedicated to the stone statue of Jizo which had been fished from the sea. He said a traveler's prayer to the traveler's guardian god and, seeing the toys piled at the altar, was reminded that Jizo was also the god of children. He felt again the sting of his own childlessness, then turned and headed for the river crossing.

One of Japan's great artists visits the Minaguchi-ya

"The sun was sinking as I waded the Okitsu River, making the scene very beautiful. Tired from sketching and the climb over Satta, I looked forward to tasting my abalone."

He was headed for the Minaguchi-ya. It may seem surprising that he would stop at a *waki-honjin*. He had neither the money nor the status associated with most of the Minaguchi-ya's customers, but he had stayed there on his first trip down the Tokaido, and he had then established such friendly relations with the Mochizukis that he had always returned there.

He had stayed at a *waki-honjin* that first trip because he was traveling as a member of an official mission. It was one of those ceremonial jaunts so dear to the hearts of the government: the Shogun was presenting a few fine horses to the Emperor, and it was the duty of the mission to escort the horses from Edo to Kyoto.

Hiroshige had been granted a minor place in the party because once he had been an official himself. He had inherited from his father, who was the third son of a samurai, a position as junior officer in the Shogun's fire brigade. Those were the firefighters who were stationed at strategic points around the walls of Edo Castle to protect the castle and its compounds.

Unlike the firemen for the city of Edo, who were kept on the run because of flimsy construction, high winds, and the use of charcoal in open braziers for cooking and heating, the Shogun's brigade seldom had much to do. With time on their hands they busied themselves with cultural pursuits like poetry-making, gambling, and drinking. Young Hiroshige early displayed a talent for drawing, and one of his father's friends began to teach him to paint.

His father died when the boy was thirteen, and at that age Hiroshige stepped into his post, an indication that the duties were not too exacting. There was an occasional fire, of course, and when he was twenty-two he was cited for his work in fighting one, but by that time he had already established himself as a print designer and five years later he transferred his officer's commission to an adopted son, and struck out on an independent career as an artist. But he kept up his old friendships in the fire brigade and it was through them that in 1832, when he was thirty-six, he was able to satisfy an itch to travel by wangling a place in the mission that delivered the horses to the Emperor.

It was his first look at the Tokaido, and he was thrilled by it. When he returned to Edo he designed the Tokaido prints that rocketed him to fame, if not fortune, for he never was paid much for his designs.

Those prints were revolutionary. They were revolutionary, first, because they reflected nature. There is a great landscape tradition in Japanese painting but it is founded upon Chinese conventions of painting imaginary landscapes in the studio. There had been some fine landscapes in Japanese prints, but even they were caught by the Chinese formula. Hiroshige went straight to nature. There were many who considered him vulgar for doing so, but the public found it a refreshing, even a stirring innovation.

That first Tokaido series was revolutionary in another way, too. Though he had traveled with official pomp, Hiroshige made almost no reference to the mission in his prints, and when he showed a daimyo's procession, there was no reverence in his treatment of it. He gave much more attention to ordinary travelers.

In behaving like this, Hiroshige was not advocating revolution. He may not even have been conscious that revolution was breeding. But certainly he recorded the beginnings of revolution.

The empire was encountering new stresses. The Western world, so long shut out, was pressing in, probing the sea frontiers, penetrating men's minds. Within Japan, there was a creeping sensation of inadequacy. Power never before challenged now appeared vulnerable. The old ways seemed fallible, the old brilliance looked tinselly. A daimyo, perhaps, was only a man, and the Shogun, just another daimyo.

Yet, confronted for the first time in centuries by an outside menace, the country drew together. There was the beginning of new unity, a feeling of nationality that had never existed before. Men with new purpose took a fresh look at themselves.

The paper world of prints echoed this search for new values. Once the public had been captivated by pin-ups of actors and courtesans,

Villagers bow to the ground as a daimyo's procession moves up the Tokaido (*a print by Hiroshige*)

glamorous figures of a gaudy scene. The new mood responded to the work that Hiroshige was best at—portraits of the land, the enduring land, portraits warm, human, and with a touch of melancholy, the melancholy that marks the end of an era.

The master of the Minaguchi-ya had been one of the first to applaud Hiroshige, at the time he stopped with the horse-escorting mission. Hearing that there was an artist in the party, the innkeeper had sought him out, for he was an amateur painter himself. When he introduced himself and found that the artist was Hiroshige, he had almost cried out with pleasure. Excusing himself, he had disappeared, to return minutes later bearing bottles of saké and a print from his own collection. Hiroshige was delighted with the saké and was bracing himself for forced admiration of another artist's work when the innkeeper proudly revealed one of Hiroshige's own recently published views of Edo. Rapport was instantaneous and deep.

That Mochizuki had been old Mohei, representing the fourteenth generation. He was a Mochizuki not by blood but by adoption. He had been born a Tezuka, of the family that operated a *honjin* and ran the upper river crossing. Through long association of *waki-honjin* and *honjin*, Mochizukis and Tezukas were very close, and when the thirteenth generation of Mochizukis had failed to produce an heir, they had adopted Mohei, the Tezukas' second son (the first son succeeded to the *honjin*), and married him to a daughter they adopted from another family.

Mohei and his wife had been no more fortunate in raising a family than the generation before them, and again the Mochizukis turned to the Tezukas to provide an heir. This time it was Mohei's elder brother's second son, Genzaemon by name. And from another family Mohei adopted a daughter, Nami, to be wife to Genzaemon.

The first time Hiroshige stayed at the Minaguchi-ya, in 1832, he became fast friends with Mohei. On his second visit, in 1834, Mohei announced that he had retired, and proudly introduced his nephew Genzaemon as his successor. The third time Hiroshige appeared, in the autumn of 1837, he learned that Mohei had only recently passed on. "We miss him very much," Genzaemon had said, "but he died a happy man. He had great news to carry to our ancestors, for we had just then learned of my wife Nami's pregnancy. For the first time in three generations, we have hopes that the Mochizukis will produce a natural heir."

Hiroshige mingled condolence and congratulation. He prayed to the memory of Mohei, and he prayed that Nami, already growing heavy, might safely deliver her child.

But on his fourth trip down the Tokaido, in 1840, he found an unhappy family. Genzaemon was not at home, and he heard the story from Nami.

"Our baby is a girl," she told him. "Of course Genzaemon wanted a son, but after his first disappointment he was very happy. He adored the baby and many people told me that they had never seen such a proud and happy father.

"His happiness melted away when we realized that the baby was not healthy. Genzaemon called in all the doctors for miles around but none of them could do anything. Then he pinned his hopes on the Dutch physician, who was soon due on his way to Edo. He was certain that the Hollander, with his Western knowledge, could make our baby well and strong. The Dutch were to stay at Ichikawa's *honjin*, and Genzaemon plotted with Ichikawa about getting in to see the doctor, and paid a great bribe to the Japanese chief of the party when they arrived. It was a risk but it worked, and after dark the Dutch physician was slipped across the highway. He examined our baby for a long time, but then he, too, wagged his head and said there was nothing to be done.

"Genzaemon was crushed. For days he sat alone. He would neither eat nor sleep. He would talk to no one. Then early one morning he told me that he had determined to appeal to the gods.

"Of course we had prayed. We had prayed at our family temple, and we had prayed at the altar dedicated to poor, disfigured, hot-blooded Kashin, and we had prayed to Jizo of Satta, who looks after children. And we had done all that the priests had told us.

"I reminded him of all this, but he said it was not enough. He said it certainly was not enough because our baby still was not well. That same morning he left, in pilgrim's garb.

"I can't tell you where he has been: far-off shrines and temples, places I never heard of. He goes deep into the mountains and he crosses turbulent channels to outlying islands. He goes on and on, through the heat of summer and the cold of winter. He goes to any place with a legend of cure for the sick, and especially of cure for sick children. He gives money to priests, he fasts until he is weak, he stands naked beneath icy waterfalls.

"He comes home only when he needs more money and stays only long enough to get it. Each time he appears he looks more like death itself."

When she had finished, Hiroshige had patted her hand. There was not much he could say.

Now as he approached the Minaguchi-ya for the fifth time, in 1842, he wondered, as he had wondered many times in the interim, what had become of Genzaemon and Nami and their baby.

He learned quickly. The maids had just installed him in his room when he was waited upon by the new master of the Minaguchi-ya, an earnest young man named Raisuke. He was Genzaemon's younger brother.

Genzaemon, said Raisuke, had never been robust. Pilgrimage and immolation had been too much for him. Ironically, death had taken him first. His little daughter followed soon after.

Genzaemon gone, the Tezukas had once more provided an heir. Raisuke had stepped into Genzaemon's place as master of the Minaguchi-ya, head of the Mochizuki family, and husband to Nami.

Raisuke made Hiroshige welcome and assured him that no change of masters could alter the affection in which he was held at the Minaguchi-ya. He himself, he added, was a great admirer of the artist's work and was deeply honored at this opportunity to be host. He hoped there would be many more such occasions.

Life was full of uncertainties, replied Hiroshige, but he was happy to be back at the Minaguchi-ya. He added, as Raisuke bowed and withdrew, that he hoped the cook would not find it troublesome to prepare the abalone he had brought from Yui. Alone, he sipped his tea and pondered the fate of poor Genzaemon.

A maid interrupted to help him undress and lead him to the bath.

"Took a bath and sat to dinner. The vinegared abalone with saké was nectar. So tired that I lost all will to go out. Went to bed."

In front of the inn the narrow street, crowded and cramped by day, widened in the darkness as it emptied and grew quiet. Shutters were closed on shops and inns, gates were latched. In the post house the night shift of runners gossiped or napped with noisy snores. In the compound two young hostlers crowded a tiny fire and talked about women. Behind the dark front of a nearby house, Shibata Taisuke, dutiful son, massaged his aged parents' slackened muscles.

One of Japan's great artists visits the Minaguchi-ya

Near the signboards interdicting Christianity and exhorting to thrift, incense burned slowly along an intricate channel carved in wood, its smoldering spark creeping past notch after notch, marking the passing hours. The watchman noted, and made his round, striking his wooden clappers to sound all's well. Inside the Minaguchi-ya, Hiroshige heard in his sleep their reassuring rhythm and burrowed deeper under the bed covers.

"19th day. Rain, occasionally sunny but cold. Went shopping, and at the post station I came across friend Tohachi, headed home to Edo. He returned to the inn with me and we passed the day drinking and talking about events in the city. Downpour at night. Drank so heavily I passed out."

A sullen morning in Okitsu: Fuji withdrawn behind a grim bulkhead of clouds, Miho blocked off by rain and mist, the sea gray and sulky behind the Minaguchi-ya. An excursion when the rain tapered off, to stretch his legs and buy some little necessary, perhaps tobacco (it could have been nothing elaborate, for Okitsu was no shopping center). He tucked his kimono up under his sash to keep it from being muddied, and the maids pressed into his hand one of the inn's oil-paper umbrellas. It was a chill rain, they said; he mustn't catch cold.

On such a day, what luck to encounter an old comrade from Edo. Easy enough to dissuade him from continuing his journey, and as rain came on again they scurried for the inn, under the umbrella's bright translucent yellow, splashed with the name Minaguchi-ya. They went under one umbrella like conspiratorial lovers, giggling like schoolboys at the comparison, plotting an attack on the inn's saké.

Tohachi had been away from Edo for weeks. He had much to catch up on, for the Shogun's chief minister had gone on a rampage of reform. Among other things there had been a great roundup of prostitutes and sodomites; women hairdressers had been banned; theatres and actors had been segregated; comic shows had been prohibited at shrine and temple festivals; and tattooing had been forbidden. The chief minister was out to elevate the city's moral tone.

Some of his strictures could be laughed off but Hiroshige groaned at the new censorship of prints and illustrated novels. Since his own specialty was landscape he was not seriously affected by the ban on portraits of beauties and actors, but he was restricted to eight colors, there was price control which the publishers used as an excuse to shrink his already niggardly fees, and there seemed always to be a censor looking over his shoulder, hunting in every picture for some hidden attack against the government. Even he was driven to portray the absolutely "safe" heroes of history.

But a reunion of two old friends and a saké bottle cannot remain a glum affair. When Hiroshige played, he played as hard as he worked. He and Tohachi were men of Edo, traditionally unable to sleep as long as there was money in their pockets. They loved good food and good wine, and both were ample at the Minaguchi-ya. They appreciated each other's company. The day slipped away.

Hiroshige, who had a name as a comic poet as well as a print designer, once spun this ditty (which, it is probably unnecessary to add, suffers in translation):

> The saké cask grows lighter and lighter,
> One's legs, heavier and heavier.

Night came on. Not only his legs grew heavy, but his head, and his eyes. Rain thundered on the roof. The room and its flickering oil lamp slid away from him and he slumped on the mats. Tohachi peered at him, drained the bottle, and then he, too, melted to the horizontal. The maids put pillows under their heads, covers over them, and a jug of cool water where they could reach it when they woke up.

"20th day. Cloudy. Parted from Tohachi, asking him to deliver a letter to my home . . ."

The truth was that Hiroshige had left home without the amenities of farewell. His wife was a strong-minded woman. She was a good

Memorial portrait of Hiroshige depicted as a lay brother in a Buddhist monastery, with a eulogy above (*a print by Kunisada*)

manager, and he recognized that she was usually right when she complained about the indignity of being poor. But there was little to be done about it, and when she became too abrasive he sometimes just slipped away for a while. Recently he had been hankering for a sketching trip. An outburst from his wife had sent him through the door. The letter he now wrote despite a throbbing head would confirm what she had already guessed.

She was his second wife. The first, a gentle creature, had died three years before. By neither did he have children. He had adopted a son to succeed him in the fire brigade; in later years he would adopt a daughter who would be a joy to him, a niece by blood, the offspring of a younger brother who was a priest and had no business fathering children.

Tohachi put the letter in his wallet and the two friends said good-bye. They solemnly promised each other another celebration when Hiroshige returned to Edo.

"... *Sketched views of Okitsu despite dull weather. Retreated to the inn to put my sketchbook in order. Had a stroll in the streets in the evening.*"

Cloudy or not, hangover or not, there was work to be done. He took up his sketching materials—his little notebook, his brush-and-ink case—and set out. Yesterday he had been grateful for Tohachi's company. Today he had to be alone, to battle with himself to catch the right vision in the right line.

All morning long he worked, serious, intent, keyed-up. He knew Okitsu well, he had sketched there many times. Each time it was different. "An old scene is new each time I see it," he often said. "A lovely landscape never bores me, no matter how many times I come back to it."

Sometime after noon he stopped, suddenly drained. He was tired and he ached. With his fist he pounded the tightened muscles in the back of his neck. He took a long look at the scene before him, grimaced at the open page of his sketchbook, and trudged back to the Minaguchi-ya.

Raisuke had a special treat waiting for him, abalone and a bottle of saké. Lunch revived Hiroshige, and afterwards he slid all the doors open to the garden and set himself to transpose rough into finished sketches. There was an accumulation of work, not only from the morning but from the past few days' journeying.

This was the second step in the discipline that might some day lead to a print. The hasty, on-the-spot notations were winnowed, refined, and developed to fill another sketchbook, planned from graceful beginning to graceful close to lure the viewer down one stretch of the Tokaido. These pages were not for the public and none was intended as basis for a print. They were simply a part of the process by which Hiroshige organized the image in his brain. He worked steadily until the light began to fail. Then he bathed, had dinner, and strolled the darkening streets of Okitsu to walk out some of the tension that was in him. Tomorrow, he decided, he would climb the long stone steps to Seikenji.

"21st day. Visited Seikenji. Looking down from the temple, saw the salt fires on the beach. Had a smoke and pondered the remarkable beauty of this place."

He sat on a bench in the temple courtyard. After a time he took out his guidebook and scanned the list of the ancient temple's notable sights. "Crawling Dragon" he had already seen. He had passed it at the base of the temple steps, a venerable plum tree that sprawled negligently along the highway. It was a famous tree, and, thought Hiroshige, it looked as though it knew it. It looked secure in its fame, secure in the knowledge that its blossoms traveled annually with daimyo's rank to the Shogun's court for New Year's.

Another of Seikenji's tourist attractions Hiroshige had seen on previous visits. It was the ceiling of the entrance to the great hall, unremarkable save for a dark stain that crept across it . . .

About thirteen hundred years earlier, the civilized clans of the southwest had at this point (then called Kiyomi, "Clear View") thrown a barrier-gate across the coastal trail to keep back the marauding tribesmen of the north. (Soon they installed a Buddhist image to make their roadblock more effective, and this might be called the beginning of Seikenji.)

History records sharp battles at this place, one in the late eighth century, another in the early tenth. The stain dates from one of these. It is a bloodstain, from the blood of men who died fighting for the barrier: wood from the old gate, which somehow had survived the fires that razed the temple itself, was used to build the ceiling of the present entrance hall. Nearby are some of the barrier's weapons, forked spears to be aimed at the throat, others with multiple points or rows of evil barbs.

Hiroshige thought of making a historical print based on one of those battles, quickly discarded the idea. Now the government was in the north at Edo, and its enemies were the clans of the southwest. No matter what point of view an artist took, any government censor would see parallels which could land a man in jail.

Today there remained only memories of battles. Hiroshige read with pleasure from his guidebook a poem written by a military inspector on a wintry night during that tenth-century campaign:

> Lights of fishing boats
> Shining cold on the waves,
> Bells of post horses
> Echoing from dark mountains.

And another, indicating that travelers by sea were also obligated to check through the barrier:

> Boats sail by without stopping
> at the barrier!
> —Lo, they are leaves blown
> by the wind from the trees.

Hiroshige's revery was interrupted by one of the priests, who wandered out from the temple, attracted by the man who sat so long in the courtyard, sketching materials at hand. Soon they were deep in conversation.

To Hiroshige's question about the temple's origin, the priest laughed lightly. "I will tell you the legend of its founding," he said. "You may believe it or not, as you wish.

"Until 1262 there was only the barrier's sentinel Buddha. Then a priest named Kansei founded a real temple here. Concerning Kansei, they tell this story.

"There was an old hermit-priest who lived in a rustic retreat on top of the mountain. He used to read the holy sutras daily, and daily a snake would come out to listen. It was an unusual snake, for it was blind in one eye. The snake failed to appear one day, and the next, and the next, and finally the old priest gave it up for lost.

"Some time later, fishermen caught a large octopus in the bay. It was an unusual octopus, for it was blind in one eye. The people of the village thought it would be unlucky to eat such a freak, so they buried it on the beach. Where they buried it, grass sprouted and grew. A spinster of the village ate some of the grass and mysteriously became pregnant. When the child, a boy, was born, he was blind in one eye.

"Despondent, the woman determined to kill herself and her baby, but the old priest who lived on the mountain stopped her, and offered to take the boy and bring him up. He did, and he taught him the lessons of Buddha, and it was this boy who grew up to become Kansei and who founded Seikenji."

Hiroshige smiled but said nothing. After a moment the priest said gently, "Would you like to see his grave?"

Hiroshige nodded, and followed his guide past the temple and up a steep path beneath towering cedars. They passed the grave of the Ryukyuan prince and came upon the burial place of the temple's abbots. The priest pointed to the first stone, the oldest stone, a very old stone, flaky and covered with lichen. It was in the stylized shape of an octopus.

They came down the path as silently as they had climbed it. "The man who made Seikenji rich and important was the warrior Takauji," said the priest when they reached the main hall. "I will show you his honorable shadow."

Hiroshige smiled a little at the priest's use of guidebook language.

The honorable shadow of Takauji was a fine wood statue in a dim recess at one side of the altar.

There the old boy sat cross-legged as he had for almost four hundred years. Hiroshige looked closely, for he could see that it was a fine piece of work and he was interested in it as a contemporary comment on Takauji's character. It had the prominent jowls which the Japanese associate with "conqueror's features" (Ieyasu had them, too), and piercing eyes in which one could see white all around the iris. People say this indicates a dark and scheming nature, and that is the usual estimate of Takauji. He was the great man of his age, but it was a dark age. Compared with his less successful but more admired adversary, Yui Shosetsu's hero, Kusunoki Masashige, Takauji was a ruthless intriguer whose promises were made to be broken, and who switched sides whenever ambition dictated. He ended up on top, and history punishes him for it: the Japanese have always chosen failures for their greatest heroes.

It was in 1335, when he was resting at Seikenji after a fine bloody victory, that Takauji ordered the temple endowed with some truly magnificent buildings. A few years later he was back to do battle with his son and his brother (it was a family that seldom saw eye to eye) and he burned those buildings to the ground. His was the usual reason: it was too dominant a point to risk its falling to the enemy. He thus became the first to burn Seikenji, as Ieyasu was the last, but both men took care that it was reconstructed.

The priest, who was thoroughly enjoying this tourist Hiroshige, now led him to the rear gallery of the main hall, and bidding him kneel, slid open the heavy wooden shutters, revealing the famous garden.

The waterfall leaped in nine stages down the face of the mountain into the pool, and the teahouse beckoned with promise of peaceful contemplation. The priest indicated the little bridge with Basho's poem carved on the underside, and then, sucking in his breath, he pointed out the five trees that Ieyasu had planted and the three stones that he had named. It was because of these that all men, even daimyo, kneeled to look at this garden.

There remained Seikenji's great conversation piece, and because Hiroshige was an artist the priest decided to bring it out. The guidebook called it "a painting from the brush of Sesshu," but in fact it was a very fine copy, and whether the original was actually by Sesshu was a matter of great contention. It was, and still is, an important question, for Sesshu is almost unanimously considered to be Japan's greatest artist.

Painter and Zen priest, Sesshu was a contemporary of Christopher Columbus. In his travels about the country he lived for a time on the mountain above Seikenji. Some years later he went to China with a commission to buy art objects for a wealthy daimyo. This was the fulfillment of a cherished dream, for China was the fountainhead of Japanese culture, and Sesshu looked forward to study with the masters.

In this he was disappointed. China had passed its peak, and the Chinese recognized in Sesshu a painter greater than any of their living artists. In Peking he was showered with requests for his work.

At one point, according to story, he was asked to paint the most beautiful scene in Japan, and drawing on memories of his retreat above Okitsu, he made our painting. He painted Fuji, looming over a screen of lower mountains. He painted the storied hook of Miho, with its wind-swept pines thrust deep into the sands. He painted the village of Okitsu, strung along the inner coast, and some of its white-sailed fishing boats scudding across the bay. He painted Satta Pass, and a glimpse of the village of Yui beyond. He painted the temple of Seikenji, planted firmly against the middle slopes of the mountain in the foreground. And then, because he was an artist, and because he felt his composition lacked a little something, he painted, behind the temple buildings, a five-storied pagoda where none had ever been.

The painting was not an end in itself. It was a study for a mural for Peking's Imperial palace, and those who believe that it is genuine point to old records that Sesshu did paint such a mural. Unfortunately, and this is the root of the controversy, the artist himself did not inscribe his painting. A friend of his, a scholar of Peking, did that, writing on it this poem:

> Fuji towers over the sea below
> Like stairs climbing to heaven.
> Even in June there is snow,
> Making it a lotus bud.
> Clouds encircle the peak;
> The famous Seiken stands in the clouds.
> The sky is high and dustless,
> Priests live there above the pollution of the earth.
> I want to fly east mounted on the wind.

After he painted the mural, Sesshu brought his study back to Japan with him. And when he next journeyed through Okitsu, he stopped at Seikenji and told them about that pagoda.

I doubt that he suggested such a thing, but so great was his fame and honor that the temple and its patrons felt that they had let him down by not having a pagoda where he felt one was needed. Straightway, they built one. It was little enough to do for an artist like Sesshu, whom even the Chinese revered.

This was the pagoda dedicated to the Buddha of medicine, the deity who handed down the formula for the salve of Seikenji. How one thing leads to another!

It was a thoughtful gesture on the part of the family who owned the original painting to commission a copy as a gift to Seikenji. It seems a pity that their generosity should have led to doubts about their treasure, for it was the scholar-painter who made this copy who raised the fuss about the authenticity of the original.

Hiroshige was grateful for a look at the famous work, and he recognized that in bringing it out, the priest was terminating his escorted tour. Anything else would be anticlimactic.

He took his leave, but he stopped at the head of the steps for one more long look down. He remembered an old saying about this view: the man galloping by will rein in his horse, the man at the oars will forget to row, the man on shank's mare will turn his head nine times in ten steps. Hiroshige sighed. It was too much to capture in a print.

He descended the steps and emerged into the stir of the highway. Before him were the salve shops of Seikenji. He had heard of the boy salesmen who had once enlivened this scene, but their day was past. He decided to stop in at the shop called Maru-ichi. He would get a packet of salve and a bowl of noodles before he went back to the Minaguchi-ya.

"22d day. Cloudy. Requested to draw a view of Okitsu. Hard rain in the evening."

The drawing was requested by Raisuke, who had approached Hiroshige the previous evening, after his return from Seikenji. In making this request, Raisuke was continuing a custom initiated by Genzaemon on Hiroshige's second visit to the Minaguchi-ya. Raisuke's motive, like Genzaemon's, was double-barreled: the Mochizukis admired Hiroshige's prints, and collected them, but they also desired things personal and unique, like drawings or paintings. More than that, they knew perfectly well that Hiroshige could not afford to stay at the Minaguchi-ya, and so each time he appeared they requested something from his brush, and they always contrived to pay for it a little more than the artist's bill at the end of his stay. No one would have dreamed of mentioning such an arrangement: it just invariably happened that way.

Much of Hiroshige's income came from work other than prints. During his career he was commissioned to paint several theatre curtains, and he made long journeys to execute them. He painted murals and theatre billboards. And of course he did paintings of the kind that the Japanese hang in the place of honor in their rooms.

Even so, it was difficult to make ends meet. His first wife had sold most of her trousseau to raise money for his sketching trips. His second wife sometimes had to borrow from their neighbors. He lived fairly well, but at his death his house would not be paid for.

"23d day. Arranged and refined my sketches. Sketched along the seashore. Watched fishermen repairing their boats."

The cultured, moneyed, art-loving upper class called Hiroshige

The sea wall at Okitsu, fishing boats, and Mount Fuji
(*from one of Hiroshige's sketchbooks*)

not artist but artisan, assuming, of course, that they knew of his existence at all. Prints were lowly things, not to be considered in the same bracket with classical painting, though that painting had become vapid and sterile.

Hiroshige knew all this. He did not aim his work at the upper class. He populated his prints with ordinary people: farmers trudging to their fields, coolies toasting their bare bottoms by a fire, tourists being set upon by the ladies of the inns. When he showed a daimyo's entourage he seems to have been most interested in the decorative effect of their banner poles and hooded spears.

He was proud that his grandfather had been a samurai but he knew very well that he himself was not one. He was a commoner, he lived a commoner's life. Wherever he went he quickly absorbed the facts of ordinary people's lives. He had visited Okitsu many times, and he knew the town well.

He knew, for example, the local heroes. There was Sankichi, a youth who, whenever his father, a mailman, was assigned to carry the mail to Yui at night, took the task upon himself, going alone over dangerous Satta. There was Taisuke, who only recently had been officially cited for his exemplary life; he loved learning and hated hedonism; he worked hard and helped the needy; and, dutiful son, he nightly massaged his parents. And there was faithful Moto: daughter of a river coolie who could not afford to keep her, she had at fourteen been sent as maidservant to the home of prosperous farmer Kambei; when Kambei became hard up, so poor he could no longer pay Moto her pittance, he had advised her to change to another family, but she had answered that she had no intention of leaving the household simply because Kambei had become poor; frequently she had walked miles to call the doctor for Kambei's sick and aged father, and after the old man died she had visited his grave every morning, rain or shine, for one hundred days (she had tried to keep these visits secret but the story leaked out when woodcutters reported seeing her at dawn); she was so admired that she received many offers of marriage but she refused them all, saying that if she married she would then not be able to visit freely Kambei's family and her own parents; and so she continued, going to the mountains in the evening to pick firewood when Kambei could not buy it, grinding grain late at night for breakfast, pawning her own clothes when

Kambei desperately needed money, smoothing children's quarrels, settling grownups' disputes, and modestly protesting when officials honored her.

Hiroshige shared the townspeople's pride in their recent capture of a notorious band of jailbreakers who had terrorized the population all the way from Nagoya, and joined in the praise of the Minaguchi-ya's quick-witted bath attendant, who, when the villains were encircled in front of the inn, leaped to the roof and pelted them with roof tiles until they dropped their swords and surrendered.

Hiroshige knew the people's great days. On the eleventh day of the first month, tenant farmers gathered at their landlords' to renew their contracts, and were entertained with a party; it was just as though they were retainers and the landowners were great lords. On the last day of winter, parched beans were flung throughout the house to rout the devil and let in good fortune. Later there were the vital days of rice-planting, which according to ancient ritual had to be done by women, and hence became the one time when women's wages soared high above men's. The seventh month brought the *Bon* festival: then the gates of the underworld opened, and the spirits of one's ancestors were welcomed to their native homes; three nights later they were sent back again on tiny boats floated out to sea, each with its lantern to light the way, and on the same night the river coolies and the priests of the town gathered at a ceremonial bonfire by the river's mouth to pray for those who had lost their lives in the river during the year. A few weeks later came the climax of harvest-time, and of course each shrine and temple had its own great fair, highlighted, perhaps, with a tournament of *sumo* wrestlers, grappling in the river bed. And, finally, there was the year-end, when all one's affairs were tidied up and the New Year greeted with special food, and visits to one's temple, and conviviality with one's friends. Hiroshige shared the feeling of each of these occasions.

He loved good food, but he knew the people's scanty diet: barley or wheat occasionally enlivened with a little rice, vegetables, a bit of fish. River coolies went into debt to buy the bean paste they

Farmers in a festival dance at Yui (*a print by Hiroshige*)

needed to keep warmth in their bodies while they worked in the icy water. If a family were lucky enough to keep a chicken or two, they would eat the eggs but never the chickens; hens were kept until natural death caught up with them, or were turned loose in a shrine or temple compound to forage for themselves; Hiroshige heard from Raisuke the scandalous episode of the villager who had eaten a chicken—he had been ostracized as a fiend.

He knew how lives were circumscribed by regulation, limiting the size of houses, dictating proper clothing (cotton only, not even decorated with silk), banning gambling, exhorting to thrift and filial piety.

He knew all these facts of people's lives. They were second nature to him, and they show in his prints, in the touch of humor, the trace of melancholy, the cast of resignation.

He left the Minaguchi-ya that morning by the rear gate, through the garden, stepping directly onto the beach. He sketched the fishermen repairing their boats and mending their nets, the urchins (those that were too young to work) playing in the sand, the women making salt. Ten years later, in one of his last full sets of Tokaido prints, he would use the salt-makers to represent Okitsu.

He sketched most of the afternoon, sometimes looking back to the mountains, sometimes out to Miho. He felt at home here, in this place, with these people.

"24th day. Fine. Took a trip. Footsore so I rode in a kago as far as Shimizu, sketching on the way. Climbed to Kuno Temple to worship. Sketched the view under my eyes . . ."

The temple was not, of course, the fortress-shrine on top of the mountain, where Ieyasu had been buried, but the original temple which old Shingen had, two hundred and seventy years earlier, moved from the summit to the lower slopes. The priests were still grumpy about that.

". . . Walked to Miho and looked across to Seikenji and the beautiful Okitsu shore. It would make a good snowscape . . ."

One of Japan's great artists visits the Minaguchi-ya

Hiroshige did not have to see snow to design a snow scene, and some of his finest snow prints were based on summer sketches.

Despite his comment, he never made a snowscape of the Okitsu shore, but the best of his dozen or more Okitsu prints was made from Miho, looking across the harbor, with a full-sailed cargo boat in the foreground, Seikenji on the mountain slopes, and Fuji dominating the horizon. Still, it must be admitted that, though he loved this bit of the Tokaido, he never made a really fine print of it.

"*. . . Remembered one of my friend's talking about the delicious flavor of sea bream cooked in steam and salt on this shore. Wanted a chance to taste this fish, so lost no time in asking a local inhabitant I found on the beach to cook it for me. He said he was afraid he couldn't do it properly; it was difficult and besides he didn't want to waste the salt, because it would be worthless after it was used on the fish. However, I persuaded him. He asked me to wait till the*

Okitsu from Miho (*a print by Hiroshige*)

fishing boats came in, so I handed him enough money and strolled about reveling in the scenery. Coming back just in time, I found three bream ready and more delicious than I had imagined possible. Never such a delicacy in my life. Decided to take some with me for a side dish with saké at dinner so I hurried back to Okitsu. Immediately after a hot bath I sat to eat, drinking saké accompanied by the salt fish. The landlord stopped by and marveled at the fish, saying, 'How did you manage to get this? Even we have not tasted it often.'"

Hiroshige traveled for scenery but it took food to make his diary sing.

The Japanese name for sea bream is *tai*. It is a handsome fish, a close relative of our red snapper. *Okitsu-tai* is famous all over Japan. It consists of fillets salted and partly dried on planks in the sun, then broiled. It was a favorite dish of Ieyasu's, and remains a favorite today.

But fresh *tai*, packed in salt and steamed on shore within minutes of its catching, was a delicacy even at the Minaguchi-ya. Raisuke was amazed that Hiroshige should have known of it. This indicates merely that Raisuke was not yet well acquainted with his guest.

In a drawing book, published "for the purpose of giving hints to children who wish to paint, though they have not yet begun to paint regularly in classes," Hiroshige told how to sketch a *tai*. He prefaced: "The way to paint pictures is to copy from nature, but adding slightly an artistic idea in the brushwork."

". . . I invited the landlord to share the fish with me and he was delighted. Bowing, he excused himself, and soon returned with two bottles of saké to express his gratitude, inviting me to drink deeply with the delicacy. Fell asleep soon after dinner."

The day's long walks, the good food and wine, made him sleep soundly. Tomorrow he would take to the road again. His return trip would bring him back to the Minaguchi-ya, but only when his urge for travel was burned out. He would not tarry then, for he would be homesick for Edo. Edo was his town.

One of Japan's great artists visits the Minaguchi-ya

"25th day. In spite of a slight headache this morning I left the inn. Arrived soon at the post town of Shimizu. Though a little too early, I took lunch there and then started for Shizuoka. Fine scenery hereabouts . . ."

Seventeenth Generation

CHAPTER TWELVE

Which introduces the Tokaido's Number One Boss

PRINCIPAL CHARACTERS

The great-grandmother of Isako, *present mistress of the inn;*
    one of the Mochizukis of Shimizu, not then related to the
    Mochizukis of the Minaguchi-ya

Jirocho of Shimizu, *the Boss*

Jirohachi, *Jirocho's uncle and foster father*

Sataro, *keeper of a cheap inn at Odawara, and an unlucky*
    gambler

Buichi, *a gambling boss friendly to Jirocho*

Yaogadake, *a sumo wrestler, later a gambling boss and Jirocho's*
    enemy

O-cho, *a maid at the Minaguchi-ya, later Jirocho's wife*

Saigo Takamori, *a samurai of the Satsuma clan, one of the*
    leaders of the revolution against the Tokugawa
    Shogunate

Ishimatsu, *one of Jirocho's favorite lieutenants*

Kichibei, *a gambler who becomes Jirocho's enemy*

Lord of Satsuma, Shimazu Hisamitsu, *head of the great*
    Satsuma clan

Katsuzo, *a gambling boss, enemy of Jirocho*

Yamaoka Tesshu, *a Shogunate official who later serves the*
    Imperial government; friend and mentor to Jirocho

Tokugawa Yoshinobu, *fifteenth and last Tokugawa Shogun,*
    afterwards Lord of Suruga

Ulysses S. Grant, *ex-President of the United States*

Amada, *Jirocho's adopted son*

and among the people of the inn:

Mochizuki Raisuke, *sixteenth master of the Minaguchi-ya*

Mochizuki Hanjuro I, *seventeenth master of the Minaguchi-ya*

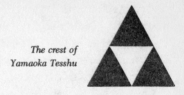

BY 1850, when Hiroshige was at the height of his popularity, Raisuke was nicely settled into his job as master of the Minaguchi-ya, and enjoying it thoroughly. He enjoyed it all the more because there were moments when he still felt a tingle of surprise at his good fortune.

For the first twenty-five years of his life he had never expected to be master of anything. His eldest brother had inherited the Tezuka *honjin*. His second brother, Genzaemon, had by adoption inherited the Minaguchi-ya. Raisuke had faced the prospect of being only a superfluous appendage to the family business. Then suddenly he had been put in Genzaemon's place. He was made head of a flourishing house, he was married to his brother's young widow, Nami. Now they had a son, a strong, healthy boy. Small wonder that Raisuke was amazed at his change of fortune. Small wonder that he took his responsibilities very seriously.

That being the case, he spent little time watching the pageant that flowed by on the highway, and there was no reason he should have noticed the little procession that passed the Minaguchi-ya one bleak wintry day early in 1850.

There were five kago, each borne by two burly men. At the post station those bearers were paid and dismissed, and a new set took their places. Shuttered against the cold, the kago were jostled towards the river and across it on the temporary wooden bridge which spanned the shallow winter channel, the bearers' heavy footfalls echoing hollowly in the river basin. The column moved through the long lane of stall-fronted houses that made up Satta village, and then,

with much heaving and grunting from the bearers, began the tortuous climb up Satta Mountain.

It is Isako, the present mistress of the inn, who tells this story,
for it was her great-grandmother who was bracing herself in the first
swaying palanquin. The old lady had had her fill of winter that year.
The chill of it was in her, and she had acquired lamentable aches and
pains. She prescribed her own remedy. It was to be a long holiday at
a hot spring, until the heat of the mineral waters and the radiance of
the first plum blossoms could banish winter from her bones. She was
now on her way from her home in Shimizu to the current-warmed
peninsula of Izu, for hot springs were always there and plum blossoms soon would be. For company in the steamy baths she had invited two favorite nieces, and her entourage was completed by a
maid and a man she had brought along as escort on the highway.

Despite the chill wind the bearers stopped even before the ascent
had fairly begun, to mop their brows and complain of the weight.
A little farther they stopped again to curse the luck that had given
them such a heavy load. And then near the top, at the loneliest spot
on the pass, they set the kago down with a thud. The women were
as heavy as stones, they said. It was ridiculous to expect men to carry
them over the mountain for the pittance specified. They would be
carried no farther. They could freeze here, or perhaps the bandits
that lurked on Satta would slit their throats. It was a matter of indifference. Such a miserly witch deserved no better.

The old lady had a quick temper and a sharp tongue. At the first
sign of revolt she unleashed the feminine invective that made her
the terror of her household, but she knew the bearers had the upper
hand. True, they didn't know there was a man in the last kago, but
certainly, she figured, he was no match for ten burly villains. She
would have to pay. Her mind was already clicking like an abacus.

The most repulsive of the ruffians had just suggested that the
kago, occupants and all, might easily go tumbling over the cliff, and
she was about to begin haggling, when she saw the man's glance shift
to the rear palanquin, whose shutter had slid softly open.

"Oh, bother!" she thought. "Let's not have any witless heroics."

And she was about to cry out to her man to stay out of this, when she saw the shock on the bearer's face. His jaw fell slack and his color drained away. Suddenly he was on his knees in the rocky path and all his cohorts were in the dirt around him. They were imploring pardon, they were begging for mercy. She looked back to find them transfixed by the icy glare of her escort, the heavy-set man who was leaning ever so slightly from his chair.

Then the bearers were scrambling to their feet, frantically hoisting the kago, and hustling them on their way. She leaned back and caught her breath in astonishment. Undoubtedly the sweating men had been startled to find a man in her party, but this alone could not account for their fright. One man could not terrorize ten with only a glance, unless he were someone extraordinary. But was that possible? He was only a town rascal, perpetually in debt to her family's pawnshop but tolerated because once, briefly, when he was a wild and ungovernable boy, he had been apprenticed to them. She congratulated herself on having brought him along, and as the palanquins rattled and squeaked down Satta Mountain into the town of Yui, she wondered about him. He must have hidden talents. He must, she thought, be quite a man.

He was. He was Jirocho of Shimizu. "As you journey along the Tokaido," sings the balladier, "the fragrance of tea and orange blossoms greets you at Suruga. Here there are many famous and historical places, but as famous even as the pines of Miho is Jirocho of Shimizu Port, the Tokaido's Number One Boss."

If Isako's great-grandmother had not heard of his exploits it was because she moved in somewhat rarefied middle-class circles. To the common people of Suruga, Jirocho was a giant. To them, the awesome machinery of government was remote and mysterious, and its law barely touched them. It was Jirocho who made thieves and cutthroats scarce, whose dominance was a shield against even the samurai's brutal arrogance. Jirocho was a gambler, but he was no pirate. He was a good man in his way, but more important he was a strong man. He was Robin Hood. He was Boss.

Raisuke knew him. Jirocho's home base of Shimizu was only the next station, and the Minaguchi-ya lay squarely in his territory. He held sway along the coast all the way from the Fuji River, two stations towards Edo, to the Oi River, six stations towards Kyoto. In this heartland of the Tokaido, not a shrine or temple held a festival, not a daimyo's retinue stopped for the night, but Jirocho's men were there with dice and a sporting chance. And in the background there would be some of Jirocho's strongmen, tough and alert.

Raisuke often thought he had reason to be grateful that Jirocho was the kind he was. Gambling there would always be, and the bosses that went with it, and an innkeeper was lucky when his stretch of highway was so well and firmly controlled. The police were remarkably ineffective, he often remarked. Mostly they did nothing, which was what they were bribed to do, but you could hardly blame them; the whole government was corrupt and panicky. Nor was this surprising: every year foreign nations were more threatening and the southwest clans more rebellious. Where would it all end? Raisuke wondered. In the meantime, an innkeeper was fortunate when there was a good, strong man like Jirocho to keep peace on the highway.

If a novelist sat down to create a character who would mirror the times between 1820 and 1893—times that began in lawlessness and near-panic before a foreign menace, times that saw the old government toppled, a new one raised, and two and a half centuries of isolation shattered, times that closed with Japan's hurling herself into the modern world—if a novelist sat down to create a character who would mirror these times, he might very well create Jirocho. This same thought has occurred to countless Japanese writers, most of whom were thereupon incited to write a book about the man. It first occurred to Jirocho himself, but he had foresightedly saved himself the anguish of authorship by never learning to write. He could express his meaning well enough in Japan's own phonetic syllabary, but he had chosen never to give any attention to the complex Chinese characters in which every literate Japanese cloaks his thoughts.

Jirocho created his book by recounting his experiences to a budding author. It is, therefore, an authorized biography, and it tells Jirocho's story as Jirocho wanted it told. It completely overlooks his worst defeats, for Jirocho took the sensible view that if the other fellow wanted to boast he could have his own book written; and it is told with considerable flair, for Jirocho had a vivid sense of the dramatic.

He began by being born on the first day of January, 1820. There is a local superstition that a New Year's baby will grow up to be either a beneficent genius or a deep-dyed villain, and his father, aware of the odds, took no chances. Annoyed by his wife's imprudence, he speedily arranged to have the baby adopted by one of her brothers, a successful rice dealer named Jirohachi, who had a daughter but no son. The baby had been called Chogoro, but now that he was Jirohachi's Chogoro, he was tagged by the first half of his foster father's name and the first half of his own. He became Jirocho.

He also became a young terror. When he was eight he was sent to a boarding school to learn reading and writing. This was his first encounter with Chinese characters. He balked, and the other boys, previously docile, followed his lead. He was sent home.

He was then put in the school of a Zen Buddhist temple (Seikenji was spared; the scourge fell on a sister temple in Shimizu). At first shunned by the other boys, he proved that he already understood the problems of leadership. He took some cake to school every day, and by dividing it among his foes he soon made them his devoted henchmen.

He did not let them down. The head priest loved to grow chrysanthemums, and he found the boys handy for watering and weeding. The boys, naturally, were indignant. When he was given the job, Jirocho pulled the flowers up by the roots. For this heroism he was expelled. His last act was to carry home all the goldfish from the temple pond.

It was then that the rice dealer apprenticed the boy to Isako's great-grandparents, the Mochizukis of Shimizu. They were used to wild young apprentices but this one was too much. After a few months they sent him back. He was now ten.

His foster father tried once more. He turned him over to one of his wife's brothers, a farmer who lived on Satta Pass, not so very far from the spot where years later the porters would stage their rebellion. In this farmer the boy at last met his match. Every step out of line brought swift and painful punishment. Eventually, in the words of one biographer, "he began to show signs of decency."

It was while young Jirocho was living in the farmhouse on Satta that Hiroshige made his first trip over the mountain, accompanying the horses being sent to the Emperor in Kyoto. Jirocho watched them go. It is indicative of some moral progress that he did not throw stones at the horses to stampede them.

After four years with the stern farmer on Satta, he was considered manageable, and he was allowed to go home to his foster parents and the rice shop. He was no sooner there than he broached plans to leave for Edo to make his fame and fortune. Refused permission, he promptly stole his mother's secret savings, a tidy little fortune of four hundred and fifty gold pieces, buried one hundred and fifty of them in the garden, and set off for the big city with the remaining three hundred.

His foster father Jirohachi caught up with him in an inn six stations down the highway and about a quarter of the way to Edo. He retrieved the three hundred gold pieces, tried fruitlessly to learn what had happened to the other hundred and fifty, and finally, taking possession of all the young rascal's clothing except the loincloth he was wearing, he left him penniless and all but naked. It was Jirohachi's hope that this drastic course would bring Jirocho both home and to his senses.

It was a vain hope, for the boy was quite prepared for this turn of events. He begged an old kimono to travel in, slipped home in the middle of the night, dug up the hundred and fifty gold pieces he had buried, and well heeled again, set off in the direction of Kyoto.

In Shizuoka he bought some new clothes and celebrated with a night in the gay quarters. He then put another fifty miles between him and the rice shop in Shimizu by moving on to the city of Hamamatsu.

In one of the houses there he discovered an appealing little harlot named Otoki. He and Otoki found something in common: they were both from Shimizu. She had been sold to a procurer by her mother, who was not one to pass up a cash offer.

Jirocho found Otoki's company delightful, but he was not so bemused by her that he failed to notice that the summer was unseasonably cold and rainy. Though he had spent very little time in the rice business, he knew perfectly well what that kind of weather would do to the crop.

Taking advantage of his foster father's name, he bought on credit all the rice he could from Hamamatsu dealers, and in Otoki's company he reveled in each new cold and rainy day. His gamble paid off. The price of rice rose higher and higher, and in a month or so, by the time he was ready to go home, he had settled with the Hamamatsu dealers and had acquired a small fortune in rice and cash.

When he reappeared in Shimizu his foster father was furious but he soon melted. It was impossible to stay angry with a son who showed so much sound business sense, and so Jirocho was pardoned and welcomed into the shop. For the first time in his life he settled down to work.

It was only the next year that the old man died, and at sixteen Jirocho inherited the business. He became even more diligent, a very model of a young rice merchant. In two years he had made the shop so prosperous that it provided an irresistible temptation for the old man's widow, who one night disappeared with her paramour and all the firm's cash assets.

It was a hard blow but Jirocho was equal to it. His name was good, his credit was good, and the Mochizukis, who had once turned him away as an ungovernable apprentice, were now happy to loan him new capital. Working harder than ever he speedily rebuilt the business, and incidentally took himself a wife. The girl

Men bailing rice (*detail from a book of prints by Hokusai*)

must have been delighted to enter a home with no mother-in-law.

If this picture of a hard-working young businessman impresses the reader as being incongruous in the light of Jirocho's misspent youth, it must have seemed even more incongruous to Jirocho himself. Within two more years he was bored to the teeth. There then occurred a fortuitous incident that gave him the excuse to do what he wanted.

One morning, as he was praying for the repose of his dead father's soul, he noticed a wandering monk standing in the doorway. He called the monk in and asked him to read sutras before the family altar. When the ceremony was concluded, the monk fixed Jirocho with such a mournful gaze that Jirocho could not help asking why.

"Ah," begged the monk, "please don't ask."

But Jirocho insisted.

"Well, then," the monk said, "—but I tell you this very reluctantly. For I clearly see that you are a young man of great ability and upstanding character, with a fine prosperous business. One would assume that yours is a rosy future. Yet I have rarely seen a more unfortunate physiognomy. Your features clearly indicate, my son, that you will not live to be more than twenty-five years of age."

Jirocho laughed as he gave the monk some money and watched him disappear down the street, but, though he fought it, the mournful prophecy became an obsession. He was now twenty. If he had only five years more to live, could he spend them in the dull routine of the rice business, in the musty atmosphere of account books, a slave to the responsibility imposed on him as head of his family?

There was another kind of life, he knew. It swirled about him in the streets of Shimizu, to the staccato tempo of the click of dice. Its heroes were the people's idols, men who lived outside the law and yet were more and more the only law that counted.

For the government was falling apart. The country and its rulers were jittery. There were sure signs that the nation's self-imposed exile was about to be shattered. The British, Russians, French and Americans were prowling Japan's coasts, and the Dutch at Nagasaki were sending frequent warnings that the government's refusal to open its ports would certainly bring war. Inside the country, the southwest clans that had for more than two hundred years lain quiet under Tokugawa dominance were now seething. The naïve among them thundered that the foreign barbarians must be repulsed. The sophisticated, who knew how impossible that was, echoed the cry, delighted at any chance to embarrass the shaky government.

Official discipline was loose. Bribery was rampant. The police who once had been the gamblers' scourge now turned to them as allies. Maintain order for us, the police said to the bosses, keep peace in your territory, and we will wink at your gambling.

Gambling had never been so unmolested, but as a result the field was overcrowded. An ambitious young man had to fight to get in and fight to stay there. Jirocho was attacked more than once, and one night, coming home from a theatre party, he was nearly killed. He was, unfortunately, drunk, and quite unable to defend himself. A stone thrown out of the darkness downed him, more stones hit him as he lay writhing on the ground, and finally his attackers emerged from hiding to beat him with clubs. He was found by passers-by in the early morning and carried home more dead than alive. His injuries took fifty days to heal. He gave up drinking.

He was no sooner in action again than he had another battle with the same gang. This time he was ready for them, and he left two bodies sprawled in the street. With arrest for murder imminent, he divorced his wife to free her from complicity, turned the rice business over to his foster sister and her husband, and, as a measure of atonement for future villainies, burned the IOUs of all his debtors. Then he fled Shimizu.

For the next three years he wandered. This was his real initiation into the underworld, whose rigid etiquette for meeting, greeting, and fighting unconsciously parodied the code and ceremony of the samurai. When one of the members of this wildly romantic world introduced himself he took a stance and intoned his own testimonial: "Allow me to give you my greetings. I am a man of the port town of Shimizu in Suruga. Chogoro Yamamoto is my real name, but people commonly call me Jirocho of Shimizu, a humble man about town."

Jirocho generally took a self-deprecating line, especially after he became famous, but others were not so modest: "A man of Hamamatsu, I was disowned by my parents when I was fourteen. Ever since, I've made my way as a rogue. I'm a born pickpocket and I steal from temples and rich men's houses. I'm on the wanted list from Edo to Kyoto, but I'm a benevolent rogue and I never harass good citizens. Nihonzaemon is my name."

In these stormy years Jirocho lived to the hilt. He lodged with various gambling bosses, and by living under their roofs and eating their food he pledged himself as their brother in arms. He helped them in their battles over territory, and in their struggles to collect gambling debts. He learned how to manipulate dice and how to handle a sword. He was able to judge men quickly, to talk them down if that were possible, or to outfight them if it came to that.

He made a name for himself by incidents like that in which he strode alone into an enemy's house to deliver an ultimatum. He found the boss playing *go* surrounded by steely-eyed strongmen. Jirocho stood over them but the game went on. He was being elaborately ignored. So he kicked over the *go* board, said his piece, and walked out as coolly as he had come in.

These were the years when he formulated the code he later lived by:

1. Justice first.
2. In gambling, don't be grasping. When others are losing, try to stop the game for a while. When you are losing, don't cheat.
3. In mediating a dispute, be impartial. Try your best to reconcile the parties, and accept no reward for success.
4. Don't try to save only your own face. Save face for others too.
5. Smile in distress. Don't be conceited in success.
6. Don't be arrogant on the street. Wear a sword only when absolutely necessary. Be courteous and pleasant.
7. Remember that a boss is more than a gambler. Help the weak and control the strong.

One day, among kago-bearers on the Tokaido, he spotted one of the men he thought he had killed in Shimizu. A little checking disclosed that the other fellow was also alive and, now that he knew there was no murder charge hanging over him, Jirocho headed home.

He had made a reputation, and the same gamblers who had fought him a few years earlier now rushed to bow to him as boss, scrambling to get under his wing and to split their winnings with him. Until he appeared, there had been no real power around Shimizu and Okitsu, creating the sort of vacuum which the underworld abhors, and Jirocho was able to move in without drawing a sword in anger.

The news reached Raisuke soon enough, for he had a sharp ear for local gossip, and though he reserved final judgment until he knew more about Jirocho, he felt a sense of relief. A strong local boss would keep the district from being fought over, with inevitable chaos and peril on the highway. Raisuke knew the value of stability.

Jirocho's prestige took another leap when he was accepted as mediator in a quarrel between two of his most powerful neighbors. This was a tribute, for it meant that both men trusted and respected him.

One regrets to say that his mediation was not a success. This was not due to ineptitude on Jirocho's part, but rather to the nature of the quarrel itself. It did not involve some simple matter like a gambling debt, or an invasion of territory. Rather, it concerned a handsome young rascal and a farmer's daughter, and, as is well known, these affairs are generally insoluble. Jirocho succeeded in reconciling the two bosses, only to have the young Lothario set the police on them all. Jirocho fled towards Edo, and began another period of wandering.

With three henchmen he first took up lodging in Odawara, safely over the Hakone Mountains, at a cheap inn belonging to a certain Sataro. Sataro was helplessly addicted to gambling. He took the rent money that Jirocho had paid him and headed for a game. He lost, but certain that his luck would change if he had another stake, he crept in at night (he had an advantage, for it was his own house and he knew which floor-boards creaked) and stole all his customers' clothing and possessions. These he pawned. Before the night was over he had lost everything.

A chastened man, he confronted his naked guests the next morning with the most profound apologies. He would repay them within the day, he promised. Jirocho shivered skeptically, but Sataro insisted he could get the money. He would, he said, sell his wife to a brothel.

Jirocho refused his offer. He had no wish to break up a marriage and, besides, he had seen the lady in question and he doubted that she would bring enough to make it worthwhile. He and his men set out in their loincloths. Sataro bowed them off, having shaved his head to express penitence.

A friendly boss soon put kimonos on their backs, and they continued their roving until they came to the territory of a brother-gambler named Buichi. Buichi welcomed them, and invited them to join a big year-end celebration which he had organized. Some fifty men were huddled over hot dice in a local restaurant when the police raided the place. Jirocho and Buichi fought off the police until the others had escaped, and then surrendered with the restaurant owner. They spent New Year's Day of 1846, Jirocho's twenty-sixth birthday, in jail.

It was six months before sentence was pronounced. Buichi, because he had once been a samurai, was released, but Jirocho and the restaurant keeper, both commoners, were awarded one hundred lashes.

The restaurant man was whipped first. With every lash of the whip on his naked body he screamed and agonized, while a sizable audience jeered. Jirocho watched coldly, and when his turn came he set his lips in a smile and bore the flogging without showing a trace of pain. The restaurant owner proved to have been the better psychologist, for Jirocho's stoicism so enraged the officials that his punishment was promptly doubled. Even after that, when Buichi tried to get him to ride home in a sedan chair, he refused. "I would not want anyone to think," he said, speaking very carefully, "that two hundred lashes made me unable to walk." But once at Buichi's house, he collapsed. It was two months before he recovered.

Jirocho and Buichi learned then who had given the police the tip that had led to the raid. Their revenge was remarkably mild, all things considered. They merely tied the informer to a pine tree in a lonely wood and plucked him bald, hair by hair.

When, years later, Jirocho recounted the story of his life for his biographer, he told it as a fighting man would, in terms of his fights. Three foes stand out. It was at this point in his life that he met the first of these, a *sumo* wrestler who called himself Yaogadake, after one of Japan's minor mountains.

Shortly after setting out from Buichi's, Jirocho won heavily in a dice session. He was resting in a teahouse when his attention was drawn to a *sumo* wrestler, a huge hulk of a man, blubbering uncontrollably in a corner. Jirocho recognized him as one of those who had just lost their money, and by kindly inquiries he learned that in order to join the game, the big fellow had pawned his wrestler's belt with its great archaic fringe. Without it he could not enter the ring, and he was desperate. Touched, Jirocho gave him money enough to retrieve his belt, and by this kindness began an association which would be a plague for more than ten years.

For the present, however, Jirocho hiked back to Shimizu. He found that the police were no longer interested in him, and he settled down again.

Inevitably the matchmakers went to work. One day he received a visit from one of his pledged brothers in Shimizu. By happy coincidence, this man announced, he just happened to have a young sister named O-cho, Miss Butterfly, who would make Jirocho a splendid wife. The girl was at the moment working as a maid at the Minaguchi-ya in Okitsu until marriage plans were set for her, but of course she could leave whenever her family gave the inn proper notice and provided a suitable replacement.

Jirocho could make no serious objections, particularly since he was on such close terms with the brother, and so the marriage was

Tying a *sumo* wrestler's belt (*detail from a book of prints by Hokusai*)

concluded. Shortly after, to humor O-cho, Jirocho went with her to Okitsu to meet her former employers, and he and Raisuke had a good talk. Raisuke was always very much interested in a gambler's life.

Reflecting her training at the Minaguchi-ya, O-cho turned out to be a good manager. This was fortunate. Jirocho's star was rising, and he attracted scores of followers, wandering men who arrived to attach themselves for board and keep, just as he had done during his own itinerancy. Often he had more guests than the Minaguchi-ya. He kept Shimizu under firm control, but nevertheless it was not easy to stretch his income as far as it had to go. There were never less than thirty men in the house. "My family," he called them.

Even Yaogadake showed up, begging protection. He was getting too old for wrestling and he had decided to become a gambler. He had almost immediately fallen into trouble, and the authorities were now after him for murder. Jirocho sheltered him until the police narrowed their search to Shimizu, and then passed him along to a pledged brother some distance away. Yaogadake had never been a very good wrestler, but few could equal him at stowing away food, a talent for which all *sumo* men are famous. O-cho sometimes caught herself watching him apprehensively as he made his way through bowl after bowl of rice, though she scolded herself for this discourtesy.

Still, she had reason to be concerned. There wasn't even enough money to buy mosquito nets in the summer. Jirocho used to send some of his "family" to cut branches from a big cedar in the compound of a nearby temple. At night they burned them in the house to smoke out mosquitoes. By the end of summer, the tree was a skeleton. People called it "Jirocho's cedar."

This was the period when Jirocho most frequently visited the pawnshop of the Shimizu Mochizukis, so when Isako's great-grandmother asked him to escort her to a hot-spring resort, he was happy to oblige. It was certainly not surprising that the bearers recognized him. It was only surprising that the Mochizukis were unaware of his importance.

A little later he received another plea from Yaogadake, who was back in his home grounds of Nagoya and in trouble again. He was at odds with a local boss and a fight was imminent. Jirocho rushed to Nagoya with seventeen of his best men, a show of force which smoothed the way for a reconciliation.

He returned to Shimizu in time to help O-cho's brother, who was embroiled with a gangster from the inland mountains. By killing a few men in his brother-in-law's behalf, Jirocho succeeded in annoying the police, and again he was a hunted man. With O-cho he wandered for months, just ahead of capture. Finally, at the close of 1858, they found refuge with a friend near Nagoya.

This was Yaogadake's territory, and Jirocho asked for help. He needed money, he needed protection from the police, and above all he needed a good doctor. O-cho, worn out from their flight, was desperately ill. No help came.

O-cho's condition steadily worsened, and Jirocho, half frenzied, went to Yaogadake and angrily denounced him for unfaithfulness. The truth was that Yaogadake was doubling as an informer for the local police, and he was afraid to help Jirocho now that there was a warrant out for him. Jirocho's visit terrified the ex-wrestler. He felt that he was caught between Jirocho and the police, and he began to scheme a way out.

O-cho died early in the morning of New Year's Day, 1859. It was Jirocho's saddest birthday.

Once her death became known, local bosses streamed in to attend her funeral. Jirocho was grateful, but Yaogadake, gripped by fear and a guilty conscience, was convinced that they meant to attack him. He tipped off the police.

In the raid that followed, Jirocho escaped but his host was seized. A few days later the man's wife tearfully informed Jirocho that her husband had been tortured to death in jail. She asked for revenge. She wanted Yaogadake dead. Jirocho nodded.

This was a formidable task, and Jirocho and his men prepared by making a pilgrimage to the great Kompira Shrine on Shikoku Island, where they prayed for success. Then they set out after Yaogadake. They caught up with him in a small town where he was promoting a *sumo* tournament. In a flashing duel, Jirocho cut him down.

Since this was only an intramural fight between gamblers the police were not much interested, and Jirocho was soon able to return to Shimizu. It was then that he paid a visit to the Minaguchi-ya, to tell them of O-cho's death.

There was a new face at the inn now. Raisuke and Nami had produced a son, but Raisuke's older brother at the Tezuka *honjin* had not. So Raisuke's son had been given to the Tezukas to continue their line, in consideration of the many sons they had given the Mochi-zukis. Raisuke had cast about for someone to take his own son's place at the Minaguchi-ya, and just that year, 1859, he had adopted a promising young man named Hanjuro from one of Kambara's best families. (It was a family rich in sons that generation, for, at almost the same time, one of Hanjuro's brothers was adopted into the family that ran the old halfway house on Satta's lower slopes in Yui, the place where Hiroshige had always stopped for shellfish.) Hanjuro would inherit the Minaguchi-ya. He was already assuming active management. Some day he would marry Raisuke's daughter, who was, however, still a little young, being now only five years old.

It was a bright December day. Jirocho, Raisuke, and Hanjuro sat in a guest room thrown open to the garden, and as the saké warmed them (Jirocho considered that this was an occasion when he should drink a little), they talked.

They praised the departed O-cho, and were reminded of other friends who had recently left them; 1858 had been a wretched year. Cholera had swept Okitsu, and seventy people had died. But in Edo the same disease had killed more than twenty-eight thousand, and among them had been Hiroshige. A man of Edo to the end, he had written his will as though it were instructions to his family before he set out on another of his journeys. Still remembering his antecedents, he asked for a funeral in samurai style, and he wanted a full and formal Buddhist posthumous name, with the temple well paid for bestowing it. "Treat those who keep the wake to a good dinner," he wrote, "but don't waste money.

"Or," he counterproposed, "you can hold a quiet service just for kinsfolk, and announce that a formal funeral will be held later. And it doesn't really matter whether you ever have the formal services or not." He ended with the last of his little poems. He was setting out, he said, without a brush, to see new scenes on a long road.

The three men drank their saké in the December sun and were saddened by their losses, but Raisuke wondered aloud if the dead weren't the lucky ones. The nation was in turmoil, and no one could tell what it might lead to.

Six years before, Commodore Matthew C. Perry had sailed into Edo Bay and delivered a message from Millard Fillmore, President of the United States. Perry had told flustered Japanese officials that he would be back next year to sign a treaty. He would be back with even more warships and he sincerely hoped that the Japanese would be co-operative, for the West meant to confer the benefits of its civilization whether Japan wanted them or not.

He had returned on schedule and the treaty had been signed. To celebrate the occasion, the Americans presented a minstrel show and the Japanese offered *sumo* wrestling. Each side was mystified by the other's entertainment, but the Americans understood saké and the Japanese understood whiskey. Both became very convivial.

For the Japanese, the hangover was awful. The country, already split over the issue of foreigners, was now in a furor. The government, cornered and confused, had taken the unprecedented step of asking for advice, first from the daimyo and then from the court. The recommendations given were unanimously solemn, invariably contradictory, and frequently ridiculous. They only added to the distress.

The opposition clans, sensing that Tokugawa rule was tottering, began to mobilize for the kill. Seizing on the cloistered Emperor as a convenient symbol, they rent the air with their cries of "Revere the Emperor—Oust the Barbarians." The government tried to rally with a slogan of its own, "Support the Government—Open the Country," but it was drowned out.

It was a period of wild confusion and fantastic intrigue. Couriers and emissaries on secret missions rushed between Edo and Kyoto. Among those who stopped often at the Minaguchi-ya was a samurai of the great southwest clan of Satsuma. His name was Saigo. He was a stocky, hearty man, a warm and friendly man with a great booming laugh that echoed through the inn. Raisuke knew he was working against the government, the Shogunate, but he could not help liking him. Lately Saigo had not appeared, and Raisuke had heard that the Satsuma elders had curbed his faction and exiled him to some lonely island. Raisuke worried about him, hoped he was safe.

It was difficult not to worry in those restless, uneasy days, and despite the Minaguchi-ya's good saké on that December afternoon, Hanjuro and Jirocho also looked glum. Suruga had been Tokugawa territory ever since Ieyasu, and all three of them were loyal to the government, though anyone could see it was staggering. Daily the uproar increased. "Where will it end?" sighed Raisuke. None of them knew, and their conversation, like others all over the country, trailed into uncertainty. As the December dusk settled over the garden, and the chill air took on the fragrance of wood smoke from fires to heat the baths, the men spoke once again of O-cho, and Jirocho left.

In the months that followed, he had always on his mind the obligation of giving thanks to Kompira Shrine for his victory over Yaogadake. In April of the next year, 1860, he succeeded in obtaining a fine sword, and he dispatched one of his lieutenants, Ishimatsu, to dedicate it to the shrine.

Ishimatsu was a great favorite of Jirocho's, a jovial, fun-loving bear of a man who commonly introduced himself by declaiming, "I am an out-and-out fool and a fool I'll be till the day I die. Just an unimportant fellow called Ishimatsu of Totomi." He had one great failing. He drank too much, and when he drank he was not responsible. Jirocho told him that under no circumstances was he to touch a drop until he had completed his mission and returned to Shimizu.

Though he became terribly thirsty, Ishimatsu stayed sober during his whole trip to Kompira. He presented the sword, which is still among the shrine's treasures, and then he started home.

He stopped briefly with one of Jirocho's allies, who entrusted him with twenty-five gold pieces to be delivered to Jirocho as a memorial gift to honor O-cho, and then he continued to the home of a gambler named Kichibei.

Kichibei held a drinking party in his honor. At first Ishimatsu was careful, remembering Jirocho's injunction, but taking one cup, and then another, he finally lost control. He drunkenly confided to Kichibei that he had the twenty-five gold pieces in his purse.

The dice had recently been unkind to Kichibei and his brothers. Insolvent as they were, the gold in Ishimatsu's belt looked like a godsend and they went to work on him. He was reluctant, but at length he loaned it to them on condition that they would repay within one or two days.

When the deadline passed, Ishimatsu became insistent. Finally Kichibei announced that he had arranged a gambling session and asked Ishimatsu to join them. He went, sure that Kichibei meant to repay him from the organizer's share of the winnings. But when they reached the lonely rendezvous on the mountain, the gamblers turned out to be thugs, half of them Kichibei's men and half of them henchmen of dead Yaogadake, summoned by Kichibei for a murder of revenge.

Alone against ten, Ishimatsu managed to fight his way out of the ambush, and, badly wounded, sought refuge in the house of an independent gambler who lived on the mountain. That man and his wife took him in, bandaged his cuts, and hid him behind their family altar when Kichibei and his villains stormed in to search the house.

Later, lying in their home in pain, Ishimatsu listened to his enemies, thrashing and hallooing through the woods. He knew that, not finding him outside, they would come back to the house. The next time he could not hope to be so lucky. They would kill him, and probably also the couple who had helped him.

Summoning all his strength, he got to his feet. His friends tried to hold him back but he threw them off. He grasped his sword and, as the blood starting fresh from his wounds began to soak his bandages, he lunged into the night.

He fought like a demon on that mountainside, dark except for thin rays of moonlight which slipped through the trees to catch flashing steel. His attackers were everywhere, above him, below him, ringing him with their swords and their shouts. He fought in the open and he fought with his back against great cedars. He parried and wheeled, a man possessed, until Kichibei, hiding, crouching low in the dark, slashed his leg. He fell and they were on him.

Thus Kichibei succeeded Yaogadake as Jirocho's greatest enemy. As soon as Jirocho learned what had happened he set out for revenge.

Kichibei attacked first. In an amphibious operation, he brought his men across Suruga Bay in boats, bypassing the outposts that would have spotted them had they come by the highway. They slipped ashore at Shimizu, but when they stormed Jirocho's house he was not there. Thwarted, they retired as they had come.

Jirocho then summoned his best men to plan a counterattack. They convened in a temple, whose priest, a good friend of Jirocho's, decided to give them a feast. From a passing fishmonger he bought globefish.

To the Japanese there is no greater delicacy than thin slices of raw globefish, pinkly, icily transparent, with a flavor as subtle as its appearance. And there are few foods as exciting, because eating it is like playing Russian roulette: the slightest mistake by the man who prepares it, and the fish's deadly, tasteless poison permeates the flesh.

It is a matter of record that the priest who prepared the fish that day was no expert. Soon after they ate, the party was writhing in agony. Because he had eaten moderately, Jirocho's case was comparatively light. The doctor was able to save him, but two of his men died.

When he heard of the poisoning, Kichibei moved into Jirocho's territory. He was so confident that he held a party one night, with plenty of food, drink, and geisha. In the merriment no one realized that Jirocho's men were gathering in the outside darkness.

The attack was quick and ruthless. Jirocho severed Kichibei's head and arms, and that same night he left with a few men to deposit his grisly trophies on Ishimatsu's grave.

It was on this trip that Jirocho was secretly approached by an emissary from one of the great court families of Kyoto. It was a sign of the times that even the ancient nobility around the Emperor, for centuries prohibited from any sort of political activity, were now recruiting private armies. And they were recruiting from the toughest fighting men of the day, the gambling bosses and their strong-arm henchmen.

The emissary was persuasive. It was vital to the country, he said, to overthrow the Tokugawas. The day was fast coming when that could be done, when the restless clans would rise in revolt and join with the court in restoring the Emperor to rightful power. It would not be easy. There would be fighting. Good men were needed—men like Jirocho. They could offer him a permanent stipend, make him a samurai.

Jirocho refused. "A frog had best stay in his puddle," he declared. "I have lived as a gambler and I shall die as a gambler." He was adamant. Many like him joined Kyoto's swelling ranks of mercenaries, but Jirocho returned to Shimizu.

There was plenty there to occupy him, for that autumn of 1862 the Tokaido was enormously busy. It began in the hot, lazy days of August, when the Lord of Satsuma, the head of his clan, traveled to Edo. Many were the times his predecessors had made the same journey, to escort the Ryukyuan envoys or to take up their alternate-year residence according to the Shogun's dictates. This time his purpose was startlingly different. He was carrying a directive from the Emperor to the Shogun.

Nothing like this had happened since Ieyasu came to power. In his time, or in the palmy days of the Shogunate, or even ten years ago, such a thing had been unthinkable. It profoundly shocked the Lord of Satsuma himself, for he was a conservative man, and though he bore the Emperor's rescript, he advised that it be rejected.

Had his advice been accepted, the Shogunate would have taken a big step towards recovery of its waning power. But so great was the confusion and timidity in Edo that the government bowed to the demands, even to the order that the Shogun come in person to Kyoto to explain his allowing foreigners into the country.

In September, the Satsuma chieftain started back with the reply. He had not gone far, only to the outskirts of Yokohama, when there occurred one of the famous clashes of those uneasy times. A party of Englishmen, three gentlemen and a lady riding out from Yokohama, refused to dismount at the side of the road when they met his procession. Instead they walked their horses along his column. Such behavior would not have been tolerated from any Japanese, nor was it from foreign barbarians. One of the men was killed, two were badly wounded, and only the lady escaped unharmed to dash to Yokohama with word of what had happened.

There was talk in Yokohama that night of landing marines from the men-of-war in the harbor for immediate vengeance, but cooler heads prevailed. The old aristocrat proceeded down the Tokaido, and three nights later, when he stopped in Okitsu, Raisuke and Hanjuro listened in silent awe as the retainers who were staying at the Minaguchi-ya told the story of their bloody encounter. For one fleeting moment the foreigner had been put in his place.

Some of the Satsuma men talked late that evening, but many slipped out of the Minaguchi-ya to a rendezvous that was whispered through the town. Jirocho's men were in action, and all night long flickering torches lighted circles of men sweatily intent on the click of dice. Odd or even, even or odd, the bets came, and guttural cries marked wins and losses. Money changed hands with savage speed, for the excitement of Yokohama was still on this band of old-fashioned warriors.

If that September night was busy, the next month was bedlam. On the seventeenth of October, 1862, the Shogunate dealt itself another great blow by abolishing alternate-year attendance. No more need daimyo post to Edo, and no more need wives and children stay as hostages in their absence. The whole system was abandoned, and a writer of that day set down the results:

"In consequence all the daimyo . . . sent their wives and children to their country residences, and in a twinkling of an eye, the flourishing city of Edo became like a desert, so that . . . the vassals of the Shogunate of all ranks, and the townspeople, too, grieved and lamented. . . . And so the prestige of the Tokugawa family, which . . . for more than two hundred and seventy years, had forced the daimyo to come breathlessly to take their turn of duty in Edo, and had day and night eighty thousand vassals at its beck and call, fell to ruin in the space of one morning."

In the emptying of Edo, the Tokaido was jammed. All down the highway, the *honjin* and the *waki-honjin* struggled to take care of their old customers, usually so regularly spaced by Shogunate planning, now demanding accommodations all at once.

At the Minaguchi-ya young Hanjuro, with old Raisuke's help from the background, often worked from dawn to dawn. At the two *honjin*, Ichikawa and Tezuka were equally harassed. And with every guest they bade good-bye they felt a chill. Would they ever see these travelers again? If this was the end of enforced attendance, was it also the end of the Tokaido's pomp and prosperity?

Two hundred and seventy years before, an Ichikawa and a Tezuka had been forced into innkeeping because they were important. Now their descendants were important because they were innkeepers— innkeepers to the daimyo. Today the exodus from Edo kept the road dusty. Would it ever be dusty again?

But though the threat was greatest at the *honjin*, it was young Hanjuro who saw it clearest. Ichikawa and Tezuka looked the other way, understandably reluctant to face extinction. It was Hanjuro of the Minaguchi-ya who saw most clearly that this was the end of an era.

Actually, the realization did not come to him that feverish autumn. He was then too busy to think. It came next spring, when the Shogun, as he had agreed to do, went to Kyoto.

At first Hanjuro was caught up in the excitement of preparation. It had been a long time since a Shogun had made this trip, not since the third Shogun's triumphant jaunt in 1634.

Now, as then, new accommodations were built and old ones refurbished all along the highway. Of course no inn was suitable. In Okitsu the ancient temple of Seikenji played host: Seikenji with its quiet little room where Ieyasu had learned his letters as a young boy, and its mountainside garden where he had planted trees as an old man. A new wing was built in the rear, a new apartment facing on that garden, and there the frail young Shogun, fourteenth of his line, took his rest. Perhaps in the quiet of the night he drew strength from old associations. More likely he felt even more inadequate.

The Minaguchi-ya, like the *honjin* of Iohikawa and Tezuka, was taken over by retainers. Hanjuro had worked hard to make his inn ready for the occasion, though he had long since learned that government patronage always had its drawbacks. This was no exception.

Long after the party had passed he was still trying to prepare his vouchers to the satisfaction of government bureaus. There was the matter of a return trip. The Shogun went to Kyoto intending to stay ten days. He would soon be returning, the officials insisted, and they intended to make one payment for both stops. Weeks went by, filled with rumors, but the truth was that the Shogun was being almost forcibly detained in Kyoto. After ninety days he was finally permitted to leave. He returned by ship, and this further upset the highway officials. It was weeks more before Hanjuro was paid.

It was this experience, embittering to any businessman, that set Hanjuro to thinking. As a merchant he was not supposed to speculate on the fate of his betters, but he had a sense of history. He had watched the daimyo desert Edo, and now he began to compare the procession of this fourteenth Shogun with the almost legendary expedition of the third Shogun more than two centuries before.

In 1634 it had been a display of pomp and power: in 1863 it was a demonstration of weakness. The third Shogun had been a mighty dictator accepting homage: the fourteenth was a submissive vassal posting to a summons. And even when Hanjuro was in a mood to question these judgments, he could not elude one incontrovertible fact—the third Shogun had been escorted by 307,000 men: the fourteenth went with 3,000.

Hanjuro kept his thoughts to himself, for he had a feeling that even Raisuke might not understand, but he decided that great changes had taken place and that more were coming. If Japan changed, the Tokaido would change, and if the Minaguchi-ya were to survive, it would have to move with the times. He began to think and to plan.

In Shimizu, Jirocho too had a problem. He had heard unpleasant rumors. People were saying that his men were out of hand, that they no longer lived by the code he professed. It was said that they had become ruthless in collecting gambling debts, and that in one case, finding a debtor ill abed, they had stripped him of household goods, of clothes, even of bedding.

Jirocho was furious that any of the men under his protection should behave this way. Government might disintegrate, but his rule—never! He set his spies to work, and that was how he discovered that his coastal territory was being raided from the inland mountains, the province of a boss named Katsuzo. The guilty men were not his but Katsuzo's.

And so Katsuzo followed Yaogadake and Kichibei as Jirocho's number one enemy. It was a conflict which had long smoldered along their common boundary. Even now there was no outbreak, for Katsuzo apologized and punished his guilty henchmen in a quite satisfactory manner. He cut off their heads.

But the rift between the two bosses deepened, and another chance for a showdown soon developed. Katsuzo killed the son of an official, and the usually phlegmatic police were prodded into action. Still they preferred not to act themselves. It was easier to call on another gambler to eradicate the menace.

They placed their demand on a boss named Tomozo, and Tomozo

promptly turned to Jirocho for help. Unlike Tomozo, who was more politician than fighter, Jirocho did not maintain subterranean connections with the police, but this happened to be a cause for which he had great sympathy. He quickly rallied his men and, setting out one night, joined Tomozo the next day near Hamamatsu. There they faced Katsuzo across the Tenryu River. There were about a hundred men on each bank, but again there was no clash. As soon as he realized that Jirocho had joined the fight, Katsuzo beat a retreat. Jirocho went after him.

Katsuzo was not difficult to track, for he kept adding to his crimes. Since it was dreary traveling without diversion, he kidnapped an attractive courtesan. He had intended to buy her, but discovering that her master was quite rich, he succumbed to temptation and ended by stealing both woman and money.

For years Jirocho pursued his campaign against Katsuzo. It ranged all over central Japan, and every gambler of any importance found it necessary to align himself with one side or the other. It culminated in a great pitched battle over the gambling rights at the sacred shrines of Ise, making the April festivals of 1865 the most exciting on record.

That was Katsuzo's last stand. The next year, having received an attractive offer from a court noble who did not demand character references, he joined the army of toughs being assembled in Kyoto.

He picked the winning side at the right moment. Goaded by repeated insubordination from the southwest clan of Choshu, the Shogun's vaunted army had finally taken to the field, and it had ignominiously failed. Everywhere unsuccessful, the generals were happy to call the whole thing off when the Shogun's death gave them an excuse: they had to observe a period of mourning.

At this point in the year 1866 the fifteenth and last Shogun, Yoshinobu, came to office. A year later he rang down the curtain on Tokugawa supremacy. In relinquishing his power to the Emperor, he wrote with dignity and perception:

"Now that foreign intercourse becomes daily more extensive, unless the government is directed from one central authority the foundation of the state will fall to pieces. If, however, the old order of things be changed, and administrative authority be restored to the Imperial court, and if national deliberations be conducted on an extensive scale, and Imperial decisions be secured, and if the empire be supported by the whole people, then the empire will be able to maintain its rank and dignity among the nations of the earth."

He had hoped that his action would clear the way for the peaceful formation of a new government representing all the clans. In this he was disappointed, for the cabal at Kyoto, the court and the southwest clans of Satsuma and Choshu, would now be satisfied with nothing less than complete supremacy.

These rebels had old-fashioned weapons but they understood psychological warfare. All over Japan, Shinto shrines were organized in pro-Imperial, anti-Shogunate activities. This was not difficult to arrange, for the shrines were guardians of the ancient religion and

A Shinto priest
(*detail from
a book illustration
by Jichosai*)

the Emperor was their head priest. They campaigned both openly and clandestinely. In Okitsu, as in many other towns, there suddenly appeared someone who called himself a divinity. It was a descent of God, people said, and they seized the talismans he distributed, and danced in the streets, beating drums, ringing bells, and giving thanks to the Emperor, for the divinity had made it clear that he had come in response to the Imperial greatness and goodness.

And in the meantime, the forces of Satsuma and Choshu, under the Emperor's banner, advanced steadily up the Tokaido. In March of 1868 they reached Shizuoka, and in that city occurred the war's most dramatic meeting. It was a meeting which Hanjuro's brother at the halfway house in Yui helped to bring about.

He had been roused from his bed at midnight, long after the house was closed and shuttered. He had asked who was there, and a man had answered that he was Yamaoka Tesshu. Tesshu was a famous officer of the Shogun's forces, and Hanjuro's brother at once opened the door. Tesshu poured out his story: he had been pushing from Edo with a small force of men; they had been ambushed in the mountains and most of them killed; he was being hotly pursued but he must get to Shizuoka on a mission of vital importance.

Hanjuro's brother lost no time. He routed out a neighboring fisherman, gave Tesshu some fishermen's clothes to change into. Then he led him down steep stairs into the cellar, out a well-concealed door, and down a dark path to the beach. Tesshu scrambled into the fisherman's boat and was away.

Imperial soldiers appeared soon after. They ransacked the halfway house and they grilled its master, but they learned nothing from him and they never found the clothes or the revolver that Tesshu had left behind. The revolver is still in the house, a heavy old gun that fired bullets more than a half-inch in diameter.

And to whom did Hanjuro's brother send Tesshu? Whom but Jirocho, for if anyone could get Tesshu through to Shizuoka, the Boss could. Jirocho could and Jirocho did. Next day Tesshu was ushered into the headquarters of the Imperial forces.

Nominal command of that army was given to an Imperial prince, but actual command lay with the chief of staff, and the chief of staff was Saigo, the same Satsuma samurai whom Raisuke had liked so much when he was dashing between Edo and Kyoto on secret missions. Saigo is the revolution's greatest hero. He had fought for it against the conservatives in his own clan, against other clans, finally against the Shogunate itself. Now he was triumphant, and to him in Shizuoka came the Shogun's envoy, Tesshu.

In the shadow of Ieyasu's castle the two men met, and Tesshu delivered the Shogun's appeal: let Edo be declared an open city and its population spared from war. Tesshu added a plea of his own, that the Tokugawa family be spared. To both entreaties Saigo nodded, and in most respects the war was over. Only a few Shogunate die-hards would continue to fight for a lost cause.

The Imperial armies marched unopposed to Edo. The servants at the Minaguchi-ya, after watching them pass, went back to work muttering a popular local prediction: "They go as soldiers but they will return as Buddhas," meaning that they would come back dead. Hanjuro said nothing but he knew they were wrong.

Ex-Shogun Yoshinobu was no longer ruler of the country but he was still a great daimyo and he still held the fief which Ieyasu had carved out for the Tokugawas, with Suruga in the heart of it. Here he came in the summer of 1868 to serve as head of his clan.

He did not come alone. Thousands of retainers followed him from Edo, some by land and some by sea. More than twenty-five hundred came on a chartered American ship, the *Golden Age,* jamming the cabins, the decks, and the holds for a stormy two-and-a-half-day voyage. So crowded they could not all lie down at the same time, men and women alike vomited and obeyed nature in open unscreened barrels, which, when they were hoisted out of the holds to be emptied, swayed and splashed stinking filth on those below. Nevertheless they reached Shimizu alive. Among them were that branch of Hiroshige's family who had continued to serve in the Shogun's fire brigade.

Another storm-battered Shogunate vessel, the warship *Kanrin Maru,* slipped into Shimizu harbor early in September to make repairs. A few days later three Imperialist ships appeared, and although the *Kanrin Maru* hoisted a white flag of surrender, it was bombarded, boarded, and its skeleton crew put to the sword. Tossing the bodies overboard, the victors set about to tow the battered ship to Edo.

Currents carried some of the bodies out to sea. Others floated in the harbor, for the population, always wary of involvement, was now afraid to show any sympathy for the losing side.

As soon as he heard what had happened, Jirocho took charge. He and his men recovered all the bodies they could find, and buried them along the river bank, where they rest to this day. (Some say it is the same spot where he used to bury his victims after gang fights.) And since no priest dared to say prayers over the graves, he gathered a cartful of stones, asked a priest to write a bit of a sutra on each, and covered the graves with them.

It was not long before word of all this came to the ears of the new Imperial government, who promptly directed the local authorities of Suruga to investigate, and if they found that Jirocho was guilty of action traitorous to the new government, to behead him.

The man who was appointed investigating officer was Tesshu. It was the second meeting between Tesshu and Jirocho. The first time, Tesshu had been a harassed fugitive. Now Jirocho was accused of criminal treason.

No doubt Tesshu looked forward to this second encounter. Having lived in Suruga for the past few months, he had come to know the power that Jirocho wielded, his reputation for a kind of lawless integrity, and his fame as a tough and wily swordsman. Tesshu was a fighter, too. He had a reputation as a strategist, and it was said of him, as it was of some of his differently armed contemporaries of the American West, that his draw was faster than the eye could see.

Summoned and charged, Jirocho protested: "Am I to be punished because I buried the dead? Whatever he may have done in life, a dead man is no longer guilty. Sir, the guilty ones are the Imperialist forces who abandoned the bodies of those they killed."

And then, seeing that Tesshu, facing him grimly, was apparently unmoved, Jirocho took the only course that he could see open to him. He rose, hitched up his kimono to free his legs for action, and slid his right arm out of his sleeve. If he had to die, he would die fighting.

Tesshu sat immobile, his eyes boring into Jirocho's. Then he spoke. "You are a little man when you fight. You are a big man when you no longer rely on force to control people."

Jirocho stared, then slowly relaxed. He sat down, and they talked.

Thirty years earlier a wandering monk had slipped in and out of Jirocho's life in the space of an hour, and a young rice dealer had become a gambler. Now came Tesshu, and the turning was even more dramatic. Tesshu demanded more of Jirocho, but he also stood by him.

Next year he publicly endorsed Jirocho's action by writing the epitaph for the grave of the *Kanrin Maru* victims. That was the year Jirocho first demonstrated Tesshu's influence in his life.

Trouble hit the little peninsula of Miho, trouble centering around its Shinto shrine. That shrine had been a key link in Imperial propaganda. Now it was a target of revenge. Many of the men who had followed the ex-Shogun to Suruga were roaming there in terrorist bands, jobless, rootless, and bitter. One night a gang of them somehow enticed the chief official of the Miho shrine to unlock his door, killed him on the spot. When they left they planted a sign by the shrine gate. It read: "This is a warning. Get rid of all shrine officials or your village will be burned to the ground!"

Not long after, a fire broke out in someone's house. This was not an unusual occurrence in winter, but this night the villagers, instead of rallying to put it out, turned into a maddened mob, hunting down shrine officials, fighting each other, while fire swept uncontrolled through house after house.

Jirocho rushed to the scene to try to break up the mob and put out the fire. At first he too was attacked and beaten, but finally, a bloody figure in the glare of flames, crying out over the screams of the mob, he succeeded in restoring order.

The next day he began a campaign to collect rice, clothing, and money for the stricken village. The Mochizukis contributed gladly.

This was a new Jirocho, still Boss but now serving his community.

Incidents like those at Miho were the tag end of revolution. They pointed up Suruga's most pressing problem—rehabilitation of the retainers who had followed ex-Shogun Yoshinobu out of Edo. The lawless fringe of the type who had terrorized Miho were easily disposed of; this was old stuff to Jirocho. The thousands of decent, talented people were a bigger challenge. Some of them entered local government or the professions, becoming town or police officials, teachers or doctors. But new enterprises were needed to absorb many more of these displaced persons, and here Yoshinobu, now governor of Suruga, found in Jirocho a dynamic, driving ally.

Jirocho promoted the cultivation of tea on the mountain slopes, helping to make Suruga Japan's greatest producer of tea. He developed salt flats along the shores of Miho. He opened up new farmland on the previously uncultivated plain that stretches away from Kunozan, and was so successful in this that he was asked to work on the rough, hard-to-irrigate lower slopes of Mount Fuji. There, with convict labor, he reclaimed an area that still bears his name. He created jobs for hundreds.

As revolution receded, Suruga saw more and more of their governor, the ex-Shogun. Fifteenth and last of the Shoguns, Yoshinobu was of course deeply interested in the first and greatest, and as relaxation from the problems of his fallen clan he began to visit the many places associated with Ieyasu. That was how he came to the farm at Mizunashi where, more than two and a half centuries before, Ieyasu had hunted and laughed with Gen'emon. He sat in the farmhouse where Ieyasu had sat, and examined some of the treasures that Ieyasu had given his jaunty farmer friend, while Isako's grandmother, the daughter of the house, served him tea and a juicy pear, the like of which had so pleased Ieyasu that he named the district after them.

To celebrate the occasion, Yoshinobu called for paper and ink, and he brushed the calligraphy which hangs today over the spot where he sat. It is typical of Yoshinobu that he alluded not to lost greatness but to a bright new future.

He visited Seikenji, too, for its many associations with Ieyasu. Raisuke and Hanjuro, formally dressed, were among the village elders appointed to receive him on that occasion, and they gave time off to almost all the Minaguchi-ya staff so they could catch a glimpse of him.

It was different a few weeks later when Emperor Meiji stopped at Seikenji. There was no thought of seeing him, for it was considered blasphemous for a commoner to look upon his person. Nevertheless it was easier to move him than the capital, and so the young Emperor, who would at least nominally head the nation for the next forty-five years while it grappled for a place in the modern world, moved up the Tokaido to the city that Ieyasu and his clan had built. Only it was not called Edo any longer. It had been renamed Tokyo, the Eastern Capital.

At Seikenji he rested in the apartment built only six years earlier for the Shogun's trip in the other direction. Wherever he looked he saw the Tokugawa crest, those three hollyhock leaves in a circle. It could not have bothered him much. The crest remained but the power had changed hands.

At the Minaguchi-ya, Hanjuro was host to some of the Emperor's retainers. He knew that this was the beginning of a new day for Japan. He was ready for it.

The adaptability and vision that he showed were not in wide supply. In those difficult days it was easier to count the fine old businesses that went smash than those which survived and prospered.

Among the dozens of inns in Okitsu, only the Minaguchi-ya made the transition. The parade to oblivion was led by those which had been greatest, as Ichikawas and Tezukas, baffled and resentful, shuttered their *honjin* and let their handsome old rooms grow musty.

Hanjuro, on the other hand, had never been busier. Perhaps daimyo would no longer parade the Tokaido as they had, but he could see no dearth of traffic. Businessmen, sightseers, and religious pilgrims continued to fill the highway. After all, he reasoned, there had never been but a couple of hundred daimyo and a few thousand well-to-do retainers. But there were millions of other people.

There were businessmen like the Itos of Nagoya. They had been stopping at the Minaguchi-ya how long now?—at least two centuries, Hanjuro was sure, even without checking the old registers. They weren't nobility, but they had taste and they appreciated comfort and good service. He resolved to make the Minaguchi-ya even better for customers like them.

But far outnumbering the Itos of Japan, Hanjuro realized, were the ordinary souls who tramped by in the thousands. Especially there were the pilgrims. Some went singly, but mostly they traveled in groups. From the northeast and Edo (no, Tokyo, he reminded himself; he must remember to use the capital's new name: it stamped him as old-fashioned not to) they were bound for Ise and Kyoto. From the southwest they streamed towards the great headquarters of the Nichiren sect of Buddhism in the mountains inland from Okitsu. They had saved money for years to make this trip, he knew, or perhaps they had been chosen by lot from the members of their pilgrims' clubs. They were decent people, they were not beggars. They had money, but how little, said Hanjuro to himself, how little they got for it when they stopped for the night. They slept in filthy bedding and ate poisonous food and, more often than not, had prostitutes forced on them at exorbitant rates.

Hanjuro knew from experience how grateful these people were after they had spent a night in clean comfort at the Minaguchi-ya. Well, he decided, he would really give them something to be grateful for. He would give these pilgrims the kind of service that a daimyo or an Ito could expect. Oh, there would be differences of course. They expected to sleep together as a group: they wanted to save money and they were sociable. But they would be treated as honored guests. The idea was so radical that it took Hanjuro a little time to put it into effect. The older servants, especially, growled and carried on. The master had gone dotty, they said; the idea of treating ordinary common travelers with the same kind of respect you'd give a samurai! The old master, Raisuke—he never would have permitted such goings-on if he were running things, but nowadays he only sat in the sun or talked with old cronies. Hanjuro put up with the grumbling but he had his own way, and the Minaguchi-ya succeeded in a climate of failure.

It was his customers who gave him his next idea. Why, they lamented, were there not other inns as good along the rest of their route?

Why indeed? thought Hanjuro. And that was when he conceived his guild. The Prestige Guild, he called it. All up and down the Tokaido he sought out inns who would adhere to his standards: cleanliness, good service, and no prostitutes. It was a new concept in operating general inns. Hiroshige would have blinked in disbelief.

Most of the candidates for the guild had to be helped with training and advice, or even with loans to cover needed improvements. But how astonishingly successful they were as soon as they could hang out front the signboard that marked them as members of Hanjuro's Prestige Guild.

Soon pilgrim associations all over the country sought contracts with the guild, and every year their groups would travel from one Prestige inn to another, with a reservation and a welcome assured each night. The Minaguchi-ya and the other inns of the guild hung out a little sign for every such association they served. Before long, dozens of such boards marched across their fronts in proud display.

The surprising thing was that catering to the pilgrims did not keep the daimyo away. Even the Lord of Satsuma, who could easily have ordered one of the *honjin* reopened for his convenience, chose now to stop at the Minaguchi-ya. This was really astonishing, as Hanjuro remarked one day to Raisuke, for they didn't come any more conservative than that crusty old gentleman. Nor any more powerful, muttered Raisuke, now that Satsuma and Choshu seemed to be in sole charge of the government. Just wherein, he wondered, was government by two clans so superior to the Tokugawa government by one? But anyway he liked one Satsuma man, young Saigo. He had led the Emperor's armies, and now he was a big man in the government. Things would go well as long as they listened to Saigo, of that Raisuke was sure.

The thing was, mused Hanjuro, who had frequently listened to Raisuke's political opinions and was a good deal more interested in his own ideas on innkeeping—the thing was that a progressive inn was a busy inn, and a busy inn was a prosperous inn, and a prosperous inn could afford to give its guests the best of everything. That was all that the Lord of Satsuma wanted, the best. That was why he came to the Minaguchi-ya.

No doubt, said Raisuke. Anyway, he was proud to have him and his retainer Saigo stop there. He was always pleased to have Saigo under their roof.

It was a bitter day for Raisuke when Saigo quit the government and marched in anger back to Satsuma. That was the last time he stayed at the Minaguchi-ya, and that time there was no sound of the big man's booming laughter. It was a tight-faced group that came and went.

There were many reasons for that first split in the government, and men of many opinions walked out with Saigo. The Tokugawa government had fallen, not because it had become militarily weak, but because of deep-rooted social and economic changes that it was unable to understand and powerless to control. The new government began with as little understanding of these problems as the old, but it had a wealth of bright young men. On the critical issue of "throw out the barbarians" they about-faced as soon as they came to power.

Japan had no choice, they said. It could stand and fight, but if it did it would be overrun, occupied, and dismembered like China. The alternative was to accept the foreigners, learn from them, and build the nation's strength for an eventual showdown. (It was what the Tokugawas had said all along.)

They moved fast during those first years, too fast for men like Saigo. The old-fashioned samurai he led had fought a revolution to defend, not destroy, the system that they knew. Their basic idea had been very simple—smash the Tokugawas and take over themselves. Now they found the old ideals tumbling before a worship of everything new, everything foreign.

The immediate cause of the split was Korea. That unenlightened kingdom took the position that Emperor Meiji was a rebel chief who had overthrown the rightful Shogunate, and refused to open trade and diplomatic ties. Saigo's group, foreshadowing things to come, had a foreign policy as aggressive as their domestic policy was conservative. Saigo himself was haunted by the plight of thousands of his own warrior class, who were offended and bewildered by a new age which had no use for them. Their warriors' solution to unemployment was to go to war, and Korea seemed to them a fine target. They had even persuaded the Emperor, when their opponents, many of whom rushed home from foreign tours which had convinced them of Japan's desperate weakness, succeeded in changing the Imperial mind. Saigo quit then, in anger and disgust.

He went back to Satsuma, and there he established a school to teach samurai ideals and warrior skills.

It was not many years before the Lord of Satsuma followed his retainer. His conservative instincts had been offended by dozens of reforms: the feudal fiefs, his own included, had been submerged in the central government; compulsory education for all the people had been instituted; military conscription had undermined the samurai by founding an army of commoners. He had borne all these things and more, but when the samurai as a class were to all intents abolished, and the wearing of swords prohibited, he could take no more. Early in 1877 he marched out of Tokyo with the same sense of outrage that had impelled his man Saigo.

Down the Tokaido he went, for the last time. But this time the swords of his retainers were wrapped in cotton bags and no heralds went before to warn those by the side of the road to prostrate themselves. The pomp and pageantry were gone. As the sullen procession marched by, it was a demonstration, if one were needed, that feudalism was dead.

The Lord of Satsuma had never said that he liked the Minaguchi-ya. Hanjuro could not remember that the old aristocrat had ever complimented any aspect of the service or the food. He had never even praised the view, and men had been doing that for at least twelve centuries. But on that last visit he gave sure evidence of how he felt. On the morning that he was to leave he summoned Hanjuro to his room and there, in the cold gray light of a winter dawn, to the music of a kettle hissing over glowing coals in a brazier, he gave to the innkeeper, his family, his successors, and the Minaguchi-ya forever, the right to use the Satsuma crest as their own.

It is a simple design, a cross within a circle. It is, perhaps, a rather un-Japanese motif, and there are those who explain the cross by pointing out that Francis Xavier first touched Japan on Satsuma's shores and that there his new religion struck deep roots. But though the origins of the crest are lost in time, the reasons that it was granted to the Minaguchi-ya are not, and they wear it there with pride.

Not long after, there came word that rebellion had broken out in Satsuma. It was a revolt of the samurai, a last desperate attempt to assert their old pre-eminence. At its head was Saigo.

"Oh no!" was all that Raisuke said when they told him, and then he went out and stood on the beach a long time, looking out over the gray breakers. A few hours later he took to bed. He died before word came that Saigo too was dead. The revolt of the samurai had been crushed by an army of commoners.

When Jirocho first heard of Saigo's rebellion he pleaded with Tesshu to mediate before it was too late. Tesshu had once been successful in talks with Saigo, when he headed the mission that saved Edo and the Tokugawas. Perhaps, Jirocho urged, he might be successful again. When Tesshu replied that he could see no possibility of success this time, Jirocho angrily told him that there could never be success in anything if one started with the idea of failure.

Tesshu sighed. "What is your plan?" he asked.

"My plan is to try," Jirocho answered, but though Tesshu appreciated this spirit he never offered to mediate.

He could see that Saigo was unable to adjust to changing times, just as he could see that Jirocho had that ability. Jirocho had a natural ardor for new things. He was one of the first in Shimizu to face that ominous instrument the camera. He was one of the first to cut off his topknot and get a modern haircut (but he always hated hats, and when someone admired one that he was wearing he promptly gave it to the admirer, though it had been a gift from Tesshu, and to Tesshu from the Emperor). He was one of the first to sleep in a wooden bed (he built it himself). And he was one of the first to eat beef (his teeth were bad so he had it minced).

Whatever he did others did after him, for he was always the Boss. His followers remained loyal and there was a general feeling that his enemies were just as staunch, so that he was accompanied by bodyguards wherever he went. Nothing emptied the public bath faster than a visit by Jirocho. It was not that he was personally feared or disliked, for he was enormously respected and he always had a joke for the men and a friendly pat on the bottom for the women, mixed bathing being the rule in those days. It was simply that the tough, sharp-eyed men who always took up positions at the entrance made everybody nervous.

Not only did his men from the old days stay with him, but he even acquired new ones. There was, for instance, a young *sumo* wrestler, who came to him for protection one hot summer. He was an apprentice in a troupe that was performing in Shimizu, but he had rebelled at his additional duties, which consisted of fanning the head wrestler whenever he went to bed with his mistress. Jirocho agreed with the young fellow that this was beyond the call of duty, and took him under his wing. The other wrestlers of the troupe moved to beat up the deserter, but when they discovered that he was now Jirocho's man they decided instead to leave town.

The interrupted war with Katsuzo flared too, after the recess occasioned by that foe's joining the Imperial forces. Despite his mantle of respectability, Katsuzo still passed orders to his gang, who now took up highway robbery—an activity which would have annoyed the old Jirocho and which incensed the new. Katsuzo himself soon abandoned his samurai status and reverted to his gangster ways. The police finally hanged him in his native mountain territory. When Jirocho heard of it he sighed, for he had lost his last enemy from the old days.

Not that he did not have enough to keep him busy. He introduced modern big-net fishing to Shimizu and, typically, he became a fisherman when he realized that was the only way to convince die-hards that the new ways were better; he built bridges; and he even (and this must have shocked some of his old associates) established a penitentiary.

He agitated for a railroad to link Shimizu and Shizuoka, and he started steamship service between Shimizu and Yokohama. He led a fight to develop Shimizu port, turning himself into a whirlwind one-man lobby, hammering at the government in Tokyo until they gave Shimizu the big modern docks he wanted.

This campaign was so successful that when former President of the United States Ulysses S. Grant visited Japan in 1879 he landed first in Shimizu.

Jirocho was not on the reception committee: the town officials considered that his presence among them would not be seemly. But when they wanted the town's fishermen to demonstrate their skill with nets around Grant's warship, it was Jirocho who gave the word. When rickshawmen thought they saw a golden opportunity and quadrupled their rates, it was Jirocho who cooled them off. And when an expedition by rickshaw to Okitsu's Seikenji had to be canceled midway because of lack of time, Jirocho was heard to mutter that when he made a schedule, it worked.

Like any visiting dignitary, Grant was given little time to talk to people. He would have found many who spoke English, for Jirocho had pioneered in bringing English teachers to Shimizu. Perhaps he was alert to the advantages of English because of his running feud with his own language, at least as it was written. He once told Tesshu, who had been writing to him in the usual Chinese characters, that he was really not so smart after all, since apparently he was unable to write letters that the recipient could understand. Thereafter Tesshu wrote to Jirocho in phonetic script. (Tesshu, incidentally, was famous as a calligrapher, but he wrote in a way that was easy to imitate, thus providing a nice source of income for his houseboy, who produced a forgery whenever he needed money.)

The winter following Grant's visit was ushered in by cold weather early in December. The night of the thirteenth was raw and blustery. At a little past midnight, in a farmer's house on the other side of the post station from the Minaguchi-ya, a cat lunged for a mouse and knocked over a rush-lamp. Oil spread over the straw mats and caught from the guttering wick. Flame roared through the little house. The farmer and his family were trapped inside.

Those in the next house were luckier. They broke out of their door just as it was wrapped in fire. The third house had already caught and the fourth smoldered. Wind swept the flames straight down the highway.

Jangling bells and screaming voices roused the village. Servants were already passing buckets of water to douse the roofs of the Minaguchi-ya, but it was no use. In thirty minutes the inn was ashes. The fire was stopped just short of Seikenji's neighborhood by an open area whose buildings had burned two weeks earlier. Seventy houses had been destroyed during the night.

No lives were lost in the Minaguchi-ya, and the maids had carried all the guests' belongings to the shore. All Hanjuro's guests that night were Tokyo-bound. He sent them with a servant to his brother's half-way house on Satta. He also sent his wife and daughter.

Jirocho was already on the scene. He sought out Hanjuro to offer assistance but the innkeeper assured him that there were others in the village who needed help far more desperately. Next morning Jirocho started a drive in the surrounding area for relief goods of all kinds.

Hanjuro's only thought was to rebuild. The day had passed when the government would subsidize the reconstruction of a *waki-honjin*, but the Mochizukis had accumulated wealth in farmlands and their cash reserve had been saved from the fire.

Before long, Hanjuro had convinced himself that the inn's destruction was for the best. It gave him an opportunity to build a new Minaguchi-ya, larger and finer than ever before. He began to visualize it, from imposing entrance through roomy kitchen and service areas to handsome guest suites arranged about a central garden. He knew just the pine tree he would transplant to be the focus of that garden. He sent out word that he was in the market for fine timber. He chose an auspicious day for the ground-breaking, when priests would intone ancient liturgies to call down the blessings of the gods and carpenters would level the earth as they chanted an ancient choric tune. He even began to plan the celebration for the day when the ridge of the roof would be set: it was the custom to throw rice cakes from the ridge beam when it was in place, and he decided that he would provide a deluge of rice cakes, enough for every well-wisher who crowded around. There was excitement and joy in him as the new Minaguchi-ya grew in his mind, and his only regret, when he looked at the ashes of the old, was the loss of treasured records: guest registers that went back more than two hundred years, family archives that chronicled generations of Mochizukis.

Whenever Hanjuro encountered Jirocho during the hectic days after the fire, the Boss was sputtering over the smallness of the government's relief fund for the village. He protested furiously to more than one official, but he never succeeded in getting it increased. It was after these encounters that he complained to Tesshu about the timidity of government officials who cowered before his stare. Tesshu, who, like most Shogunate officials, had been brought into the new government soon after the civil war had ended and was now a trusted chamberlain to the Emperor Meiji, replied that not all officials were that easily intimidated, and the two immediately held a contest to see which could outglare the other. It was Jirocho who surrendered, whereupon Tesshu gave him a scroll on which he wrote, "Penetrating eyes are the symbol of greatness."

It was Tesshu who convinced Jirocho that since he had no children of his own he should adopt a son. Tesshu nominated a young man named Amada, a samurai's son. It was in some ways a strange choice, for Amada's tastes were scholarly and literary, but it worked out well in one respect, for it was Amada who wrote the biography based on Jirocho's own stories.

Before it could be finished, however, there occurred one of the most mortifying interludes of Jirocho's life. In 1884 there was a nation-wide roundup of gamblers, and despite the fact that, personally, he had long since given up gambling and had been loyally serving the law and his community, the new governor of the prefecture arrested him and sentenced him to seven years' imprisonment.

It was a distressing turn of the wheel but he bore it nobly. He was, of course, well treated, the warden being no fool. During the year or so it took Tesshu and other friends to get him out, he bossed the prison from within and, not one to waste his time, he promoted a new prison industry, raising silkworms.

His biography was published while he was still in prison and, that task finished, his adopted son cut the ties between them. He was probably right to do so, for he was not the type to have become Jirocho II. Instead he entered the priesthood and made a modest reputation as a poet.

After he was released from prison Jirocho opened a restaurant near Shimizu port. He called it Suehiro, which translates as "The Folding Fan" and signifies good luck. It is a name which has always been popular with restaurants in Japan. At the opening he distributed a thousand fans bearing calligraphy by Tesshu, and hundreds of towels printed with the same design.

Next April he came to Okitsu to help dedicate a monument to the *Kanrin Maru* victims. It had been erected with his support on the grounds of Seikenji Temple, overlooking the harbor where the attack took place. After the dedication a banquet was held at the Minaguchi-ya, and Jirocho and Hanjuro had their first chance in years for a good talk.

There was much to talk about. There was a completely new Minaguchi-ya. The huge entrance had a flaring curved roof, like a temple, for which the inn was sometimes mistaken, and behind it, handsome suites were disposed around the garden which fronted on the sea.

But Hanjuro was still unhappy over the loss of old records. He showed Jirocho the scroll he had commissioned, tracing the family tree back as far as anyone then living could remember. Memories had been prodded until six generations were filled in. If only Raisuke were still alive—Hanjuro was certain he could have pushed back still further into the past.

Jirocho met the personable young man that Hanjuro had adopted to marry his daughter and become next master of the Minaguchi-ya. Hanjuro called too for his eldest granddaughter, on whom he doted, and held her in his lap while the two men talked on into the evening. The little girl went to sleep in her grandfather's arms, and today, more than seventy years later, she cannot remember that she ever met Jirocho. She cannot remember, either, that later that year her grandfather took her to Shimizu to see a play about Jirocho, whose life was being dramatized while he was still around to see it.

The next year Tesshu died in Tokyo. The telegram with word of his critical illness reached Shimizu after the day's steamship for Yokohama had left, and Jirocho stayed fretfully awake all night worrying about his friend.

When they told Tesshu that the end was near he insisted on getting out of bed and being dressed in the pure white kimono of death. He breathed his last sitting upright in a chair, properly clothed, and smiling.

Jirocho was too late to say good-bye but he led the funeral procession with two hundred of his men. Bareheaded in a driving rain they marched slowly through the center of the city and past the Imperial palace, where the Emperor Meiji was in mourning.

Thereafter Jirocho lived quietly at his restaurant. The *Kanrin Maru* incident had made him a particular favorite of the Navy, and whenever a naval ship put in to Shimizu its officers would come to pay their respects; sometimes he rewarded them with tales of his old life. Whenever he took a walk he was surrounded by a swarm of children; they were rewarded with candy and kites. He died in 1893 at seventy-three. In his last delirium he talked only of Tesshu, but on his body they found a dagger. Some old habits had persisted to the end.

He was buried at the temple where he once almost lost his life eating globefish. Hanjuro, getting old himself, was one of the thousands who mourned at his funeral. Every year thousands still visit the grave where he lies with his followers, his "family." Nearby, posed against a rough stone wall, is a great bronze statue of him. The pose is forceful, as the man was.

At the foot of Mount Fuji there is another kind of monument. The farmers who work the land that he reclaimed have built a shrine. There they have deified him, and there they offer prayers to him. The Tokaido's Number One Boss has become a Shinto god.

Eighteenth Generation

1889–1940

CHAPTER THIRTEEN

In which the inn successfully makes the transition into modern times

PRINCIPAL CHARACTERS

Count Goto Shojiro, *an early politician of the new regime, who gave the Minaguchi-ya its other name*

Marquis Inouye Kaoru, *another leader of the new Japan, one of the Genro, elder statesmen; he built a villa in Okitsu*

Prince Ito Hirobumi, *greatest of the early statesmen, a Genro*

Prince Yamagata Aritomo, *his perennial opponent, also a Genro*

Prince Saionji Kimmochi, *the last Genro, who lived in Okitsu from 1919 till his death in 1940*

Prince Konoye Fumimaro, *Saionji's protégé*

Baron Harada Kumao, *Saionji's private secretary and spokesman*

Nakagawa Kojuro, *another secretary to Saionji*

and among the people of the inn:

Mochizuki Hanjuro I, *seventeenth master of the Minaguchi-ya*

Mochizuki Hanjuro II, *eighteenth master of the Minaguchi-ya*

Mochizuki, *son of Hanjuro III, who becomes secretary to Baron Harada*

Isako, *his wife*

The crest of
Saionji Kimmochi

IN 1889 the lengthening railroad, pushing from Tokyo towards Kyoto along the old Tokaido highway, reached Okitsu, and trains began to make travel on foot seem slow and arduous. Hanjuro took part in the ceremonies opening Okitsu station, as befitted his position in the town, but he was a far-sighted man, and as he watched the first train come puffing in, he wondered to himself if this meant the end of the Minaguchi-ya. He had brought the inn safely through the disintegration of the old regime and the birth of the new. He had saved it when daimyo suddenly quit their lavish journeys, and he had rebuilt it when fire destroyed it. But it seemed to him that this iron monster might finally defeat him. He was sure that the travelers who now tramped past his inn by the thousands would soon ride by without giving Okitsu a thought. Certainly they would not be looking for an inn to spend the night.

He was quite right about most travelers, though for several years Okitsu remained a stopping-off place for tourists who wanted to break their journey with a side trip to Miho. And when the Minaguchi-ya put its sightseeing guests in their rickshaws for the swing around the harbor to the Pacific side of the long sand spit, it was always with an introduction to the guild inn that sprawled in the lee of bent pines and dunes of black sand.

But elsewhere the guild that Hanjuro had founded began to break up, and many of the member inns that once had bustled with travelers every night of the year were now empty for weeks on end, growing dusty and musty until at last their gloomy owners shut their doors forever. Closer to home, the Ichikawas had given up their *honjin*. The Tezukas were bankrupt, and the last of that line came to the Minaguchi-ya to live out his days. The Seikenji medicine shops went out of business one by one, Dragon King tobacco and steamed shellfish were no longer sold on the river bank, and the myriad stalls that had offered noodles or cakes disappeared.

One might have guessed, with Hanjuro, that the Minaguchi-ya was in for bad times, that perhaps it had reached the end of its usefulness. But such a guess would have been reckoning without the instinct of that first Mochizuki of Okitsu, sixteen generations earlier. The warmth and beauty of the sheltered shore that had so attracted him now saved the inn which he, against his will, had founded. The Minaguchi-ya did not decline. It entered one of its most prosperous periods. For as the pilgrims abandoned Okitsu, the politicians discovered it.

Hanjuro had prepared for this transition, too, though perhaps with more luck than plan. An innovator in business, he had nevertheless followed tradition in family affairs: he had failed to produce a son. He did have a daughter, however, and to marry this daughter and become head of the family he had adopted one of the young sons of a well-to-do landowner from Fuji town, twelve miles and four stations towards Tokyo. There had been times when he had regretted his selection, for the young man was not entirely predictable. On his wedding night, for instance, he had disappeared, and he had not returned for two weeks, while Hanjuro faced a mounting domestic crisis. Then the groom came swinging down the highway, his kimono indicating that he hadn't slept under a roof since he'd left, and he resumed life at the inn as though he had never been away. He never offered an explanation, and of course it would have been unthinkable for his bride to request one, though she never quite forgave him.

But despite, or perhaps because of, this streak of wayward independence, the young man proved to be a good choice as next master of the Minaguchi-ya. Hanjuro II, for that is the name he assumed a year or so after his foster father's death, was ideally suited to cope with the political luminaries of new Japan. He was affable but he did not fawn. He was hearty without presuming. And he never abused a confidence.

One of the first of the new pashas to discover the Minaguchi-ya was Count Goto. He came from Tosa, a clan which offered the government many capable leaders. Long before the fall of the Shogunate, for example, Goto had studied the parliamentary system of England and was able to discuss it intelligently with the British ambassador. But the men of Tosa, like those of most other clans, found themselves gradually frozen out by the alliance of Satsuma and Choshu. It soon seemed to many men that they had helped throw out one clan, the Tokugawa, only to rivet on Japan a dictatorship of two other clans.

When Saigo disgustedly resigned from the government in 1873, Goto was with him. They had little in common, these two, for Saigo thought the government was too radical and Goto thought it was too conservative, but they agreed on one thing, that Japan should at once invade and take Korea. They were among the nation's first militant nationalists.

Goto did not join Saigo's ill-fated rebellion a few years later, for he was not that kind. Instead, he helped organize Japan's first political party, and he spent most of his life battling for government that was a little more representative.

He was popular with the people. As far as they understood his ideas, they approved of them, and they applauded him because, like very few others of the old samurai class, he was willing to speak from the same platform as commoners: this was democracy in action. But the ruling clique had no intention of turning the government over to the people, and Goto's campaigns could never bring him real political power.

Goto came often to the Minaguchi-ya. He loved the sea, and he loved the view of it from Okitsu. It was he who gave the inn its other name, Ippekiro. It is a name which to Western ears is even more unalluring than Minaguchi-ya, but, with its heavy freight of Chinese learning, it has a distinguished ring to a Japanese. The phrase must have occurred to Goto as he lounged at peace, looking out over the bay in the haze of morning or of early evening, times when everything is blue—the sea, the sky, the mountainous profile of Izu, the pine-softened hook of Miho. Since then, the inn has been officially known as the Minaguchi-ya Ippekiro: Minaguchi-ya, the Mansion of the Blue View.

Another of the makers of new Japan liked Okitsu so much that he bought a large tract of land just west of town and built a villa there. Marquis Inouye was from Choshu, which meant that, unlike Goto, he was "in." True, he did not garner all the honors that came to those other Choshu giants, Ito (no relative of the merchant family of Nagoya) or Yamagata. He never was Prime Minister, as they were (for a time they alternated in that position), but he served often in the cabinet, and like them he was one of the four or five elder statesmen, the Genro, who steered Japan's course as the Emperor's advisers and had the final word in any change of government.

Inouye was on Ito's team, meaning that he was identified with the "civil" faction in the government, as opposed to Yamagata's "military" faction. This was a fissure that appeared early and ran deep. It split the leadership of Japan almost until Pearl Harbor.

Inouye built his villa in 1896, incorporating a wing of his Tokyo residence, which was torn down and reassembled in Okitsu; the wing was Western-style, redolent of a decade which took its name from an international club dubbed the Baying Stag. This club was the symbol of the first great wave of cosmopolitanism that hit Japan, when the elite vied to display their newly acquired European tastes, manners, and clothes. Ito as Prime Minister and Inouye as Foreign Minister led the parade. Partly the whole business was an attempt to show foreigners how really very civilized the Japanese had become, as an argument for altering the unequal treaties which the Western powers had forced on Japan when the country was first opened and quite helpless. But mostly it was just for fun: the Japanese were going through one of their crazes for everything foreign, and having a wonderful time while it lasted.

Of course there was a reaction. There always is. The conservatives in their kimonos were outraged, and moralists muttered darkly that Japan had come to the decadence of the Roman Empire without first reaching its glory.

The wave of nationalism that accompanied the war with China in 1894 and 1895 effectively put an end to the Age of the Baying Stag, and it may have been that Inouye was happy to get the cosmopolitan wing of his mansion down to Okitsu, where it was less conspicuous.

The land that Inouye bought had its history, too. Plump in the middle of his spacious garden rose the pointed hill called Rice Bran Mountain. Everyone knew how it came there. Four hundred or more years ago, the land belonged to the Millionaire of Seikenji. The hill was formed from rice bran cast away from the daily hulling of rice for his table. Only the rich could afford to eat rice in those days, and a thoughtful inspection of the big hill is enough to convince anyone that the Millionaire was not only wealthy but must have been very stout. It is also recorded that he was full of good works, for he was the main supporter of the temple of Seikenji. Unfortunately, his vision of the future was clouded. He bet on Shingen, and when Shingen's son was crushed by Ieyasu, the Millionaire went down to ruin.

There was a clear stream at the foot of Inouye's land, and he diverted water from it to fill the pools he had dug at the foot of Rice Bran Mountain. The garden was knit by a mossy path which wandered among trees and by beds of iris, and crossed on rounded little bridges to miniature islands accented with stone lanterns.

For a more strenuous ramble one could climb the path that wound up Rice Bran Mountain, pausing at frequent vantage points to look out to sea or up the valley towards tangerine groves. After Inouye died they put a great bronze statue of him on top of this, his very own mountain, and set monumental slabs of stone along the path, engraved with suitable tributes from his contemporaries. He would have liked that.

Inouye was not very popular in Okitsu. He was thought arrogant.

He had a habit of stopping express trains for his personal convenience, though Okitsu was not an express stop. He didn't even stop them at the station, but right at his villa.

Of course Hanjuro II came to know him, but the innkeeper was not impressed. Inouye spotted the fine old tree in the garden of the Minaguchi-ya, that superb pine which the first Hanjuro had selected and moved there, and he decided it was just what he needed in his own garden. To ask was to receive, in Inouye's vocabulary, and he was shocked and angered when the second Hanjuro told him the tree would remain where it was. However, both men mellowed, and when, some years later, Inouye admired a pet monkey at the Minaguchi-ya, Hanjuro graciously presented it to him.

But of all the statesmen who were attracted to Okitsu none lived there as long or became as deeply identified with the town as Prince Saionji.

Saionji moved to Okitsu in 1919, a few years after Inouye's death. His house was built for him while he was in France, a country he loved, serving as Japan's chief delegate to the Peace Conference of Versailles. He moved in when he returned, and for the next twenty years Okitsu was the country capital of Japan. For Saionji was the last Genro, the last of that little group of elders who had made Japan into a modern nation, and on this reluctant, aging man fell a great burden.

Prime ministers and would-be prime ministers, men with an idea and men who wanted one, streamed to Okitsu for a few minutes at his villa. While they were waiting—and sometimes he made them wait a very long time—they stayed at the Minaguchi-ya.

Hanjuro II spoke often of the contrast between Saionji and Inouye. It could be summed up in their homes. Inouye's proud mansion stood aloof from the town and sea on its big tract of land. Saionji's modest house faced directly on the bay, shouldered by fishermen's homes larger than itself, fronting the shore cluttered with fishing gear.

To build his home, Saionji brought a carpenter from Kyoto. He was a Kyoto man himself, and the quiet taste of the old capital was his taste. He was a comparative rarity among Japanese statesmen, a member not of one of the feudal military clans, but of the old aristocracy of the Imperial court. As innkeepers of an earlier age had learned so well when they had to put up with the tantrums and knavery of some of these courtiers on their excursions to Edo or Nikko, it was an aristocracy which had decayed through centuries of enforced idleness, but it still produced a few men of great talent, and Saionji was one of these.

In his youth he had been poor, as the Emperor and all his court were poor. (Another courtier had made a living by letting a local boss like Jirocho use his house for gambling; it was a good spot for such activities, since the palace precincts were out of bounds to police.) Saionji never in his life had a great deal of money, or desired it, but it must be added that his younger brother, who became head of the great financial-industrial house of Sumitomo, saw to it that he never wanted for anything.

And lest it be thought that the Mochizuki family was unique in their frequent adoptions, it may be remarked that Saionji himself was an adopted son. His older brother, heir of their own Tokudaiji family, became the Emperor Meiji's most intimate personal adviser, Grand Chamberlain and Lord Keeper of the Privy Seal. His younger brother was adopted by the Sumitomos and became one of Japan's great businessmen.

By the time he moved to Okitsu, Saionji was seventy years old and had had a full career. In the not very savage war of revolution, he had, at the age of twenty, commanded one of the Emperor's armies. It is true that a member of the court was wanted as only a nominal commander and that actual campaigning fell on troops provided by the clans. It is also true, however, that the court passed over many older men to choose Saionji, that he managed to hold together a force drawn from several clans whose dislike of the Tokugawa was only slightly exceeded by their distrust of each other, and that he accomplished his mission.

The doors of the new government were wide open to him then. He might have stepped immediately into a position of power and authority, but he was in no hurry. He had two things on his mind: some fun and a chance to study abroad.

The first he took care of by moving to Tokyo and taking up residence in what the Japanese call a teahouse, but which foreigners know as a geisha house. As for the second, he began a campaign to get himself sent to Europe as a government student. The Western world excited him. He wanted to study it first-hand. In 1870 he was ordered to France.

He and about thirty other students went by way of the United States, sailing from Yokohama on a side-paddle American steamer. In Washington, President Grant invited them to the White House, and in a letter home, young Saionji, who had never been girl-shy, recorded his shock at the women's low-necked dresses.

In Paris he quickly recovered his poise and acquired a mistress. He confided to a friend that the best way he had found to keep awake while studying dry lessons in a difficult foreign language was to keep an attractive girl at his side, mingling scholarship and kisses.

He lived in Paris for ten years, and became more Parisian than the natives. But more than that, he became deeply imbued with the spirit of French law and French liberalism, and this spirit guided him all the rest of his life.

His return home in 1880 was chilling. After ten years in Paris, he found Tokyo raw, which it was, and the government despotic, which it was. He was restless and discontented. He and some friends started a liberal newspaper, which the government quickly suppressed. He went back to his old haunts, the teahouses. He found a young geisha who had charmed him before he went to Paris, and he fell in love with her all over again. Her name was Okiku, Chrysanthemum.

There is a legend about the Saionji family. Each family in the Imperial court had its special pursuit, like poetry, or soothsaying, or football. For a thousand years or so, the specialty of the Saionjis had been playing the lute, and when he was a boy Saionji mastered this instrument. The legend about the Saionjis says that the goddess of the lute is fiendishly jealous, that she will not tolerate a licit rival, and that should any head of the house take a legal wife she will suffer early death.

Saionji laughed at the legend, but it existed, and it was, as he said, a great convenience to a man who did not want to be tied down. Saionji had a weakness for a pretty face and figure, but he did not want to be tied down. He did not marry Okiku, but they lived together for many years and had a lovely daughter, to whom Saionji was devoted, and who of course was raised as a Saionji. Eventually there came the time which Okiku must always have known would come, and she moved out to make way for a fresh young thing. There were others after her, but none ever quite took Okiku's place.

But this is getting ahead of the story. At the time when Saionji was courting Okiku in his favorite teahouse, statesman Ito sought him out and put him to work. Ito also liked women and wine, but he did not intend to let a talent like Saionji's become quite so specialized.

Working with Ito, Saionji learned politics, the practical politics of a practicing politician. There was the time when one of the older leaders, Kido, told Ito that he was worn out with anxiety and anger over the course of the government, and that he was going home to die. Ito pointed out to Kido that it would be better for the country if he died in Tokyo, for if he went back to the provinces nursing such feelings he would attract all kinds of dangerous malcontents, and no telling what trouble might arise. So Kido died in Tokyo.

Those were days when things were simmering. There was much talk of a constitution. Should it be drawn up by representatives of the people, or come down from the Emperor? And what kind of government should it establish?

The first question was answered soon enough. The constitution would come down from the Emperor. The present oligarchy would create it and the public would not concern itself.

Ito went to Europe to study the structure of governments there, and he took Saionji with him. Saionji was sent to France, to his great pleasure, but Ito himself knew exactly what he was looking for. He headed straight for Bismarck's Germany, and in the end it was a Prussian-model constitution that Japan got.

While Ito worked on his constitution, Saionji was given a taste of diplomatic life. In 1885 he was made Minister to Austria, and then to Germany. In 1891, when he came home, he counted that nineteen of his past twenty-two years had been spent abroad. He headed for the teahouses.

But once again Ito dug him out of those delightful pleasure haunts and put him to work. In 1894, during the war with China, Ito brought him into his cabinet as Education Minister, and Saionji received his baptism of fire. In the whole bureaucracy there was no more stubbornly reactionary group than that which controlled the Ministry of Education, and from that vantage point ladled out their potent blend of nationalism and Emperor worship. Saionji's ideas of individual liberty and international co-operation were anathema, and he was savagely attacked. They called him "cosmopolitan," a very nasty word, and there were those who suggested that a little assassination might be a good thing. But he stuck it out and, if he failed to make much headway against the entrenched reactionaries of his ministry, there was probably no man who could have done more.

Later, when the Foreign Minister fell ill and resigned, Saionji took over that portfolio as well, and here he ran into some of Ito's back-seat driving. For instance, the Prime Minister liked to touch up all official notes sent abroad. Saionji was equal to this problem. He submitted his notes not in Japanese but in English. Ito knew some English but he did not have enough confidence to make revisions in that language.

Ito went out of power in 1896, and Saionji with him, but both were back a year or so later. All through these years, Ito and Yamagata shuffled the premiership back and forth between their two camps. And though Ito was a great admirer of Bismarck and Germany, and though the constitution, which he had drafted, carefully insured that the powers granted to the national assembly—the Diet —and the people were all shadow and no substance, he was a pillar of representative government compared with Yamagata. That hard-headed general had only contempt for the Diet. When they defied him, he had two methods of bringing them into line: hired thugs and bribery. The second proved more effective, for there are always some men who hit back harder after being beaten up. Recognition of this was about the extent of Yamagata's education in democratic processes.

Ito did not share Yamagata's utter distrust of democracy, but he genuinely believed that "the public" was not ready to govern itself. He wrote: "Our people are still childish and simple; childish, simple people, like white silk, are easy to dye various colors." The trouble was that Ito could not bring himself to train the people for responsibility. He had fought to throw out the Tokugawas, but he could not get over the Tokugawa idea that government was to be obeyed, not understood.

Inevitably there came the day, in 1901, when Ito and Yamagata retired from active politics to become Genro, and their protégés took over. Ito's man was Saionji. Ito also turned over to Saionji the fledgling political party he had founded. Yamagata hated parties.

Through the twelve years that Saionji and Yamagata's heir, Prince Katsura, alternated in the premiership, they fought from long-established positions. Like Yamagata, his successor favored a "strong" foreign policy, increased armaments to back it up, and heavier taxes to support the armaments; he repressed civil liberties and strengthened the old bureaucracy. Saionji, when his turn came, worked for a conciliatory foreign policy, limitation on armaments, and reduced taxes; he widened civil liberties and tried to build representative government.

Saionji's second cabinet fell in 1912. There had just been a general election and his party had swept to a clear majority in the Diet, but under the constitution that was not enough. The Army, at Yamagata's instigation, demanded two new divisions. Saionji refused, and the War Minister resigned.

Under the constitution, each minister was responsible not to the Prime Minister or even to the Diet but directly to the Emperor. Moreover, a policy established by Yamagata decreed that the Ministers of War and Navy must be chosen from active officers of those services. The consequence was clear. If the Army or the Navy refused to furnish a minister, no man could form a cabinet.

There was a way out, a way Ito would have used. Saionji could have obtained from the Emperor an edict that the Army must furnish a minister.

Saionji would not do this. He saw the Emperor as a constitutional monarch: as a constitutional monarch he should not be used in political manipulations, and certainly he should not be led to exert power in a way that might lead to absolute monarchy. Saionji's reasoning prevented him from acting. He and his cabinet resigned.

Had Saionji known at sixty-three what he knew at eighty-five, he might have made a different decision. He might have realized that the military were seceding from the government, shattering every instrument of control. He might have led a fight to reassert government supremacy over the armed forces. At sixty-three he did not, and at eighty-five it was too late.

Three years later Saionji retired from active politics. He joined the dwindling ranks of the Genro. He became an elder statesman.

Reluctantly, he came back into the limelight to head Japan's delegation to the Peace Conference of Versailles, though he was happy at the thought of returning to Paris and seeing his old friend Clemenceau. He took his daughter and her husband, whom he had adopted as his son. He took a young protégé of his named Konoye, for whom he had great hopes. He also took his current young lady. There were those who criticized him for this, but Saionji replied that if at seventy he had to drag himself halfway around the world in the service of his government, he would at least make up his personal party as he saw fit.

When he returned to Japan he moved into the house at Okitsu. He called it Zagyo-so, a name that connotes a retreat aloof from struggle for power, with a Chinese allusion to "one who sits quietly fishing while others clamor for the catch." Zagyo-so signified his plan for the rest of his life. There, in Okitsu, with the fresh smell of the sea in his nostrils, and the lovely bay before his eyes, he hoped to spend his last years in peace. He had his books, his Chinese classics and his French novels, and for lighter entertainment he could listen to the gossip of fishermen's wives.

There are those who say that Hanjuro II sold Saionji the piece of land on the shore, and there are others who say that he helped Saionji buy it from a third party. One day I asked for the truth from Hanjuro's grandson, the man who is today Hanjuro IV.

"Well, I'll tell you," he replied, gazing out towards the sea. "He gave the land to Saionji."

He smiled. "Of course, grandfather wasn't as generous as that sounds. He knew that by giving it he'd get more for it."

Despite his grandson's polite depreciation, there is no evidence that Hanjuro II ever tried to use Saionji. It was not in the inn-keeper's character to try, and it was not in Saionji's character to let him get away with it if he had tried. The gift of the land was simply a generous act which Hanjuro camouflaged, for his wife and the world, as a shrewd bit of business.

Of course, the Minaguchi-ya did profit from Saionji's presence. The Genro's staff and his visitors stayed at the Minaguchi-ya, but that was because Hanjuro kept it not only the best inn in Okitsu but a very fine inn by any standards.

Had Saionji had his choice, there would have been no staff and no official visitors. He would have liked to resign as Genro, and he thought the time was nearing when he could. The Genro was strictly an extra-legal institution, he pointed out, not even hinted at in the constitution, and it should be allowed to disappear as soon as the government could function without it. That day was coming, he was sure, for the political parties were growing stronger. Soon the choice of Prime Minister would be automatic. He would be leader of the party that held a majority in the Diet, and there would be no need of a Genro working behind the scenes to nominate him or to pull him down when he lost the Diet's support.

Things looked bright after the Great War, as people called it. There was a whole new Age of the Baying Stag, with Woodrow Wilson as its hero. The Crown Prince, Emperor Meiji's grandson, toured Europe, something that would have been unthinkable a few years earlier, and Saionji's adopted son accompanied him. But perhaps nothing symbolized the passing of the old order quite as eloquently as the death of Prince Yamagata, hard, ruthless, autocratic old Yamagata, who had devoted his life to building a militant Japan, and to fighting democracy because it got in the way.

Still Saionji never could persuade the Throne to accept his retirement, and so he continued to serve as the last Genro. And his would-be confidants continued to fill the Minaguchi-ya.

Living quietly in Okitsu, Saionji needed eyes and ears and a voice in the capital, and he found them in Baron Harada. Harada was the perfect secretary, selflessly dedicated to Saionji and the things he believed in. In Tokyo, where he spent about two-thirds of his time, he had a constant round of appointments, lunches, dinners, quiet conversations with men of importance in government and business. Here he sought a scrap of information, there he dropped a hint. Tirelessly he ran down rumors. Always he did as Saionji would have done.

In Okitsu, his days were quieter. He lived at the Minaguchi-ya, where his suite was always ready for him. He spent hours with Saionji, passing on the information he had gleaned, absorbing the old man's reactions, weighing men, pondering moves.

Saionji himself never went to Tokyo except in crises. All over Japan, people knew it was serious when the Genro boarded a train for the capital.

There were others on Saionji's staff, though none functioned in politics as Harada did. There was, for instance, Nakagawa, handsome, dashing, and, like his chief, apparently irresistible to women. He left a trail of conquests wherever he went, including the Minaguchi-ya. Isako remembers him with special affection. When she came to the inn as a young bride she faced not only a mother- and father-in-law but a grandmother- and grandfather-in-law. This put her under about as many thumbs as a Japanese bride can be, and she remembers kindness like Nakagawa's. He gave her ten yen as a wedding present. "It was the first money of my own I'd ever had in my life," she says. "I spent it all on books, and received a terrible scolding from my mother-in-law because I didn't save it."

The early years in Okitsu were the best for Saionji. They were the peaceful years. When he awoke very early in the morning, as an old man is apt to do, he sometimes rose in the gray light of dawn and climbed the stone steps to the old temple of Seikenji to watch the sunrise. Sometimes he talked with the head priest after the priest had sounded the morning bell, and they became friends.

In the evening he might walk through the village streets or along the shore, and often he stopped in at the Minaguchi-ya, to sit in the entry and sip a cup of tea, and chat. He liked to talk with Hanjuro II, for the innkeeper seemed always to have a new story, and a re-

Suruga Bay seen over the roofs of Seikenji (*a print by Hiratsuka*)

freshing flow of good, man's talk. And unlike the politicians who were always about, Hanjuro had no ax to grind. Sometimes the two men met in Hanjuro's cottage, a retreat about halfway between Saionji's house and the inn, for a few bottles of sake. It was here they toasted the new Emperor when Meiji's grandson assumed the throne.

Those were peaceful years, but they did not last. By the mid-twenties, Japan, which had overexpanded when the war removed all competition from her overseas markets, was in the depths of depression. Western liberalism had turned sour, and the country was swept by confusion and unrest. Ominously, this unrest gripped the Army. No element of the nation was quite so susceptible. Most of its junior officers were peasants' sons who had risen from the ranks, and the suffering of their families back on tiny farms tore at them. Trained, like the rest of the population, to read but not to think, they lashed out at everything about them—at the economic system that was squeezing them, at the shadowy Diet that failed to provide leadership, at the corruption that linked politicians and big business. Every day brought them closer to open violence.

The upper echelons of officers watched their juniors' flaming resentment and schemed to use it. They were heir to the old system of clan government, government by military men. They detested the fumbling slowness of cabinet and parliament.

They moved to strike early in 1931. They plotted a great *coup d'etat* which would sweep away the government and impose military dictatorship. While their conspiracy was being nurtured, it was countenanced by no less than the Minister of War. At the last moment, he had qualms and ordered the plot quashed, but the damage was done. His action enraged the ringleaders and did nothing to restore discipline. Mutiny had been condoned by the Army's highest officers.

Details of the affair leaked out slowly, and it was a hot August afternoon before Harada was able to piece together the whole story and give it to Saionji.

Saionji was shocked. He had not known things were so serious.

The Emperor must be told, he said. And the ringleaders must be made to resign from the Army.

But the Emperor was not told, and nothing was done. Saionji's words were drowned in a sea of caution. Other men said that forced resignations might stir things up. Better let the moderates in the Army handle it in their own way. Give us time, they said, and we will work it out.

Creeping paralysis numbed the government, and a month later the Army struck. It staged a hoax bombing of the Manchurian railway and, using it for an excuse, swept through Manchuria. It was the "Manchurian Incident."

In Okitsu, a private car was hooked onto a train, and Saionji set off for Tokyo. He invited Hanjuro to ride along. It was an unfortunate experience for the gregarious master of the Minaguchi-ya, because this day Saionji did not want to talk. He sat silent and depressed, staring ahead, his chin propped on his hands which rested on the head of his cane. Hanjuro appreciated his old friend's anxiety but he had a horror of silence. He put up with it for as long as he could, and then about halfway to Tokyo he excused himself and took a train back. Even his return was disconcerting. As usual when he was traveling alone he kept falling asleep. On this occasion, he slept through Okitsu three times, east and west, before a friendly conductor put him off at his station.

In Tokyo, Saionji found the Emperor determined: the Army must be checked. Saionji spoke with the new Premier, and the Emperor made himself clear, but in the end nothing was done. There was even talk of a direct order from the Throne that the Army should cease operations in Manchuria. The order was never issued, for as Saionji pointed out, it was very probable that the Army would not obey, and then Imperial prestige would be shattered. It was already too late, even for such measures.

The Army's mutinous success in Manchuria was not Saionji's only worry. The military had good reason to be unhappy with the present Emperor, and there were many who thought that perhaps the Tokugawa solution had been best after all: return His Majesty to Kyoto, and box him there in tight seclusion. In the meantime, the Army lost no chance to discredit the Emperor. One of their stories reached Saionji in Okitsu before Harada heard it in Tokyo. It seems that a patriotic young recruit had been assigned to the palace guard. Seeing a light late at night in the Emperor's room, he was overwhelmed with gratitude at the thought that His Majesty was hard at work. But drawing closer he was shocked and disillusioned to find that, on the contrary, the Emperor was engaged in trivial recreation while his armies were in the field: he was playing mah-jongg with the Empress. Things like this proved, said some officers, that the Emperor was "a mediocre person."

There was not long to wait for the next "incident." On the fifteenth of May of the following year, a group of young officers broke into the Prime Minister's residence and shot him in the stomach. It was their third assassination that spring. There were to have been others, twenty in all. Saionji was on their list, but his intended assassin, after keeping watch for a couple of weeks from the heights behind Seikenji Temple, gave up. By the time of their trial a year later, the assassins were being favorably compared with Oishi and the others of the forty-seven *ronin*.

From the fifteenth of May, 1932, terrorism was always in the air. It corroded men, it ate away their will, and coupled with military successes from which there could be no drawing back, it worked irresistibly on all but the strongest characters. Two men, in particular, were not affected—Saionji in Okitsu and the Emperor in Tokyo, but Saionji watched glumly as they were progressively isolated. Even his protégé Konoye was saying that Saionji was too old and out of date.

No longer could Saionji climb to Seikenji's quiet precincts before sunrise, or take an evening walk through Okitsu. The risk was too great, his guards said, and now there were always guards around his house.

In 1933 he must have felt a personal loss, for that year Hanjuro II died. At seventy he was fourteen years younger than Saionji, but now he was dead, and there would be no more relaxing chats with him.

Hanjuro's death left the Minaguchi-ya without an active master, for Hanjuro III had been an invalid for ten years, and his eldest son, who showed little interest in the inn, had been working in a bank since finishing college.

That was the year this young man changed jobs. By this time Saionji's secretary Harada knew the Mochizukis well and he had kept his eye on this eldest son. Now he asked him to be his secretary.

It meant that young Mochizuki would be in Tokyo most of the time, and could spend only a few days a month with his wife and their two young boys at the Minaguchi-ya, but the family admired Harada almost as much as they admired Saionji, and there really was not much need for discussion. For his part, young Mochizuki was no more excited by banking than he was by innkeeping, and he was happy to accept Harada's flattering offer. And so he joined Saionji's official family in the same year that his grandfather bowed out of the unofficial one.

The Minaguchi-ya was operated committee-fashion. Hanjuro III, though bedridden, could supervise money matters, and the chief clerk knew the business well. Mostly, the inn was run by three women representing three generations: the still active widow of Hanjuro II; her daughter, the wife of Hanjuro III (for like the five preceding masters of the inn, he was an adopted son); and their son's young wife, Isako, from Shimizu, who knew nothing about innkeeping but was rapidly learning from two hard taskmasters. She also looked after her two small boys, the older of whom sometimes went to call on the pleasant old gentleman who lived up the beach in the house with policemen in front of it, and once, on a last day of winter, energetically assisted his host in the traditional rites of that day, tossing dried beans about the house to rout any skulking devils and let in good fortune.

Among other miscellaneous skills, Isako learned to operate the telephone switchboard. The farm girls usually assigned to that job found the little switchboard a formidably complex mechanism at best, and when some frightening notable like Harada or the current Prime Minister was at the inn, telephone service in the girls' hands was likely to disintegrate into a hopeless tangle of misdirected, interrupted, and unanswered calls. Reactions to this varied. Suave, handsome Nakagawa, who always stayed in the Ivy Room, would wiggle a black eyebrow, close his eyes, lean back, and wait for order to be restored. Saionji's adopted son, ensconced in the Hollyhock Room, would lose his temper, and roar at some innocent maid until she dissolved in tears. Harada was more direct. He simply insisted that when he was at the inn Isako take over the switchboard. In her hands it was docile and well behaved, he pointed out, and, besides, she knew the private numbers and code-names of all the people he usually called in Tokyo, and could be trusted not to listen in. Of course he had his way.

Isako was not on the switchboard the morning of the twenty-sixth of February, 1936. In the first place, Harada was not at the inn to demand it, though Nakagawa was installed in the Ivy Room. In the second place, Isako had given birth to her third son on the fourth of the month, and though the traditional three weeks had elapsed, and the twenty-sixth was the day for her to be up and about, she had other things on her mind.

Everyone was agog over the weather. It was snowing. Even a flurry of white flakes is unusual in Okitsu, but this was a real snow. There were inches of the stuff on the ground and it was still falling. There wasn't a graybeard in town who could remember when such a thing had happened before. It was such a startling occurrence that it named the new baby. They first thought they would call him Yukizo, *yuki* meaning snow, but eventually they hit on a shorter version, Yuzo.

Since Isako was not on the switchboard, it is not surprising that the call from Tokyo that exploded in the operator's face that chill white morning was misdirected. The girl meant to call the Ivy Room, but her trembling hand missed the mark, and so it was not

Nakagawa but a dignified old gentleman visiting the inn for a rest who first heard the horrifying news.

Fourteen hundred men of the crack First Division had mutinied, had seized a large group of buildings just west of the palace, had butchered the Prime Minister (it turned out later they had killed his brother-in-law instead), the Minister of Finance, the Lord Keeper of the Privy Seal, and the Inspector-General of the Army. They had seriously wounded the Emperor's Grand Chamberlain. And a party of murderers was on its way towards Okitsu and Saionji.

The old gentleman who had received Nakagawa's call burst out of his room in a state of shock, his body trembling, his white beard quivering. Someone took him in hand, and Isako redirected the call to Nakagawa.

No one had ever seen Nakagawa excited before. He was out of his room without a coat, his necktie streaming. He yelled for his shoes, and Isako laid her baby down in the entry to get them and help him into them. He ran through the snow to Saionji's house.

A little later police reinforcements arrived from Shizuoka. They judged it impossible to defend the little seaside villa, and that evening they bundled the neuralgia-racked old man into a car and started for Shizuoka. Just out of town another car swung in behind them. The police increased their speed but the headlights flashing on the snow at their rear kept pace. They careened over the slippery road, nerves taut, revolvers drawn, until they slid through the gate of the governor's official residence. It was hours later before they learned that the car behind had been filled with newspaper reporters.

Next day things seemed quieter. At least the mutiny had not spread, and Saionji was brought home to an Okitsu swarming with police. The next morning he headed for Tokyo, grim, slushy, immobilized Tokyo, the hushed center of this storm of violence. A panicky nation took heart from an indomitable old man.

He found the Emperor aroused and, for once, in control. His Majesty refused to dignify the revolt by any name but mutiny. He insisted that it be crushed unconditionally. He refused to parley over politics until that was done.

This once the Emperor had his way. The mutineers surrendered and their punishment was swift and secret. But in the end it was the Army that won. No government thereafter was formed without its approval. No politician thereafter lived without terror as his close companion.

The Army's victory was complete. From then on it was the only real government of Japan. It set the nation's policies, it conducted the nation's diplomacy. What passed for the government was only façade.

It was not in Saionji's nature to stop trying. He persuaded Konoye to accept the premiership, and his protégé's behavior was perhaps the final, crushing blow. Harada, who had been less hopeful, was less disillusioned. "I have known Prince Konoye for a long time," he said. "He is of weak character . . ."

A month after Konoye took office in 1937 the Army staged its "Second China Incident." Konoye tried to stop it, wavered, then authorized reinforcements. "We are like marionettes in the Army's hands," he moaned. It was the beginning of the last act, the war with China that couldn't be won and couldn't be stopped, that mushroomed into global conflict and final, total defeat.

Saionji was close to giving up. "There is nothing to do," he said. "At present there is nothing to do but endure this."

But he could still defend his Emperor. There was a fifth column in the palace now, for the Army saw that it was the Emperor who had defeated them on February 26, and they stepped up their personal attacks. They abused him for his hobby of marine biology: "he should be studying Confucianism." Time and again Saionji intervened to keep the palace safe, but the attacks continued. The Emperor was a scientist, a liberal, and a lover of peace, the generals said, and they spat the words.

Konoye journeyed to Okitsu, took over the Minaguchi-ya, begged Saionji to let him resign. "After a year of this," he pleaded, "I could be excused." He was.

There were more assassination plots. In 1940, Harada was on a list, but escaped.

In July of 1940, Konoye, having thought it over and decided to hitch his wagon to the Army's star, returned as Prime Minister. This time Saionji refused to give his approval. Konoye came once more to Okitsu. He reported that the Emperor had endorsed the Tripartite Alliance with Hitler's Germany and Mussolini's Italy. The old man listened coldly, knew better than to believe.

Prince Saionji's last illness came before the end of the year. He died on November 24, 1940, in the little villa he had named Zagyo-so because he had hoped to find peace there.

Young Mochizuki rode with the body on its last journey to Tokyo. A little more than a year later he would be glad, with others who had been close to Saionji, that the prince had not lived to see the war with America and England. But for the moment there was only grief, grief in every corner of Japan, grief in Okitsu, and grief at the Minaguchi-ya.

Twentieth Generation

1940–1957

CHAPTER FOURTEEN

In which the inn survives the war and the Occupation

PRINCIPAL CHARACTERS

Among the people of the inn:

Mochizuki, *twentieth master of the Minaguchi-ya*
Isako, *his wife*
Mochizuki Ryozo, *Isako's father, of the Mochizuki family of Shimizu*
Yasuo, *eldest son of Mochizuki and Isako*
Obaasan, *Mochizuki's mother, widow of Hanjuro III*
Yoshi, *bath attendant at the Minaguchi-ya*

The crest of
the Minaguchi-ya

AFTER SAIONJI'S DEATH, his staff disbanded. Harada went into semi-retirement, and Mochizuki came back to the Minaguchi-ya. Somewhat reluctantly he took over business affairs from his invalid father. For the first time in seven generations the Mochizuki family had produced a son and heir, and he took only a grudging interest in the inn.

A few months later the radio blared announcement of war. "When I heard it," said Mochizuki, "I remembered a conversation from my days with Baron Harada. One Saturday afternoon, he and I went to the huge naval base at Yokosuka to visit Admiral Yamamoto Isoroku. Yamamoto was not a great sailor; he was an administrator. He was profoundly opposed to the nation's course towards war, and he was sent to sea to save his life: had he been kept in the government in Tokyo, he would have been murdered by extremists.

"He was lonely and unhappy at Yokosuka, and Harada's visit was an attempt to cheer him. We had a good dinner aboard the flagship, and a long talk that evening.

"Yamamoto was gloomy. He was one of the few who really understood the strength of the United States and Britain, and he lamented that so many in the Navy thought Japan could defeat those powers. He said that if war came, the Japanese Navy could only assemble in the Inland Sea and stay there.

"When the radio screamed war, I remembered what he had said, and I really expected the Navy to head for the Inland Sea. But of course it didn't. It sailed out to some smashing successes. Most of the nation seemed to think that victory was certain. I had no such hopes. I began to stockpile food and make plans for evacuation; in Shimizu, Isako's father was doing the same thing. I had only one thing in mind: how to bring my family through the war alive."

Mochizuki was able to concentrate on that aim because the Minaguchi-ya was soon requisitioned as a residence for the swollen staff of a big aluminum plant across the bay, and he was freed of operating responsibility.

In the meantime, his anti-war views and his long association with Saionji and Harada made him a target for the military police, the dreaded Kempei-tai. Three times he was hauled to Tokyo, threatened with prison, grilled from morning till midnight. "They weren't interested in me," he says, "they were trying to pin something on Harada. I refused to talk, and then when Harada suffered a disabling stroke they lost interest in him."

In July, 1944, the war began to come home to Japan. Mochizuki packed up Isako and the children and moved them back into the mountains, about ten miles from the exposed coast. Their refuge was a big, thatch-roofed, decrepit old farmhouse. The farmer took satisfaction in the extensive repairs made by the Minaguchi-ya's carpenters, and the farmer's wife soon found ways of easing all the housekeeping onto Isako. This, and taking care of her six children, who ranged from twelve-year-old son Yasuo down to one-year-old daughter Chikue (born on the Empress's birthday and named after her), kept Isako occupied and left her little time to brood.

Mochizuki himself stayed at the inn with his mother and father, for his father was quite helpless now, and it was thought best not to move him unless it became imperative. They constructed three bomb shelters underneath the garden, complete with *tatami* floors and electricity. One of them was close to the old man's bedroom. They had occasion to use those shelters, for incendiary bombs fell with increasing frequency. Inouye's big villa was hit and burned to the ground, and that same night two bombs fell in the garden of the Minaguchi-ya. "It was as though the sky was filled with fireworks," Mochizuki recalls today, "and more incendiaries burned harmlessly on the surface of the bay. It was beautiful."

The inn survives the war and the Occupation

Mochizuki, his mother, and his father lived with this beauty until the last weeks of the war, when the Japanese Navy had been swept from even the Inland Sea, and Allied warships were able to sit offshore and lob shells onto the defenseless coast. Finally, and with great difficulty, for no vehicles were available, they carried the invalid several miles inland.

"I listened to the Emperor's speech announcing surrender," Mochizuki goes on, "and like those around me I wept. I wept with relief that the war was over, and with anxiety for the future. The Minaguchi-ya was intact, but the country was knocked out. We dreaded being occupied, especially by the Chinese or Russians. Late in September, a team of two American officers came to inspect this area and stayed with us. They were kind and understanding, and then I knew that we were safe. I brought my family back. The officers gave us K-rations, bananas, and chocolates. The children didn't know what bananas and chocolates were.

"Still we were apprehensive when, in October, the Minaguchi-ya was placed 'on limits,' meaning that it was opened to members of the Occupation. We were one of the very first inns to be approved. That was partly because the Minaguchi-ya was mostly a one-story structure. Occupation authorities were afraid of fires, and obviously escape is easier from a ground-level building."

Those fears were not baseless, for the Americans speedily demonstrated that they were even more adept than the Japanese at burning hotels, and many a fine old resort hostelry, taken over and operated as a recreation billet, was reduced to ashes in a vain attempt to approximate central heating.

The Minaguchi-ya was spared this fate, for it was not requisitioned. It was merely approved as a retreat for those who wanted to sample Japanese ways.

"Conditions were chaotic," says Mochizuki. "It was hard to get enough to eat, even for our family, and the Occupation flatly prohibited our serving food to its people. At first, like the inns of four hundred years ago, we could do little but warm the food that travelers brought with them."

And yet we Americans came, in great numbers. On weekends we filled the inn, and Isako's father, summoned from his home in Shimizu, would leap onto his bicycle and pedal to Okitsu to try to explain to some probably irate American that unless he had a reservation there simply was no room for him. It was unenviable duty at best, and it was not made easier by the elder Mr. Mochizuki's tendency to confuse the words "yesterday" and "tomorrow." Many a disappointed weekender, trying to keep calm in what he considered disastrous circumstances, finally dissolved in rage on being advised that there would be a room for him if he would come yesterday.

Isako's father also found himself thrust into another role for which he was totally unprepared. He has not forgotten the first occasion. A group of men arrived, and he was summoned to their room. Their spokesman, a baby-faced blond, was disarmingly direct. "Papa-san," he said, "get us some women."

Despite a great desire to be helpful, Mr. Mochizuki protested. Protests were in vain.

He then phoned the police, for Japanese police are supposed to be able to cope with any situation.

"Send them to a brothel," the chief commanded.

"I'll bring them to you," Mr. Mochizuki suggested hopefully, "and you can direct them."

"Under no circumstances!" roared the chief. "You keep them away from here!"

And that is how Mr. Mochizuki came to be regarded as a sort of patron saint in several of Shimizu's better bagnios.

The Occupation authorities had, of course, prohibited this sort of thing. They had prohibited all unofficial contact with the Japanese people, and consorting with the opposite sex was clearly unofficial. But this was not one of the most successfully enforced of Occupation orders, and American men frequently brought their Japanese girl friends to the Minaguchi-ya.

Innkeeper Mochizuki remembers the attendant difficulties. "Sometimes in the middle of the night we'd hear a Military Police jeep, and then, while I found it very difficult to unlock the door, Isako and the maids would run to the rooms and get the girls out of bed. Sometimes we hid them in our own closets, and sometimes we slipped them through the garden and along the beach walk to some other houses we owned." He sighed. "An innkeeper has all sorts of problems."

Occupation officials also went through the inn and placed neatly lettered signs over every faucet. "This water," they announced, "is unfit for drinking or brushing teeth."

There were, generally speaking, two reactions to this. There were those who regarded with cynicism any pronouncement by any military agency. They sampled the water reflectively, and failing to drop dead on the spot, continued to drink it copiously whenever they felt thirsty. There is no record that any of them suffered any ill effects.

There was another group, about equally large, who accepted the dictum joyously, without reservation. With MacArthur on their side, they took no liquid but bourbon or Scotch during their stay, and found a new thrill in brushing their teeth.

As for food, almost everyone arrived laden with snacks from the Post Exchange—Vienna sausage, cheese spreads, and cookies—but again there were two methods of using these indigestibles.

Some ate them. This group consisted largely of bachelor girls, forlorn specimens who had swarmed to Japan to type for and minister to thousands of lonely soldiers on a hostile shore, only to find that the enemy had lost the war but won the men. Already bitter, they were ready to believe the worst of anything that came out of a Japanese kitchen and they refused to relinquish their rations even to be warmed. They ate cold snacks for lunch, for dinner, and again for breakfast. The gentler ones brushed their teeth with Coca-Cola. As the weekend wore on, they looked increasingly bilious.

The other group summoned Isako as soon as they were installed in their rooms, loaded their PX treasures into her arms, and, making it clear they never wanted to see them again, threw themselves on her mercy. After the first distressing weeks, she never failed them.

Difficult though it was to get food, her guests ate well: sukiyaki, succulent strips of beef simmered with vegetables; *tempura*, fat shrimp golden-browned in sweet oil; and for breakfast, fresh eggs.

"The MP's scolded us for serving food," says Mochizuki, "but we couldn't help ourselves. These people were our guests, and they begged for *tempura* and sukiyaki. Sometimes they even missed their trains for it. I remember a man named Fleming who refused to leave his sukiyaki to catch the last local back to Tokyo. By the time he finished, it was even too late to go to Shizuoka to catch the last express, so he and Isako's father flagged down the express here at Okitsu. It was the first time an express had been stopped in Okitsu since the days of Inouye, and the railroad was very upset about it. After that, every time the station master saw Fleming arrive, he would beg him not to do it again."

One thing that made it easy for members of the Occupation to come to the Minaguchi-ya was that it was so cheap. In the postwar inflation and shortages that gripped Japan, money lost its value and only things mattered. With well-stocked Post Exchanges at their disposal, Occupationaires had things in abundance, things exciting and desirable to people who could scarcely remember good candy, good soap, and good cigarettes. Many an American discovered that he could convert two or three cartons of cigarettes, purchased tax-free at sixty or seventy cents, into a weekend of freedom and luxury. It was illegal, of course, but all the more interesting for that.

Some of us regulars came to know the Mochizuki family. Isako first, because she was our hostess; she greeted us all, and made us feel that the Minaguchi-ya was a warm and friendly place.

Her children, bright and attractive, played in the garden or on the beach. Those of us who kept returning to the inn sometimes badgered the oldest boy, Yasuo, into walking with us: one bucolic day he escorted me to the national experimental farm, home of the cherry trees which adorn the city of Washington. Over the years we watched Yasuo fill out his navy-blue high-school uniform; congratulated him as he changed to the scarcely distinguishable uniform of his university in Tokyo; smiled bravely with his mother when, degree achieved, he put on the monkey suit of a bellboy to start at the bottom in Tokyo's newest chrome and marble hotel; and sighed with pleasure when he progressed to gray flannel and a place behind the reservation desk.

We took the same delight in watching his younger brothers and sisters grow up, all the way down to Chikue, a baby of four when I first saw her. We fed her candy and cake, which she survived to become, one day when our backs were turned, a pert and pretty teen-ager.

We will never forget the children's grandmother, Isako's mother-in-law, the Queen Mother of the Minaguchi-ya, who years ago as a little girl nestled in the arms of her grandfather, Hanjuro I, while he chatted with Jirocho. She is *Obaasan*, Grandmother, to the family, and she is *Obaasan* to us. A visit to the inn never seems complete until she finds time to stop by and greet us. She enters softly, a little figure in dark kimono, and she drops to her knees, more slowly than she used to, and bows very low. Her hair is white and brushed straight back, and her skin is soft and clear as a child's. When she straightens up, her face is dimpled in a smile.

"I was very frightened of Americans at first," she said once, "but no longer. I remember one man especially because he seemed so big and fearsome, until we became acquainted. Like me, he had false teeth, and he gave me a special brush for cleaning them. I still use it.

"Americans have never caused us any trouble," she goes on, "though some complain when we close the shutters at night." I wince, for over the years no one has complained more loudly than I about this Japanese habit of shuttering the windows even in mid-summer.

Obaasan is approaching eighty, "but a person has to keep working." She rises every morning at five, and begins the day by wiping her body with cold water. She opens the doors and prays to the life-giving sun, and then, at the altar in her room, to Buddha and her ancestors, making a little offering of rice and tea. In her prayers she always includes Prince Saionji, "because he has no relatives around here and we considered him part of our family." After these prayers she frequently visits the five small Shinto shrines in the inn and garden; though she may sometimes delegate this duty to the oldest maid, she never fails to make the rounds in person on the first, fifteenth, and twenty-eighth of every month, when each of the gods is offered a cup of saké. She worries a little about the continuation of these religious observances: of the younger generation, the girls are amenable but the boys seem indifferent.

Without any real responsibility, she nevertheless keeps a sharp eye on the ten maids. "In my mother's time we had many more," she says, "but no inn can afford such a large staff today. In the old days, servants felt a greater responsibility than they do now. They never complained in the busy season, and before a girl resigned she always found someone to take her place. Still we seldom have servant trouble, and I can't remember having to scold a maid—just an occasional reminder about manners, like going to one's knees to open a door. We never hire girls from Okitsu, and farm girls, though it takes longer to train them, usually turn out better than city girls.

"Used to be, most of the maids were older women, probably widows. Then, girls married at fifteen or sixteen. Now they marry at twenty-two or twenty-three and most of our maids are young girls saving money for marriage. In their spare time, some of them take lessons in the old arts of homemaking, like flower arrangement. Of course, the backbone of the staff are women who have been with us for twenty or twenty-five years."

Among the staff it is always Yoshi who springs first to my mind: stocky, bald-headed Yoshi, who seizes our bags the moment we appear at the gate, who puts away our shoes and brings them to us when we leave, who summons us to the bath, tempers the water for us, and scrubs our backs. Yoshi, too, has served at the Minaguchi-ya a quarter of a century.

We guests never mingled much, even those of us who came repeatedly. A Japanese inn has little use for public rooms and in Occupation days the Minaguchi-ya had none. (Today, bowing to the times, it has a small television lounge.) In a country as densely populated as Japan, few things are as desirable as privacy, and that is what a good inn offers. A guest's suite is his living room, dining room, and bedroom. This was fine with those of us who sought out the Minaguchi-ya, for generally we wanted a respite from the rest of the military population. Long, lazy days brought many of us out to investigate the neighborhood, but we remained with the companions of our choice.

In summertime we swam, or lolled on the sand while almost naked kids played around us or splashed in the surf. If we were caught in the water by MP's come to patrol this forbidden beach, we simply swam far enough out to be unrecognizable and, floating on gentle swells, outwaited the intruders.

We strolled along the beach where men were building fishing boats to replace the fleet worn out during the war. We saw women, each under a yoke of wooden buckets, carrying water from the sea, making salt just as they had in Kaempfer's day and long before. In those early postwar years, salt was expensive, if you could buy it.

In midsummer on that same beach we watched the end of the *Bon* festival. While young people ringed a musicians' tower in centuries-old folk dances, the souls that three nights earlier had been welcomed back to their earthly homes by little fires before each doorway were now returned to the realm of spirits on hundreds of tiny boats, each with its lantern, floating through the surf and out to sea until their lights disappeared in the darkness.

I began to feel that I was discovering Japan . . .

A friend and I walked along the Tokaido, found Saionji's little villa between its fishermen neighbors, and stood in the rooms where a tired old man had fought a losing battle. We went further, to the edge of town, and came upon the burnt-out ruins of Inouye's mansion, and climbed his Rice Bran Mountain to the raw concrete base on top, put there for his bronze statue. The statue is gone, hauled away and melted down during the war.

We climbed the hills behind the town. With Fuji looming over us we wandered among tangerine groves fragrant with blossoms in June, heavy with fruit in December.

At a *Bon* festival young people ring a musicians' tower in centuries-old folk dances (*a print by Maekawa*)

The inn survives the war and the Occupation

We pushed up the dusty old road along the Okitsu River and were rewarded by finding a two-hundred-fifty-year-old saké brewery, founded by a family who, like the Mochizukis, had been retainers of the Takeda clan, and who had settled here when that clan went down to defeat. The head of the present generation welcomed us, showed us the fastidious way in which saké is made, and in the dim light of the aging room, drew from a vat a big cool cupful of his finest wine. We floated back to the inn.

We climbed the stone steps to Seikenji, and sometimes, while my companion offered a prayer, I felt that I could sense the thrust of thirteen centuries of Buddhism on the lusty story of Japan. We saw the little room where Ieyasu studied as a boy, and the apartment where the last Shogun passed a night on the road to surrender, and where the Emperor Meiji stopped on his way to Tokyo to lead his nation into the modern world. We stood where the steep, tiered side of the mountain forms a natural amphitheatre, and looked up at the stone statues of the five hundred Rakan, those disciples of Buddha who were appointed to save the world; weather and mold have softened their features, and some of them are chipped and battered, but they sit in the dim light that filters through great cedars like a silent audience following the course of a drama. We played the fortune-telling game with the Rakan: one starts at random and counts as many of the figures as he is old; ending on a happy face means a happy future, ending on a grim face is equally prophetic. It seemed to me that the results were ambiguous. As we left Seikenji we halted at the top of the steps and looked across the bay towards Miho.

We skirted the bay to reach Miho, its crashing surf, its black sand, its rugged pines bent by incessant wind from the sea. We saw the very pine on which the angel hung her feathered robe when she went for a swim, we walked the beach where she danced to recover it from the fisherman who made off with it (there are memorials to single out these points of interest). We got sand in our shoes, and we found the perfect view of Fuji.

We came across the place where in midwinter they grow strawberries as big as eggs—the sheer face of Kunozan, with plants wedged in chinks between flat rocks so that they draw warmth through the night from sun soaked up during the day. And having thus found Kunozan we climbed its one thousand and thirty-nine steps to the medieval stronghold on its summit, and the place where Ieyasu was laid to rest.

We hired a charcoal-fired taxi whose rear-mounted conversion unit belched smoke and kept the back seat deliciously warm in winter, and, climbing through undulant rows of tea that crawl along the slopes like great green caterpillars, we came to the high plateau of Nippon-daira and found stretched out at our feet one of Japan's most breath-taking panoramas: the slender hook of Miho, the harbor it encloses, the softly curving coastline and its gray tile-roofed towns —Shimizu, Okitsu, Yui, Kambara, and on towards Tokyo along the Tokaido—the wall of green mountains that shoulders those towns against the ocean, and, above and behind it all, the sheer bewitching force of Fuji.

Returning to the Minaguchi-ya, we were welcomed back with tea and courtesy, and once again the inn's warm familiar walls created for us a private world . . .

We guests didn't realize it, but the facts of early postwar economics that permitted us a sybaritic weekend on the proceeds from a couple of cartons of cigarettes showed another, harsher face to our host at the Minaguchi-ya.

"Before the war," says Mochizuki, "we were rich enough so that it was a matter of indifference whether or not the inn had customers. The income from our other properties was more than enough.

"But after the war, things were different We lost our farmlands in the agricultural reform. Taxes became so heavy that we had to sell piece after piece of our other property. The inn itself was old and obsolete, much of it having been built by my great-grandfather, Hanjuro I. All at once, we were comparatively poor.

"It was a shock but now I know that it was good for us. It was good for me and it was good for my sons. We developed a new sense of purpose and self-reliance.

"It didn't come at once and it didn't come easily. When I finished my work with Baron Harada and took over the inn I had little interest in it. During the war it was inactive. For a year and a half after the war ended I didn't even apply for an innkeeper's license, and our only guests were members of the Occupation. I watched unhappily as our estate slipped away, and it seemed to me that the best course would be to sell the inn and live on what was left. I thought I might take up golf.

"I can't say exactly when the inn began to take on meaning for me. I give much of the credit to friends—old patrons, and people like Isako's father—who kept urging me to keep a tradition alive. Somehow, slowly, the Minaguchi-ya became important to me, and making it successful again became a challenge. I didn't have money to rebuild, but I borrowed and went ahead. It was a new experience. Once bankers bowed to me. Now I bowed to them. I found it invigorating."

Mochizuki made a master plan for reconstructing the entire inn. First the central portion was demolished and the heart of a new inn rose in its place. Three or four years later the right wing was replaced, and, recently, the left wing. As a new Minaguchi-ya emerged and prospered, Mochizuki took a step which was at once a pledge and a fulfillment. He took the hereditary name of Hanjuro, to become fourth of the line begun by his great-grandfather, the man who piloted the inn through its transition from feudal to modern times.

As I watched the old rooms disappear I am afraid I sometimes grew a little sentimental. I revel in the new tile pool, but I remember with special affection the big wooden tub I climbed into for my first Japanese bath.

And the Hollyhock Room: it was so long the inn's finest suite, and I remember how proud I was, years ago, when Isako first ushered me into it; I felt that I had been accepted at the Minaguchi-ya. Now it has been extended and rebuilt into a sleek banquet hall, big enough to accommodate two hundred people. It is still called Hollyhock Room, a triumph of tradition in which I take some small pride, though probably I had nothing to do with it. The name derives from the crest with which the room is decorated, the hollyhock crest of Ieyasu and his line. I argued that this was a link with history which must be maintained. My adversary, whom I never met, was a wealthy businessman and good customer of the inn. He pointed out that the Japanese word for hollyhock, which is *aoi*, also means blue or green, and, by extension, the pallid face of someone who has drunk too much. To try to hold a gay party in a room named *Aoi*, he maintained, would be to labor under a hex. But the room is still called *Aoi*, though Saionji's son-in-law, who so often lost his temper there, would no longer recognize it.

Other things have changed at the Minaguchi-ya, too. There came the day when Yoshi packed an old straw suitcase and reluctantly departed. He promised to come back for visits, but he was going a long way and a good many tears were shed as he said good-bye. "I hated to see him go," said Mochizuki. "He liked working here, and we liked to have him around. But he was seventy, and his son and daughter-in-law thought it reflected unfavorably on them to have their father working at that age. He finally gave in to their insistence . . . He was very unhappy. He also had to say good-bye to a girl friend in Shimizu."

Patrons have changed, too. The Occupation and Occupationaires have receded into history, though foreign guests still appear from time to time: people who make Japan their home, and ambassadors, and occasionally a tourist who escapes the standard tours. The New York Giants baseball team stopped by, too, during a post-season exhibition tour of Japan back in the days before they emigrated to San Francisco. One of their stops was the city of Shizuoka, at which point the young men let it be known that they were tired of bathing in tubs, and yearned for a shower. Frantic researchers discovered that the Minaguchi-ya boasted the only showers in the area, so Mochizuki invited the team over for a garden party and shower baths.

But once again, most of the Minaguchi-ya's customers are Japanese. They are not altogether the same people as came before the war: the old nobility no longer show up, for their fortunes have slipped away from them along with their titles. More than ever, businessmen are the inn's most important guests.

"When I was debating whether to sell the inn," says Mochizuki, "I remembered some of our long-time patrons. I remembered the Itos. I remembered that diary I had seen at their house in Nagoya, record of an Ito who stopped here almost three hundred years ago.

"Our own family records have been swept away by fire, and more than ten generations back we are uncertain of our ancestors' names or exactly when they were born and died. But the Minaguchi-ya exists to prove that they lived and worked here by the Tokaido. All those years travelers have sought shelter here, and found rest, and gone on their way refreshed."

The twentieth master of the Minaguchi-ya tapped his cigarette and watched the smoke spiral upward.

"I didn't want to break the chain," he said.

1957

CHAPTER FIFTEEN

In which the Emperor and Empress of Japan honor the inn as its guests

PRINCIPAL CHARACTERS

The Emperor of Japan
The Empress of Japan

and among the people of the inn:

Mochizuki Hanjuro IV, *twentieth master of the Minaguchi-ya*
Isako, *his wife*
Yasuo, *their eldest son*
Obaasan, *Mochizuki's mother*
Yoshi, *formerly bath attendant at the Minaguchi-ya, invited to return to the staff during the Imperial visit*

The Imperial crest

RUMORS WERE HEARD in July, consultations began in August, and official notification came on the sixteenth of September. The Minaguchi-ya had been chosen to play host to the Emperor and Empress of Japan when they came to Shizuoka City for the National Athletic Meet of 1957. It was an event which would bring young athletes from every section of the country. Their Majesties would open the games. They would arrive at the Minaguchi-ya on the twenty-fifth of October for two days.

No greater honor, no greater responsibility, can come to any Japanese inn. From the day of notification, there was little rest for the staff of the Minaguchi-ya or for the Mochizukis themselves.

They divided the work. Mr. Mochizuki, Hanjuro IV, took charge of preparing the rooms. His wife, Isako, arranged for the day-to-day requirements of service.

Their Majesties' apartment would be the Minaguchi-ya's finest, the suite called *Akebono*, Dawn. It lies at the base of the wide flat U of the inn. Though the wings of the Minaguchi-ya rise to two stories, *Akebono*, in the middle, is on ground level, commanding a view of the whole garden as it sweeps towards the sea. Behind its two spacious living rooms are a dressing room, a tiled lavatory, an airy bath, a compartmented toilet, a big foyer, and a large waiting room facing a pleasant inner garden. *Akebono* adds up to quiet luxury.

On the first of October, *Akebono* was taken out of use. Workmen moved in.

The inner doors, which set off the rooms from their enclosed terraces, were lifted from their grooves and carried away to a work-room. The paper was stripped off, the wood was cleansed, and new paper, soft, strong, and white, was meticulously pasted on the frames.

The straw *tatami* mats of the floor were taken up. They would come back with new covers, made, like the paper of the doors, in remote villages famed for centuries because their craftsmanship has been the finest in all Japan.

Men mounted ladders to wash the ceiling, the wide boards of natural pine that stretch, without knot or flaw, from one end of the room to the other. They scrubbed with soap, and they scrubbed with disinfectant, and they gave the same treatment to the wood-work of the walls.

Every square inch of plaster was ripped off, from the foyer straight through to the terraces. Every wall was newly plastered, and sur-faced in the Japanese way with the warm texture of fine brown sand.

In the bath, the sunken tub of tile was ripped out and replaced by a new tub of satiny white cypress. A tub of tile is coolly hand-some modernity; a tub of cypress is warm and timeless indulgence.

All this renovation was Mochizuki's responsibility.

Isako was busy too. She kept a watchful eye on the seamstresses as they made new bedding, three thick pads for each Imperial bed, two light quilts for covers. They fluffed the softest cotton, and sheathed it in rich white silk softly figured in felicitous designs.

They made new uniforms for all the staff: kimonos for the maids in the deep purple of ripe eggplant, with obi sashes of golden yellow; starched whites for the chef, his four cooks, and his kitchen helpers; and navy-blue jackets for the other men, with the inn's name on the lapels, and its crest, given by the Lord of Satsuma, on the back.

They made an extra jacket for Yoshi. His years of service had earned him the right to be on hand for these triumphant days, and so he was called back from retirement. He came quickly, glad to be back at work, proud to be wanted.

Isako summoned the suppliers and ordered new dishes. The soup bowls would be the house's old and treasured lacquer, but all the china had to be new.

The menus were planned. This was the chef's responsibility and he rose to it nobly, but there were long and earnest consultations between him and Mochizuki. What local specialties should be included? What seasonal delicacies would be at their peak? And since the Emperor is a teetotaler, what subtle adjustments to create dinners at which no saké would be poured?

"We appreciated that the Emperor prefers Western foods," Mochizuki said later, "but the Minaguchi-ya is a Japanese inn, and it would have been quite out of character for us to serve Western dishes, even if we could have prepared them properly. What we tried to do was to create Japanese menus which would appeal to a Western palate." (The complete menus that they worked out, from the first evening's dinner to the final basket lunch, are shown in the back of this book.)

It is not only in the matter of food that the Emperor's tastes have been trained away from things Japanese: the whole style of life at the palace is Western. Nor in this new, secular age would it seem proper to accommodate the Emperor, as his forebears were accommodated, in temples; indeed, the temples, having lost their government subsidies, are scarcely in a position to dispense lavish hospitality. For years, whenever the present Emperor traveled, he was housed in the temples of our times—prefectural office buildings, schoolhouses, or public halls, temporarily fitted out with beds and other furniture. It can be assumed that the Emperor was made reasonably comfortable, but there were never enough beds for his chamberlains, and those travel-weary attendants finally tried the daring experiment of an inn, which could offer Japanese-style comfort to the whole party. The Emperor, who had not stayed in an inn since his boyhood, was so pleased to rediscover their allure that thereafter inns were prescribed for all Imperial jaunts.

There have been other changes as well. Before the war, ordinary people were afraid to gaze on the Emperor's countenance. He could scarcely appear before his own people. Since the war, millions have seen and cheered him as a symbol of national unity.

On October 9, palace officials came to the Minaguchi-ya to check the menus, and pronounced themselves pleased. They made one change: they added fresh milk. With this they succeeded in startling the chef, for most Japanese still do not consider milk a food for adults. They might also have succeeded in prostrating the local health department, had not Mochizuki speedily called on prefectural officials for help; they made arrangements to have milk rushed twice daily from their model research dairy, an hour away.

Even without the milk problem, local health authorities were almost overcome by their sense of responsibility. To Mochizuki, there seemed to be an inspector behind every door. They tested the water and found it clean and pure, but they insisted that the well be newly concreted anyway. They poked into the kitchen and were unable to make a suggestion of any kind: the chef snorted with satisfaction.

The police, too, were everywhere. They scanned blueprints, went over the grounds, checked the neighborhood, working out their plans to guard His Majesty.

In the flutter from morning till night, only Junzo and Chikue, the youngest children and still living at home, remained cool. Teen-aged, modern, and emancipated, they chided their parents for becoming so excited, and when they came home from school to find that no one had remembered to prepare their supper, they were indignant; their protests went unheeded as arrival day grew closer.

Obaasan, their grandmother, was as busy as anyone, and she worked the same long hours, but she found time to unearth an old book with a record of other visits by members of the Imperial family since the revolution—not the Emperor, of course, but at least his sisters and his cousins and his aunts, and his male kin as well. When visitors came, on business or merely because they were curious about the great preparations, she would sometimes seize the chance to rest a few moments. She would bring out the old book, turn its pages, and read the great names. "No one else thinks this book is important," she would murmur, not quite accurately, "but I've kept it all these years. See, Princess Arisugawa used to spend a month here every spring . . ."

Red carpet arrived and was cut and fitted to cover the polished floor and *tatami* mats of the entrance. There had to be carpet because, like no other guests the inn had ever received, the Emperor and Empress would wear their shoes into the foyer, where a chair and a bootjack would be provided.

The workmen in *Akebono* suite finished and moved out, leaving it fresh and glistening. Furniture was moved in, new tables, chairs, and mirrors for the dressing room, new stools and buckets for the bath, and in the living room, a radio, a television receiver, sofa and chairs (all new, of course): there would be that much concession to the Western living habits of Japan's sovereign.

Into the other room, which at night would become bedroom, went the Minaguchi-ya's treasured old gold screens, to be placed around the Imperial beds. The Imperial bedding was laid in the closets.

In the garden, curried and combed, the autumn-softened green was brightened with a clump of huge yellow chrysanthemums, a gift from one of the inn's long-time patrons.

More chrysanthemums were delivered for the inn's entrance hall, prize plants from members of the Okitsu Flower Club, big blooms standing proudly erect, miniatures cascading from their pots.

On the twenty-third of October the inn was closed to the public. Every room gleamed. The first of the palace chamberlains arrived, vanguard of the staff that would bulge the inn. Once more everything was checked.

On the twenty-fourth the four oldest children left their work or their college classes and came home from Tokyo. The family was together. Morning coats and trousers were pressed, kimonos were laid out, and the chamberlains gave their final drill in the demanding etiquette of the occasion. They emphasized that none of the inn's family or servants would be permitted to speak directly to Their Majesties, not even a word of greeting or farewell. Preferably there would be no circumstance requiring words, but if something had to be said it was to be said through a member of the palace staff.

Mochizuki wrestled a problem. It was he, the host, who would, wordlessly, welcome the Emperor and escort him from his car to his rooms. A critical moment, the chamberlains pointed out, would come in the entry, for there Mochizuki was to shed his shoes but the Emperor was not to remove his. There were any number of dire possibilities, said the chamberlains, none of which must be allowed to happen. Mochizuki must not let the Emperor get the idea that this was the spot to remove the Imperial shoes. Mochizuki must not fumble with his shoes and keep the Emperor waiting. And the chamberlains didn't even have to say what any Japanese gentleman would know, that it would be a nasty bungle if Mochizuki were not to get out of his shoes neatly and gracefully, if a shoe were to fall over, or, heaven forbid, land across the other.

Mochizuki's problem was that his shoes were tight, and it is not easy to step smoothly out of tight shoes. Of his sons' shoes, he could wear only Yasuo's, but they seemed loose, so loose, in fact, that it occurred to Mochizuki that he might walk right out of them while guiding the Emperor in from the street. On the night of the twenty-fourth, Hanjuro IV was still pondering this problem when he went to bed.

The twenty-fifth was warm but overcast. Early in the morning every house along the highway put out the national flag and a paper lantern likewise blazoned with the Rising Sun, though there were sprinkles of rain which sometimes made shopkeepers scurry to bring these emblems briefly under cover. The gate of the Minaguchi-ya was bracketed by flags and lanterns.

At 11:25 a special train thundered through Okitsu bound for Shizuoka City, flags streaming from the locomotive. There were coaches for railway officials, for palace officials, and the press. Then came a car marked with the Imperial insignia, the sixteen-petaled gold chrysanthemum. Railwaymen who work this car have their fingernails specially clipped so they will not mar its delicate lacquer-work.

The train crew, had they been asked, could have furnished insight into the tension that had been building up behind the gray wall of the Minaguchi-ya. "Supervising this train is hard on the nerves," the man in charge has said. "Once we tightened the springs too much, and the result was most embarrassing. The Empress became train-sick and had to move to another coach."

The engineer has confided: "At departure time my throat is dry, my voice is hoarse, my heart beats fast. My nerves are taut until we are safely at our destination."

In *Akebono* suite health officials had decreed a last-minute chore. The door fittings, the faucets, the light-switch covers were being wiped with alcohol. There was grim determination that the Emperor pick up no bug in Okitsu.

Since the athletic meet would not open until the following day, Their Majesties were scheduled to spend the afternoon visiting a hospital endowed by the Emperor's mother, and a factory considered a model of its kind. The factory was in Kambara, and so they motored back along the Tokaido and through Okitsu before they stopped for the night. The Emperor passed the house of his old ally, Saionji. He passed below Seikenji, the gray old temple flag-bedecked but silent and withdrawn as if remembering earlier days when sovereigns rested within its gates. The Emperor passed the Minaguchi-ya, moved down the flag-lined highway.

The crowds were sparse for this unheralded passage, and jovial policemen urged those on hand to step up to the curb so they could get a good look. The old folks shook their heads. This was a far cry from prewar days when it was almost an act of treason to look at all.

After the motorcade passed by, onlookers were rewarded with another pageant. More than two weeks earlier, the flag of the national athletic meet had been borne from Kobe, scene of the previous year's games, and, in a ritual based on that surrounding the Olympic torch, runners had since been carrying it towards this year's site. Their route had been a tortuous one, designed to take the flag through almost every town in Shizuoka Prefecture, so that they had doubled around Shizuoka City and now were approaching it from the direction opposite to Kobe.

It had been carried by relays, a new team taking over at every town and village. By this means, according to officials, 12,325 men had been involved during the 875-mile course. There had been such a scramble for the honor that it had been necessary to break the short trip from Yui to Okitsu by setting up two intermediate stations so that extra teams could go into action. This decision also had its humane overtones, in view of the number of elderly athletes who insisted on doing their bit.

Now the flag passed through Okitsu to applause from the small crowd. Tomorrow it would be trotted into the stadium, with the Emperor in attendance, and the games would begin.

It was still two hours before the Emperor would return, but slowly the sidewalks began to fill. Schools let out, and children lined the curb, each youngster clutching a small flag. Grownups began to jockey for good positions but, despite the obvious advantage, no one appeared at second-story windows. An old taboo against looking down on the Emperor remains strong.

The reserved spaces close to the Minaguchi-ya's gate began to fill, each section distinguished by the color of ribbon worn in the lapel or on the breast. Red denoted officers of the town, stiff and proper in their cutaways. Purple marked families of war dead. Pink designated club officials, those who headed the time-honored fraternities of fishermen, of farmers, and of youths, and the new but formidable association of women. There were yellow ribbons for men and women over seventy, and an especially good spot for them, for age is a certain passport to respect; many of them arrived on the arms of children or grandchildren, but once they were suitably installed with old friends, the younger generation slipped away to unreserved space down the line.

At frequent intervals the police loudspeaker boomed a report on the Imperial progress and the latest estimate of arrival time in Okitsu. Police jeeps rolled slowly down the street, each one causing an abortive flutter of flags. All regular traffic had been halted outside the town.

The police were at their stations in front and back of the inn, linked by walkie-talkie radios. In addition to the entire Okitsu force, there were seventy prefectural policemen among the crowd, plus an undisclosed number of roving plainclothesmen.

Now, between the patrolmen who flanked the Minaguchi-ya's gate, Mochizuki appeared, backed by some of the palace staff. The original plan had been that the Emperor's car would be driven through the gate to the inn's entrance, but town officials had pleaded for a more intimate encounter, and it was finally agreed that the car would be halted in the street, giving at least a few people a chance to see the Imperial couple as they crossed the sidewalk. A loud-speaker truck moved past: "The Emperor has entered Okitsu." There were ominous drops of rain but no one left.

The crowd strained to see down the street, its steady murmur growing louder, every flag in motion. A police jeep, and then another, went by very slowly. Two motorcycle policemen appeared, moving just fast enough to keep their machines erect.

And then it came, the big Mercedes-Benz, a regal automobile with a regal disdain for fashion. Its angular black top loomed a foot higher than the submissively curved sedans that crawled behind, its maroon body was big and boxy. It bore the gold chrysanthemum.

It glided to a stop at the Minaguchi-ya's gate and a footman opened a door. A motherly woman and a little man in gray flannel climbed out.

Mochizuki bowed low, the town dignitaries bowed low, and their Emperor bowed in return. They straightened, and there was a moment's paralysis as the leaders of Okitsu shifted mental gears to meet the still alien requirements of the new age. Then their cheer went up, self-conscious but sincere, and over their heads the crowd saw a gray felt hat raised in acknowledgment, a gesture equally self-conscious and equally sincere.

Mochizuki, bowing again, caught the Emperor's attention, guided him through the gate. The entire family and staff of the inn, lining the drive, bowed their greeting. In the entrance hall, Mochizuki stepped nimbly out of his shoes and kept the Emperor in motion.

"The chamberlains complimented me on that moment," he reminisced later. "I had finally worn my own shoes, tight as they were, but I laced them very loosely. And, fortunately, I wasn't nervous. I have nerves of steel."

He smiled, remembering that small triumph, and then continued. "I showed the Emperor to the chair and bootjack, expecting he would sit down, but he only stood against the back of the chair and pulled his shoes off in the jack. I caught my breath. Instead of landing neatly, they rolled half across the room. For one ghastly moment my impulse was to retrieve them, but I restrained myself and showed him down the corridor to his suite. I bowed him into the rooms—I never did see his face that first day, I was so busy bowing—and then I retreated."

Until the Emperor and Empress left, two days later, no member of the family or of the staff of the inn entered those rooms, for Their Majesties, as is the custom, were served solely by their own servants from the palace. Food was delivered to the door by Isako and the two senior maids. By decree of the health authorities, the trays were draped in white cloth and the women carrying them wore surgical masks.

Isako made the first trip almost at once, bearing the welcoming tea and sweets. The cakes were the first of the local products to which the Emperor was treated. Said Mochizuki, "The easy thing would have been to order sweets from one of Tokyo's famous shops, but I knew that the Emperor gets those all the time, and I wanted to give him something different. That first day we served miniature cakes originated in Okitsu, and called *miyasama manju*. About fifty years ago they were served to an Imperial prince when he stopped at Seikenji, and that's how they got their name, *miyasama* for prince and *manju* meaning sweet bean-cake. The prince liked them and I'm happy to say that the Emperor did, too."

As dusk settled over the town, Rising Sun lanterns were lighted in front of every shop. As far as the eye could see, from the river, past the Minaguchi-ya's guarded gate, and down around Seikenji's curve, the highway was lined with friendly, festive pods of light.

Inside the inn, there was bustle and intentness. Every room was filled with palace functionaries. Even the old Ivy suite, still comfortable but now almost lost behind newer buildings and relegated to being a sewing room and maids' bedroom, was brushed up and once again held guests, the palace chauffeurs.

At six-thirty a little masked procession delivered the first course of dinner to *Akebono* suite. The Emperor and Empress, dining alone, praised the food, and, like Ieyasu, three and a half centuries before, they particularly liked the *Okitsu-tai*, sea bream partially sun-dried, broiled over charcoal.

After dinner the town proclaimed its welcome with fireworks, rockets over the beach and a set-piece mounted on a boat offshore. Unfortunately, the Emperor, having briefly retired from the living room, missed the whole display, but the Empress watched it and expressed her pleasure.

The Imperial couple, early to bed, were up at six, but the inn's staff was hustling long before that. There was, for instance, the matter of the newspapers. All the Tokyo and Shizuoka dailies were rushed to the Minaguchi-ya, but the health authorities, doggedly alert, had ordered that before being delivered to the Emperor they must be sterilized with steam or disinfectant solution. Either method resulted in very soggy journals, and it took several of the maids, using all the electric irons in the laundry room, to press them dry and smooth again.

After breakfast, the Emperor went out the garden gate to check first-hand this bit of ocean. A marine biologist by inclination, the Emperor of Japan by fate, he was now in his element, and he moved nimbly across a rocky beach, his chamberlains scrambling unsteadily behind. At ocean's edge he was a scientist, and none of his entourage intruded with poetic remarks about the pines of Miho, or pointed out, down the beach in front of Seikenji and Saionji's house, the cluster of offshore rocks where a stele proclaims that his father often swam. When he had used up the little time that was his own, the Emperor returned to the inn, and minutes later, when the big Mercedes-Benz swung out of the gate, he was back in frozen-faced character as the Emperor of Japan, waving stiffly to his people as he rode with the Empress at his side to open the games.

They returned in the afternoon for another night's rest at the Minaguchi-ya. That evening the Grand Chamberlain met with Mochizuki to present gifts from the Emperor in return for the hospitality which had been shown him. There was a ceremonial saké cup, in brilliant red lacquer with a gold chrysanthemum heavily embossed in the shallow bowl: it would become one of the Minaguchi-ya's cherished possessions. There was a box of cigarettes, cardboard-tipped and bearing the Imperial emblem but filled with notably cheap tobacco (a little economy the Imperial household can indulge since the Emperor does not smoke): these would be smoked by Mochizuki and favored friends. And, carefully wrapped in the finest vellum-like paper, there was money—not much, it is true (a sum "about the size of a sparrow's tears"), but Mochizuki had not entertained his Emperor with thought of remuneration.

When Mochizuki returned to his office with the Emperor's gifts, the family and staff pressed in to see them. They were pleased with themselves, for everything had gone beautifully. They had another, more intimate, reason for elation: there was a letter from Yoshi's son saying that he had come to understand his father's desire to continue working at the Minaguchi-ya; there would be no more objections; he could stay as long as he wished.

Next morning all the people of the inn lined up before the entrance, and when the Emperor emerged he spoke to them there. For the Empress and himself, he expressed appreciation for their stay, and for all the kindly labor that had made it possible. *Obaasan* wept with gratitude.

Their Majesties climbed into their limousine and rolled away. Once again, most of the population of Okitsu had gathered in the street. They cheered their Emperor and Empress off that morning as they had welcomed them two days before, but now they did not disperse. Only a few went back to tending shops or to household chores. Most of them turned through the gate of the Minaguchi-ya.

They came by the hundreds. They filed through the entrance, across the red carpet, past the chair and bootjack, down the gleaming corridor, into the Emperor's suite. They gazed at the bedding on which he had slept, the bath in which he had bathed, the rooms in which he had lived.

The name of those rooms was changed now. It was no longer *Akebono,* but *Miyuki.* The new name proclaims one more chapter in the fabled history of the Minaguchi-ya. In the pageant of the Tokaido, sometimes turbulent, sometimes peaceful, the inn had sheltered many travelers and now it had sheltered their Emperor. *Miyuki* is a name that breathes good fortune and high honor. It means Imperial Visit.

As the curious continued to press through the doors, the inn's staff settled down to work. Hanjuro IV retired to his office. Yasuo left by the family entrance to board a train which would take him back to the marble and chrome hotel in Tokyo. Isako waved good-bye to her son, and then began to check the linen.

But an inn is truly an inn only when it has guests. Half an hour after the big maroon and black limousine had disappeared down the highway, a saucy little taxi thrust through the gate. Horn blasting, it pushed aside the crowd, achieved the entrance, deposited its passenger. A maid dropped to her knees to welcome him, Yoshi rushed out to take possession of his bags. The Minaguchi-ya was in business again.

The Menus for the Emperor and Empress

Minaguchi-ya, 1957

Each meal served at the inn was accompanied by a menu, hand-written by Mochizuki Hanjuro IV, and a palace attendant was on hand to explain the dishes to Their Majesties.

DINNER, *OCTOBER 25*

HORS D'OEUVRES

Kuri-shioyaki
(chestnuts, oven-browned and salted)

Uzura-dango
(patties of minced quail, simmered in soy sauce, flavored with sugar and salt)

Sazae-tsuboyaki
(turbo, cubed and baked in its own shell with parsley)

Daidai Ayuko Uruka

(fresh caviar of brook trout, salted and served in the half-shell of a bitter orange; this is the type of dish which was served with saké in the days before Western hors d'oeuvres came into fashion)

Daikoku-himejitake Karashi-misokake

(tiny boiled mushrooms in mustard-flavored miso *[fermented bean paste])*

Ikikakimi Taikami-shio-jime Ikura-iri Kaki-namasu Harikuri

(raw sea bream, sliced very thin, delicately salted,° and garnished with red caviar of salmon and fine slivers of persimmon and chestnut)

° The fish must be very fresh—alive when carving begins; it is sliced very thin, and each slice is covered with a sheet of thin, fine, handmade Japanese paper; the paper is sprinkled with salted ice water; when the fish has absorbed a delicate flavor of salt, the paper is removed and the fish is served as indicated above.

SOUP

Supu Shitate Jimaru Kimimaru Tsukane-negi Tsuyu-shoga

(clear soup° with cubes of turtle meat, hard-boiled turtle eggs, chives, and a dash of fresh ginger juice)

° The basic Japanese clear soup is made from shavings of dried bonito, called *katsuobushi;* in this case it was simmered with turtle bones; the meat and eggs were cooked together and added to the soup with tiny, threadlike chives.

SASHIMI
(Raw Fish)

Ise-ebi Botantsukuri

("peony lobster"; lobster tails dipped in boiling water, then sectioned and arranged in the form of a peony flower)

The Menus for the Emperor and Empress

Kampachi Ito-tsukui
(raw slivers of kampachi, *a much-prized fish of the horse-mackerel family)*

both garnished with:

Suisenji-nori
(chopped fresh-water moss unique to an old pond at Suisenji in Kumamoto)

Sutori-myoga
(tiny flowers of the myoga *plant, lightly vinegared)*

and both served with:

Tosa-joyu
(soy souce thickened by boiling with shavings of katsuobushi*)*

MAIN DISHES

Hinadori Momijiyaki Irina
(thin slices of chicken sautéed with finely chopped green tops of white radish in slightly sweetened soy sauce)

Amatai Okitsuboshi Nishoga
(charcoal-broiled fillets of sea bream*)
* Partly dried in the sun; a famous local product called *Okitsu-tai.*

Buta Shojoni Hosone Daikon Karashi-aji
(Nagasaki-style pork; pork round in slices alternating fat and lean, simmered for one day in water flavored with soy sauce; garnished with thin slices of white radish boiled in the soup, topped with a bit of mustard, and served in a covered bowl with some of the soup)

RICE

Hakuhan

(boiled white rice)

served with the following pickles:

Nasu

(salted baby eggplant)

Nishoga
(fresh young shoots of ginger, lightly vinegared)

Narazuke
(slices of small yellow melon called uri, *pickled in saké lees)*

FRUIT

With this first dinner a large tray of fresh fruits in season—Chinese pears, persimmons, and tangerines—was placed in the Emperor's suite, and thereafter fruit was not served with the meals.

BREAKFAST, *OCTOBER 26*

SOUP

Aka-shiro Miso-shitate Shiromiso Shinshu-miso Taiuwami Oroshi-gobo Kiri-goma
(potage made from miso of both red and white beans; in the soup were choice bits of sea bream and grated gobo, a kind of burdock, and just before serving it was sprinkled with sesame seeds)

352

The Menus for the Emperor and Empress

Kikuna-bitashi Hanakatsuo

(kikuna, *a leafy green vegetable similar to spinach, boiled in Japanese clear soup flavored with soy sauce, garnished with shavings of* katsuobushi)

MAIN DISHES

Kisu-rikyoboshi Choji-nasu

(fillets of a small, sweet, white sea fish called kisu, *marinated in a sauce of* mirin *[sweet saké], soy sauce, and lemon juice; then skewered, drained, and charcoal-broiled; served with baby eggplant, boiled for a few moments and flavored with cloves)*

Kikka-kabu-fukumeni Tama-miso Kiku-noha

(small white turnips cut to look like chrysanthemum flowers and simmered in water slightly flavored with soy sauce; served with a bit of miso *and garnished with chrysanthemum leaves)*

Ondo-tamago Hana-sansho

(steamed whole yolks of eggs, garnished with the tiny flowers of sansho, *a Japanese pepper)*

RICE

Hakuhan

(boiled white rice)

served with the following pickles:

Kiuri-nukazuke

(sliced cucumber, lightly vinegared)

Misozuke-daikon

(slices of long white radish pickled in miso)

353

LUNCHEON, *OCTOBER 26*

MAKUNOUCHI-BENTO
(Japanese-style box lunch, packed to be eaten away from the inn)

Kuri-kinton
(whole boiled chestnuts in beaten sweet potatoes, sweetened with honey and sugar)

Namagatsuo Saikyoyaki
(fillet of pomfret,° marinated in white miso,† *saké, and* mirin, *and then charcoal-broiled)*
° From western Japan, the Inland Sea and Fukui districts.
† From Kyoto.

Kotobukimaki-tamago
(an omelet flavored with Japanese clear soup and sugar, rolled and sliced like jelly roll)

Yakinuki-kamaboko
(loaf of fish paste, sliced and toasted)

Kamo-no-kuwanamaki
(breast of wild duck, roasted with a sauce of mirin, soy sauce, and sugar)*

Kyo-koimo
(small whole taro from Kyoto, boiled in water flavored with soy sauce and sweetened saké)

Shin-takenoko
(slices of fresh young bamboo shoot, cooked in water flavored with soy sauce and sweetened saké)

The Menus for the Emperor and Empress

Sasaudo
(a kind of asparagus, cooked in water flavored with soy sauce and sweetened saké)

Namashiitake
(flat mushrooms which grow on tree trunks, cooked in water flavored with soy sauce and sweetened saké)

Shirauo-no-shirani
(whitebait, cooked in water flavored with white soy sauce and sweetened saké)

Sayamame
(chopped boiled Chinese peas)

Sudori-shoga
(fresh young shoots of ginger, marinated in sweetened vinegar)

O-Nigiri
(small rolls of white rice sprinkled with sesame seeds)

Narazuke
(slices of small yellow melon called uri, *pickled in saké lees)*

Bananas

DINNER, *OCTOBER 26*

HORS D'OEUVRES

Uzura-hamori
(boned leg of quail, grilled with a sauce of soy sauce and sweetened saké, and served garnished with quail feathers)

Yurifukuji
(sliced lily root, cooked in water flavored with white soy sauce and sweetened saké)

Ebi-kimi-zushi
(egg balls° rolled in a shrimp tail)
° The eggs, flavored with *mirin* and a dash of vinegar, are scrambled hard, then grated, and pressed into balls.

Matsukasa-ginnan
(pan-browned ginkgo nuts, each served with a pine needle stuck into it for easy handling)

Ayunoko-karami
(fresh salted caviar of brook trout)

Kisu-sasajime Dairinkigiku Suisenji-nori Wasabizu
(raw fillet of kisu *marinated in vinegar and a dash of lemon while pressed between slices of kelp [the kelp is removed before serving]; served with yellow chrysanthemum petals which have been dipped in vinegar and lemon juice, slivers of* suisenji-nori, *and the green horseradish called* wasabi)

SOUP

Fukiyose Uni Matsutake Hamotofu Me-mitsuba
(clear soup made from shavings of katsuobushi, *with cubes of egg tofu,° sliced pine mushrooms, cubes of fish paste made from sea eel, and the buds of a kind of parsley)*
° Egg *tofu* is a sort of mousse made by steaming whipped whole eggs; it was topped with bits of sea urchin.

SASHIMI
(Raw Fish)

The Menus for the Emperor and Empress

Tai Shimofuri
(fillet of sea bream, the skin scalded with boiling water to blister it, and then sliced thin)

Kanoko Akagai
(ark-shell, a bivalve mollusk, scored with a knife and marinated in vinegar)

both garnished with:

Mizutama-udo
(thin slices of udo, *a celery-like vegetable of the asparagus family)*

Hana-jojiso
(the stem of this small plant is frequently used as a garnish when it is covered with buds; in this case the specially selected stems were in bloom with tiny yellow flowers; both buds and flowers may be added to the soy sauce for their delicate scent and flavor)

and both served with:

Wasabi
(green horseradish)

Tosa-joyu
(soy sauce thickened by boiling with shavings of katsuobushi)

MAIN DISHES

Ise-ebi Shioni Matsutake Sakamushi
(whole boiled lobster, right side up with the tail shell loosened, garnished with mushrooms dipped in saké and then steamed, and served with lemon juice and a mayonnaise sauce)

Kamo-rosu-ni Burokkuri
(roast duck, served whole but carved, with broccoli)

Imozuiki Oroshi-imo Age-suiton
(sliced fresh sprouts of taro cooked in water flavored with white soy sauce and sweetened saké, and salt; grated taro and white radish pressed into balls and cooked in deep oil; the two served together with the hot sauce in which the sliced taro was cooked)

RICE

Hakuhan
(boiled white rice)

served with the following pickles:

Narazuke
(slices of small yellow melon called uri, *pickled in saké lees)*

Moriguchi Daikon
(slices of white radish pickled in saké lees)

Hanarakkyo
(small white onions pickled in vinegar and mirin*)*

BREAKFAST, *OCTOBER 27*

SOUP

Aka-shiro Miso-shitate Kyokoimo Shiitake
(potage made from miso *of both red and white beans, with tiny whole taros from Kyoto, and sliced flat tree mushrooms)*

The Menus for the Emperor and Empress

Udo Karashizuke
(a celery-like asparagus, boiled and flavored with mustard)

Horenso Gomayose
(a bouquet of boiled spinach, topped with sesame seed)

MAIN DISHES

Tai-kazaboshi Hanasansho
(charcoal-broiled fillets of sea bream, garnished with the tiny flowers of sansho, a Japanese pepper)

Imadegawa-tofu Uchi-saya Nori-an
(a fillet of sawara, a kind of mackerel, is placed between two pieces of tofu [bean-curd custard], covered with kelp, and steamed; the kelp is removed, the fish and tofu are transferred intact to a serving dish, covered with a white sauce flavored with mirin, and garnished with flakes of dried seaweed)

SIDE DISH

Otafuku-mame-no-kanroni
(boiled broad beans, flavored with salt and a dash of sugar)

RICE

Hakuhan
(boiled white rice)

served with the following pickles:

Asazuke
(sliced large white radish pickled in salt and fermented rice)

Hakusai
(Chinese cabbage pickled in salt and fermented rice)

LUNCHEON, *OCTOBER 27*

OCHUJIKI
(Western-style box lunch, packed to be eaten away from the inn)

Sandwiches of white bread (roast ham, pimento cheese, sardine, and cucumber) garnished with shredded cabbage

Persimmons

Postscript

OKITSU is a real town and the Minaguchi-ya is a real inn. But, as I have stated, the records of the inn and of the Mochizuki family were destroyed by fire during the time of Hanjuro I, and most of my story of the inn prior to that time is what I have reconstructed from other contemporary documents.

The account of the inn's founding conforms to family legend, but most of the links with historical personalities, all of whom I have tried to present faithfully, are my own invention. This is true up until the time of Prince Saionji: Saionji's relationship to the inn is given as it was.

There are certain exceptions to this fictionalizing. The Ito family of Nagoya have been patrons for generations, and Mochizuki Hanjuro IV did see the old travel diary which made reference to the Minaguchi-ya. Old registers of the Ichikawa *honjin* still exist and I have drawn on them for details. The excerpts from Hiroshige's diary are drawn from some of his own travel diaries, now in the collection of Abbot Shutara Ryocho of Jogyoji Temple in Tokyo. The Mochizuki family tree is diagrammed according to current records beginning with Mohei, adopted from the Tezukas. Among Isako's forebears, the Mochizukis of Shimizu, Ieyasu's friendship with Gen'emon is factual, as is Jirocho's bond with that family, and the incident of the kago-bearers on Satta Mountain.

I have told how Edo became Tokyo. But there were other name changes which I did not mention because I was reluctant to introduce any more names than I had to. Thus the next post station after Okitsu, which I have referred to as Shimizu, was really called

Ejiri until it was incorporated into the modern city of Shimizu. And the city of Shizuoka has been variously known as Sumpu and Fuchu. Changing names is an old habit with the Japanese: Ieyasu was born as Matsudaira Takechiyo, became Matsudaira Motonobu at his coming of age, changed this to Matsudaira Motoyasu at sixteen, changed Motoyasu to Ieyasu at twenty, and at twenty-seven obtained the Emperor's permission to change his family name from Matsudaira to Tokugawa, thus becoming Tokugawa Ieyasu.

I have drawn my material from so many sources that I could not possibly name them all here. Most of them are written in the Japanese language. But anyone familiar with A. L. Sadler's brilliant biography of Ieyasu, *The Maker of Modern Japan* (London, Allen and Unwin, 1937), will realize my indebtedness to him, and among the general historical works on Japan it would ill become me not to acknowledge my reliance on G. B. Sansom's *Japan, A Short Cultural History* (New York, Appleton-Century, 1943) and *The Western World and Japan* (New York, Knopf, 1951). Because Saionji's era is very recent and is still viewed with contemporary bias, I should like to name the chief works from which I have drawn my facts: Shigemitsu Mamoru, *Japan and Her Destiny* (New York, Dutton, 1958); Richard Storry, *The Double Patriots* (London, Chatto and Windus, 1957); Robert A. Scalapino, *Democracy and the Party Movement in Prewar Japan* (Berkeley and Los Angeles, University of California, 1953); and two biographies of Saionji, Omura Bunji, *The Last Genro* (Philadelphia and New York, Lippincott, 1938) and Takekoshi Yosaburo, *Prince Saionji* (Kyoto, Ritsumeikan University, 1933). But my interpretation of events is my own.

Again, so many individuals have helped me that a full list would fill pages, but I must name Tanaka Hideo, ex-mayor of Okitsu and now head of its citizens' hall and library; Norizuke Toshiro of the Shimizu Public Library; Priest Mizuno Hakushu of Seikenji, Abbot Saito Kenze of Yokaiji, and the late Abbot Imai Koshun of Rigenji, all of Okitsu; Kuwabara Makoto, Oda Yasumasa, and Furuno Tateo of the National Diet Library in Tokyo; Akimoto Shunkichi, who gave me many valuable suggestions; Kamei Tanejiro, who translated much material for me; Margaret Gentles of the Art Institute of Chicago, who helped me find most of the illustrations; Toda Kenji, who assisted in determining the proper family crests; Glenn W. Shaw, who not only permitted use of his translation of the inscription on Sesshu's painting of Seikenji, a translation which first appeared in Mr. Shaw's book, *Living in Japan,* published in Tokyo in 1936 by the Hokuseido Press, but also assisted in the problem of crest designs; and Uchima Ansei, who was at my side during most of the long interviews that helped form this book.

Most of all I am grateful to the Mochizukis—to Hanjuro IV and his mother, whom I call *Obaasan,* to Isako and her father, Ryozo. Without their friendship and their help I could have done nothing.

My story of the Minaguchi-ya is in part fiction, but my affection for the inn and its family is very real.

Oliver Statler

MANCHURIA

KOREA

JAPAN

KYOTO

PUSAN

KOMPIRA SHRINE

HIROSHIMA

AKO

OSAKA

KUMAMOTO

NAGASAKI

FUKUOKA

INLAND SEA

SHIKOKU

KYUSHU

SATSUMA
(Province)

PACIFIC

SIBERIA

HOKKAIDO

SEA

HONSHU

Tokaido Road

Okitsu

NIKKO

YUI

KAMBARA
NUMAZU
Mt. Fuji
ODAWARA

EDO (Tokyo)

NAGOYA

SHIMIZU
SHIZUOKA

KAWASAKI
YOKOHAMA

SURUGA BAY

Hakone Mts.

Izu Peninsula

YOKOSUKA

HAMAMATSU

KAMAKURA

SURUGA (Province)

OCEAN

Picador

☐	**History of Rock and Roll**	ed. Jim Miller	£4.95p
☐	**Lectures on Literature**	Vladimir Nabokov	£3.95p
☐	**The Best of Myles**	Flann O' Brien	£2.95p
☐	**Autobiography**	John Cowper Powys	£3.50p
☐	**Hadrian the Seventh**	Fr. Rolfe (Baron Corvo)	£1.25p
☐	**On Broadway**	Damon Runyon	£3.50p
☐	**Midnight's Children**	Salman Rushdie	£3.50p
☐	**Snowblind**	Robert Sabbag	£1.95p
☐	**Awakenings**	Oliver Sacks	£3.95p
☐	**The Fate of the Earth**	Jonathan Schell	£1.95p
☐	**Street of Crocodiles**	Bruno Schultz	£1.25p
☐	**Poets in their Youth**	Eileen Simpson	£2.95p
☐	**Miss Silver's Past**	Josef Skvorecky	£2.50p
☐	**A Flag for Sunrise**	Robert Stone	£2.50p
☐	**Visitants**	Randolph Stow	£2.50p
☐	**Alice Fell**	Emma Tennant	£1.95p
☐	**The Flute-Player**	D. M. Thomas	£2.25p
☐	**The Great Shark Hunt**	Hunter S. Thompson	£3.50p
☐	**The Longest War**	Jacob Timerman	£2.50p
☐	**Aunt Julia and the Scriptwriter**	Mario Vargas Llosa	£2.95p
☐	**Female Friends**	Fay Weldon	£2.50p
☐	**No Particular Place To Go**	Hugo Williams	£1.95p
☐	**The Outsider**	Colin Wilson	£2.50p
☐	**Kandy-Kolored Tangerine-Flake Streamline Baby**	Tom Wolfe	£2.25p
☐	**Mars**	Fritz Zorn	£1.95p

All these books are available at your local bookshop or newsagent, or
can be ordered direct from the publisher. Indicate the number of copies
required and fill in the form below   11

....

Name_____
(Block letters please)

Address_____

_____

Send to CS Department, Pan Books Ltd, PO Box 40, Basingstoke, Hants
Please enclose remittance to the value of the cover price plus:
35p for the first book plus 15p per copy for each additional book ordered
to a maximum charge of £1.25 to cover postage and packing
Applicable only in the UK

While every effort is made to keep prices low, it is sometimes
necessary to increase prices at short notice. Pan Books reserve
the right to show on covers and charge new retail prices which
may differ from those advertised in the text or elsewhere